CONTROVERSY
AND
COALITION,
Revised Edition

*The New Feminist Movement across
Three Decades of Change*

Revised Edition

SOCIAL MOVEMENTS PAST AND PRESENT

Irwin T. Sanders, Editor

CONTROVERSY AND COALITION

Revised Edition

The New Feminist Movement across Three Decades of Change

Myra Marx Ferree and Beth B. Hess

Twayne Publishers
An Imprint of Simon & Schuster Macmillan
NEW YORK

Prentice Hall International
LONDON · MEXICO CITY · NEW DELHI · SINGAPORE · SYDNEY · TORONTO

Controversy and Coalition: The New Feminist Movement, Revised Edition
Myra Marx Ferree and Beth B. Hess

Copyright © 1995 Simon & Schuster Macmillan

Twayne Publishers
An Imprint of Simon & Schuster Macmillan
1633 Broadway
New York, NY 10019-6785

Library of Congress Cataloging-in-Publication Data

Ferree, Myra Marx.
    Controversy and coalition : the new feminist movement / Myra Marx Ferree and
Beth B. Hess. — Rev. ed.
        p. cm. — (Social movements past and present)
    Includes bibliographical references and index.
    ISBN 0-8057-3881-9 (alk. paper). — ISBN 0-8057-3882-7 (pbk. : alk. paper)
        1. Feminism—United States. I. Hess, Beth B., 1928– .
II. Title. III. Series.
HQ1426.F475 1994
305.42'0973—dc20   94-14318
                                                                                 CIP

The paper used in this publication meets the minimum requirements of American National Standard for Information Sciences—Permanence of Paper for Printed Library Materials. ANSI Z3948-1984.⊗™

10 9 8 7 6 5 4 3 2 1 (hc)
10 9 8 7 6 5 4 3   (pb)

Printed in the United States of America

Contents

Introduction

When we decided to do a second, revised and expanded edition of our 1985 book, we thought primarily about adding a chapter to cover the important changes we saw the movement going through in the past decade; however, we found ourselves rewriting much of the book for several important reasons. First, feminist scholarship has continued to grow vigorously, adding new insights and producing different views of all phases of the history of the women's movement. We tried to take account of this new scholarship, and this has led to some reassessments of the relative significance of past events. Second, social movement theory has also been undergoing important transformations. Some of the theoretical gaps of a decade ago have since been covered with an array of new concepts, and we have tried to bring these theories to bear on the developments we describe. Finally, our own feminist perspectives have undergone shifts as the movement itself has changed and grown. What we appreciate and what we view critically have been modified by our own experiences as participants and as observers in the decade since the first edition was published.

Although this volume is one of a series on social movements, we have taken as our topic a much broader and deeper phenomenon; the new feminism. It is, in fact, impossible to write of the organized feminist movement without placing it in the context of many diverse strands of feeling and action. In one sense, these underlying currents are "the movement," of which organized feminism is only one highly visible element. This diversity is our central theme. Throughout the book, we shall speak of multiple feminisms: movements with a common conviction that the present social system does not recognize the value of women or act to promote women's good.

Oversimplification characterizes much of what has been written about the contemporary women's movement, in both the professional and the popular press. In large part, this stems from the need to make order out of the seeming chaos of movement ideas and actions. In part, also, there has been a real failure to appreciate either the value of diversity or the capacity of movement organizations to absorb conflict. And, lastly, there is always the tendency of observers to impose their meaning on events rather than to attempt to understand them from the point of view of diverse participants.

Although we have been participants as well as observers for more than twenty years, we cannot claim to have captured all facets of the new feminism, or even to have interpreted correctly those aspects described in this book. But our own backgrounds and experiences with feminism are very different, and in coming to appreciate each other's perspective, we feel that we have come to understand the diversity of feminism in new ways. Our goal is to present each form of contemporary feminism in its own terms and in relation to the whole in a way that incorporates both an insider's and an outsider's perspective.

We are also attempting a fresh look at the status of American women and of feminist thought, actions, and organizations in the seventy-five years since the passage of the suffrage amendment. In this we benefit from three decades of feminist scholarship, itself an outgrowth of the trends we describe. Many long-accepted assumptions can be shown to rest on superficial impressions repeated so often that they become a kind of "truth." A revisionist view of the new feminism does not require a wholesale disregard of previous research; rather, we shall highlight previously overlooked aspects of women's experience in society and in the movement, and integrate these into the more conventional scenario.

One crucial point, all too often overlooked, is that feminism has a long and diverse history. In dealing with the New Feminist Movement, that is, with American feminism after suffrage, and the organizational forms it has taken in recent years, we are tackling a broad subject, but one that is only part of an even larger historical phenomenon. Eleanor Flexner's classic study, *Century of Struggle* (1959), provides an introduction to the first and second waves of feminist thought and action that preceded the current movement. It is important to remember, as we consider the goals and struggles of the third wave of American feminists, that women were not simply *given* an education or the right to vote, but that earlier feminists struggled, at great personal cost, against political repression and social ridicule, to gain each victory. The conditions that so many women take for granted today were the hard-won fruits of decades of sacrifice and activism. Nor were the earlier feminists able to gain all they sought; many of their goals remain issues for the new feminists: reproductive freedom, genuine equality in male-female relationships, changes in the occupational structure and the workplace, and socially recognized personhood. These are not new goals. By looking at the New Feminist Movement, we are concentrating at relatively new attempts to articulate and achieve some comparatively old goals.

Several stylistic devices deserve comment. As feminists, we are generally more comfortable using the pronoun "we" to refer both to feminists and to women as a group. This usage, however, led to continued awkwardness in the text. Making we-they distinctions among different types of feminists and different subgroups of women seemed antithetical to our goal of presenting the ideas and actions of each group in their own terms, yet we could not honestly claim membership in all of these groups. We reluctantly decided that it would be wisest to use "they" consistently, reserving "we" for reference to ourselves as authors.

Secondly, to distinguish the two threads of our topic we use the word *feminism* to refer to changes in consciousness and *movement* to denote organizational activity. Clearly, there are many women and men who share a new perception of gender-based oppression and opportunity, but who have not taken part in organized efforts for change because they have not had the time or occasion to do so. There are probably also some movement members whose participation in a specific movement organization is based on immediate self-interest more than on their consciousness and commitment to the feminist cause. And then there are those many individuals who have benefitted from the changes wrought by the movement, yet who are quick to declare, "I'm not a feminist, but . . . ," disavowing any relationship to the organized movement, but identifying to a greater or lesser extent with its goals. In some way, all these persons are part of our story—as are those who have fueled a powerful countermovement backlash. For there can be no doubt that the New Feminist Movement represents the most broad-based critique of traditional social arrangements, from the interpersonal to the institutional, of any contemporary social movement. This challenge has been developing over the past two hundred years in the United States and Western Europe and has now spread throughout the world.

The scope of this book does not permit an overview of the contemporary women's movement in its true international diversity, so we recommend that students of feminism consider some of the excellent research done on women's movements in Latin America (Jacquette 1989), Canada (Adamson, Briskin, and McPhail 1988), France (Duchen 1986), and in the Third World (Jayawardena 1986). Comparative studies (e.g., Gelb 1989 on Britain and the United States; the articles in Katzenstein and Mueller 1987; and the analytical work in Chapman 1993 and Margolis 1993) seem to us to be a most fruitful direction to pursue to gain an understanding of the significance and specificity of the developments we chronicle in the United States.

It seems clear that feminist movements are now a global reality that is here to stay. As much as recent decades have reminded us of the fragility of particular gains and the power of antifeminist interests, the broader truth that we hope this book will convey is the continuity of feminist struggles across the years. Controversies have been present in abundance, of course, and we do not wish to disguise them. Struggle within the movement, among competing perspectives and factions, will no doubt continue. But the coalitions among feminists and their many organizations and the changes in mainstream culture that have already been produced are the basis for our optimism about the future of the movement.

Eleanor Roosevelt, second from left, with close friends, including Marion Dickerman, the first woman to run for elective office in New York State. From the 1920s to the 1960s, Eleanor Roosevelt was at the center of a network of women activists in and out of government. Fittingly, in 1960 John F. Kennedy appointed her to chair the Commission on the Status of Women, from which one part of the New Feminist Movement would emerge. *Photograph courtesy of the F.D.R. Library.*

Chapter 1

Setting the Stage

Where Did All the Feminists Go?

This is the question often posed by those who examine the history of American women following the passage of the Suffrage Amendment in 1920. A powerful coalition of women's groups had been forged in the early decades of this century to press for the right to vote, yet by 1924 little remained of a nationally organized women's movement. The common wisdom is that only a shared focus on the amendment held such a diverse collection of groups together, so that once suffrage was gained, few other issues or interests linked women across regional, class, age, and cultural divisions. Leaders of the suffrage movement never generated a broadly feminist consciousness among its various constituents and failed to attack the roots of women's inferior status in all areas of social life, particularly in the family. For these and other reasons, broad-based organizations for women's rights ceased to be a major political and social force throughout the next four decades.

Yet we must distinguish its organizational form from the deeper impulses that constitute a "social movement." As defined by McCarthy and Zald (1977), "social movements" consist of opinions and beliefs in favor of changing the structure of a society and its system of allocating scarce rewards. "Social movement organizations"

1

are the formal structures designed to achieve the goals of the movement. In this latter sense, feminists and feminism did not fade away
even in the 1920s. Rather, the movement survived the "doldrums" in
several elite (as opposed to mass-membership) organizations such as
the Business and Professional Women's Clubs and the National
Women's Party (headed by Alice Paul), and through informal networks of like-minded activists (Rupp and Taylor 1987; Harrison 1988;
Buechler 1990). In addition, many individual women pursued feminist
goals outside of explicitly women-oriented organizations—in political
parties and professional associations, for example. But it was the
major demographic and social trends transforming the life of
American women between 1920 and 1960 that produced a new feminist consciousness rooted in everyday experience (Cott 1987). The
most important of these changes occurred in the areas of employment, education, and family life.

Employment Trends

Labor Force Participation. One of the most significant and star-
tling trends of the past half-century is the increased participation of
women in work outside the home. In 1920, women composed 20 percent of the civilian labor force, compared to over 45 percent today.
Similarly, about one-fourth of all women were in the labor force in
1920, a figure that had more than doubled by 1990. While the sheer
magnitude of this increase is impressive, changes in composition of
the female work force may be even more significant. In the 1920s, 77
percent of women workers were young and single, mostly from immigrant and poor families, although many young middle-class women
were also entering the labor force. Typically, these women left work
when they married. Black women, however, were an exception; in
1920, 43 percent of black females age sixteen and over were
employed, whether married or not, most often as domestic servants,
replacing live-in white immigrant "girls" in middle- and upper-class
homes (Katzman 1978). Unmarried young white women, in turn,
flocked to jobs in the newly expanding worlds of office work and retail
sales, in which they saw an opportunity to gain an independence and
status their mothers had never known (Goldin 1990).

   In contrast, among women in the labor force today, 55 percent are
married, 20 percent divorced or widowed, and only 25 percent are single, as shown in Table 1.1 (U.S. Bureau of the Census 1993). Indeed,

the most rapid increase in labor force participation today is among women of childbearing years, unlike the pattern of the period 1940–60, when the increase was largely due to the reentry of women who had left work for child raising and only returned in middle age for "second careers" (Blau 1979). Between 1960 and 1980, however, the expansion of the female labor force involved women under age forty-five. This pattern can be characterized as "limited departure" rather than "reentry," as mothers interrupted employment for increasingly shorter periods of child raising, or simply shifted to part-time work. Despite such changes, the great majority of women's jobs are still in the office and retail sectors.

Nonetheless, a female labor force composed of married women, many of whom are middle-aged and middle class, is something very different from one populated by young nonmarried women. In proposing a "sociotechnological theory of the Women's Movement," Huber (1976) claims that "only after married women entered the labor force on a long-term basis did the Woman's Movement develop into a force that could not be reversed" (371). If prestige and power come from control of the exchange of goods outside the household, Huber suggests that married women can use these resources more effectively than the nonmarried "working girls" of half a century ago.

It would be an oversimplification, however, to think of women's labor force participation as a consistent long-term (secular) trend. During the Great Depression (1928–39), for example, married women in white-collar jobs were thought to take jobs from married men; thus, for example, the many rules against hiring married women as schoolteachers. Yet most of the jobs held by women, even white-collar ones, did not appeal to men, and employers were content to pay the lower wages that women tolerated (Kessler-Harris 1990). Although women did not withdraw from the labor force in large numbers during the Depression, they were limited in the type of employment available, and tended to lower their aspirations accordingly (Scharf 1980; Goldin 1990). The only acceptable reason for their working was economic necessity, leading to a denial of individualistic goals or the need for personal fulfillment (thus also reducing the possibility of a feminist consciousness emerging from the workplace). The Depression years can best be interpreted as a period of retrenchment—in terms of promotions, aspirations, and moving into male-dominated occupations—rather than of withdrawal from the workplace.

The Great Depression ended with American involvement in World

TABLE 1.1
Marital Status of Women in the Civilian Labor Force, Selected Years, 1940–1991

Year	Percentage Distribution, Female Labor Force			Female Labor Force as Percentage of Female Population			
	Single	Married	Other*	Total	Single	Married	Other*
1940	48.5	36.4	15.1	27.4	48.1	16.7	32.0
1944	40.9	45.7	13.4	35.0	58.6	25.6	35.7
1947	37.9	46.2	15.9	29.8	51.2	21.4	34.6
1950	31.6	52.1	16.3	31.4	50.5	24.8	36.0
1955	25.2	58.7	16.0	33.5	46.4	29.4	36.0
1960	24.0	59.9	16.1	34.8	44.1	31.7	37.1
1965	22.8	62.2	15.0	36.7	40.5	35.7	35.7
1970	22.3	63.4	14.3	42.6	53.0	41.4	36.2
1975	24.3	57.3	18.3	46.3	59.8	44.3	40.1
1980	26.1	54.9	19.0	51.5	64.4	49.9	43.6
1985	25.8	54.6	19.6	54.5	66.6	53.8	45.1
1991	25.1	54.8	20.1	57.3	66.5	58.5	46.8

Source: U.S. Bureau of the Census, *Statistical Abstract of the United States: 1992* (Washington, D.C.: U.S. Government Printing Office, 1993), 387.

*From 1960 on, this category includes widowed, divorced, and separated women; for earlier years, separated women were included in the "married" category.

War II and the subsequent absence of young male workers. At the same time, the demand for labor in defense industries rose dramatically, and women were encouraged to do their "patriotic duty" by temporarily replacing "their men" on the production line (Rupp 1979). As a result, married women's participation rates increased by almost 50 percent between 1940 and 1944, with most new entrants being older (35+) married women. As seen in Table 1.1, married women's share of the female labor force rose from 36.4 percent in 1940 to 45.7 percent in 1944, while that of single women declined.

Employers and unions considered this situation a temporary wartime necessity; the concept that there was "men's work" and "women's work" remained intact, regardless of how often it was contradicted in actual experience (Milkman 1982). At the start of the war, most women workers accepted this definition of their labor, but by war's end they had become increasingly attached to their works roles. A survey by the Women's Bureau in 1945 found that over 75 percent of women workers indicated that they would prefer to stay on rather than hand over their jobs to returning men (Chafe 1991). But without a feminist movement to support them, the women could not resist the pressure to leave the labor force, much less challenge either job segregation or the ideological underpinnings of gender distinctions in the workplace (Milkman 1982). Not all went quietly, however. Unionized women auto workers in Detroit protested militantly, but union leaders were not prepared to help women keep their jobs or to fight against the sexual division of labor (Gabin 1990; Amott and Mathaei 1991.) Nonetheless, women in trade unions continued to press for changes both in the workplace and within the labor movement, so that when the New Feminist Movement emerged in the 1960s, there were networks of working-class women prepared to participate.

The ideology of this period was perfectly expressed in a best-selling book, *Modern Woman: The Lost Sex* (Lundberg and Farnham 1947), which claimed that the idea of an "independent woman is a contradiction in terms" because it violates the laws of nature (Chafe 1991). Not only were there few cultural supports for working women, but many material ones were also withdrawn; for example, federally funded day care was phased out by 1946. Nonetheless, large numbers of women remained in the labor force, even as they bore and raised an unusually large cohort of offspring. Thus, by the 1960s, a generation of young women from intact middle-class homes had grown up with the experience of a working mother.

But we must not exaggerate the work experience of American women even during the war years. As Table 1.1 shows, even at the height of the war—1944—only 35 percent of the female population fourteen years and older was employed. This proportion dips to under one in three by 1947 but increases steadily from that point on.

Nor did women forsake the workplace altogether during the 1950s for the benefits of home and hearth. To the contrary, the percentage of wife-mothers in the labor force rose steadily. This trend is hardly surprising, since the number of children born during the Great Depression and reaching adulthood in the postwar period was not sufficient to meet the labor force demands of the 1950s. There were jobs enough for men in those fields defined as "men's work," leaving the world of "women's work" open to married women who supplemented family income to meet expanding consumer needs.

Public reaction, as always, was ambivalent: on the one hand, there was the need for the kinds of paid work typically done by women; on the other, the strong belief that family care is a woman's most important responsibility (Kessler-Harris 1990; Bradley 1989). Employed wives and mothers are simultaneously accepted and condemned, a contradiction that leads many women to define their work as an extension of family obligation, and others to challenge the idea that work is of secondary significance to women.

Neither disapproval nor lack of opportunity for advancement stemmed the flow of women into the labor force as jobs opened up in offices, stores, educational institutions, and health-care facilities. The expansion of women's education reinforced this trend. The mainstays of white female employment before the 1920s (and of black female employment until the 1960s)—factory, domestic, and farm work—have largely been replaced by occupations that require formal education but still pay poorly.

Women in Higher Education.   For the past one hundred years, the proportions of boys and girls enrolled in elementary and secondary schools has been roughly similar. In higher education, however, more men than women have enrolled and many more stayed through graduation. Only in the 1980s did the number of women entering college exceed that of men, with increasing proportions completing college and entering graduate schools. But the trend toward higher education for women has not followed a simple unilinear pattern, as shown in Table 1.2.

TABLE 1.2

Women in Higher Education: 1900–1991

Year	Women as Percentage of Undergraduates	Women with Bachelor (or First Professional Degree)	Women as Percentage of Doctorates	Women as Percentage of Full-time Faculty
1900	35	19	6	20
1920	47	34	15	26
1940	40	41	13	28
1960	36	35	10	22
1970	41	41	13	25
1975	45	43	21	24
1981	50	48	31	26
1991	55	54	37	27

Adapted from Graham 1978, 766; U.S. Bureau of the Census 1993: 164, 173; Chronicle of Higher Education 1993.

In 1920, twice as many men as women received bachelor's or master's degrees, and five times as many earned doctorates. Of course, in 1920 undergraduate education was an elite undertaking; less than 8 percent of the "college-aged" population actually went to college, compared with almost 50 percent today. A college-educated woman in 1920 was thus aware of being a member of a small privileged group. She was also more likely than noncollege women to remain unmarried and to pursue a career, one reason why parents often opposed women's education—they wanted a "normal" daughter.

By 1970, four women received bachelor's and master's degrees for every five men, but the ratio for doctorates remained fewer than one in six. After World War II, higher education became increasingly available to the mass public, as the number and size of colleges and universities expanded to accommodate the wave of veterans offered a subsidized education by a grateful nation. The influx of veterans initially tilted enrollments in favor of men, but it also "normalized" going to college. Sending a daughter to college became a logical extension of parents' aspirations to middle-class status, but going on to graduate school implied more career commitment than was proper for women. Nonetheless, many women proceeded to obtain professional degrees, although only in the last few years has women's share of doctorates reached even one in three (U.S. Bureau of the Census 1993.) Although by 1990 women were a clear majority of bachelor's degree students, the percentage of women on the faculty was no greater than it had been in 1940.

Perhaps because of rising educational levels, career aspirations among women did not decline between the 1920s and 1960s, as so often has been assumed (Stricker 1979). Women's interest in medicine, law, business, and college teaching remained high, but there were many barriers to their participation, including opposition from male-dominated professional gatekeepers and the extraordinary difficulties of combining a career and family. Feminists in the postsuffrage years were unable to change the social structure that forced women to choose between children and a profession. Thus, the few middle-class women who succeeded in high-status careers in the early decades of this century typically remained unmarried or without children, stranded on the shore of social change rather than at the edge of an incoming tide, and sometimes disappointed that other women failed to follow them (Cott 1987).

Although the proportion of women physicians, attorneys, professors, and business executives remained low between 1930 and 1970, the absolute number of women entering professions actually increased throughout this period. Increasingly, also, professional women were married rather than single; when they left the labor force it was because of institutional requirements or the absence of encouragement and support (particularly from husbands), rather than in response to the irresistible appeal of family life. Many remained but were caught in positions of little mobility or prestige. Stricker (1979) concludes that "domesticity had not conquered the minds of American women, even in the 1950s. . . . What was missing through all these years was not a base of discontent or significant numbers of career women, but a feminist movement to interpret these discontents as collective phenomena, rooted in fundamentally inegalitarian social and economic structures" (490). As long as each woman thought herself an exception or suffered alone, the guilt of being "unnatural," the dominant ideology—or "feminine mystique" (Friedan 1963)—remained unchallenged.

Higher education and labor force participation were essential but not sufficient conditions for the re-emergence of a broad-based feminist movement. The experience of women in the workplace, earning their own money, making new friends, and expanding their skills, but also encountering prejudice, discrimination, humiliation, harassment, and outright hostility, helped produce the two fundamental prerequisites for a new feminist movement. On the one hand, paid employment and unpaid volunteer work provided women with resources—skills, friendship networks, money, professional contacts, and experiences that would help in organizational development. Typing and running a mimeograph machine, for example, are skills that are trivialized and underpaid in the business world, but were invaluable assets to the fledgling organizers of the 1960s.

On the other hand, the negative experiences of exclusion, devaluation, and grudging acceptance in the labor force and higher education produced what sociologists call "marginality"—being partly in and partly out, simultaneously accepted and rejected, at the edge or margin of an institution or society in general. Marginality produces stress but also permits creativity, including criticism of existing arrangements. Such marginality for women provided the opportunity to build the ideological base of the new feminism. A sense that the taken-for-granted world is neither legitimate nor inevitable is the psychological precondition, just as a resource base is the social precondition, for forming an organized movement for change.

The Postmaterialist Ethic.   The unprecedented affluence of the 1950s and 1960s also encouraged important changes in infant socialization that heightened women's experience of marginality. Under the influence of child-centered psychologies of the postwar period, parents became increasingly aware, often to the point of severe anxiety, of the effects of their child-rearing practices. Beginning with middle-class parents and gradually filtering through the strata of society, child rearing became characterized by an intense concern with the development of each child, greater permissiveness, an emphasis on the child's emotional rather than instrumental value, and a dependency on "experts" (Zelizer 1985). While much expert advice (e.g., Spock 1945) prescribed different ways for handling daughters and sons, the basic trend was toward increased equality (egalitarianism) in parent-child relationships, between parents and among their children. In the middle-class family where the timing and number of offspring were most often planned, daughters were now likely to receive the same amount of parental attention as sons, and they were expected to do well in school, develop self-esteem, and go to college. To be sure, achievement after graduation was to be sought in raising a family and providing emotional support to one's husband, but socialization to self-assurance and competence cannot be so easily limited.

The cultural climate of the 1950s, which had nurtured the suburban homemaker and the baby boom, gave way in the 1960s to a "postmaterialistic" ethic that challenged the assumptions of postwar America, at least among middle-class youth. In opposition to what they perceived as the narrowness of their parents' values, many young people rejected materialism and status seeking as the primary goals of life. If happiness were not to be found in work for its own sake or in worldly possessions, it must be sought elsewhere—in personal relationships, social awareness, and political activism, and in community-building rather than individual striving. Because such a viewpoint can be most easily adopted by those who already have a secure material base, young college-educated middle-class white women were caught between the attraction of newly opened career opportunities, on the one hand, and their generation's mistrust of material success, on the other hand.

Rather than achievement, the word that came to symbolize the new ideal was "liberation," defined as freedom to "do one's own thing" and to transcend artificial constraints on expressiveness. The concept of liberation was understood to mean more than the personal freedom of affluent college youth. National prosperity, in this era of low unemployment, seemed potentially available to everyone, and barriers based on race and gender seemed foolish and antiquated. All forms of arbitrary restraint were called into question—not only those of social class, but also those of race and gender. It is difficult today, after a decade and a half of difficult economic times, resurgent materialism, anxiety over downward mobility, and new appeals to racism and sexism, to evoke the exhilaration of the 1960s generation, the openness and generosity with which it embraced the goal of social transformation, and the challenges it raised to prevailing values.

Family Trends

Sex and Marriage.   No less than the 1960s, the 1920s were a decade of profound change in sexual mores and family relationships. Victorian morality gave way to unprecedented liberties for "flaming youth": sexual freedom, the ability of unmarrieds to live away from home, less constricting clothes to symbolize this newfound casualness, and, most enticing for young middle-class women, the chance to work at a "glamour job" in an office or shop. The new morality that had been an elite life-style in the early years of the century became a mass phenomenon after World War I. In the excitement of breaking old taboos, few young women were aware of the grime behind the glitter: the dead-end nature of their jobs and their increasing vulnerability to sexual exploitation. They saw neither the need nor the necessity for political organizing on behalf of women's rights since they saw themselves as already occupationally and sexually liberated as well as enfranchised.

At the same time, ideals of family life were being transformed, from an authoritarian pattern to one emphasizing companionship and romantic love. In essence, family life was made increasingly attractive to young women who ultimately became disillusioned with their new-found freedoms and jobs. As a career actually offered less than it once seemed to promise, particularly in terms of income and mobility, having a family may have seemed more attractive than before, especially since the women who came into adulthood after World War I could expect a family life different from that of their mothers.

Not only was mate selection freed from parental control and the ideal marriage made more egalitarian, but couples increasingly exercised choice over the number and spacing of their offspring. During the Great Depression, birth rates fell dramatically, without the inexpensive and effective legal contraceptive devices available today. Disillusion with this new sort of "partnership" family as it operates in reality (with women always the "junior partner") took some time to emerge, but emerge it did. By 1947, Lundberg and Farnham were blaming women for their discontent and exhorting them to try harder to be happy.

In contrast to the "sexual revolution" of the decade following World War I, particularly the freedom enjoyed by young women, the Great Depression brought a renewed emphasis on sexual control, largely in the interests of reducing family size. During World War II, sexual abstinence was one of those "sacrifices to the war effort" expected of women whose husbands were in the armed forces, although the same demands were rarely made of men. In general, then, the years between 1930 and 1945 were marked by a relatively puritanical view of sexuality. Yet the companionate ideal of marriage was also based upon a mutuality of sexual fulfillment, at least implicitly recognizing the sexual interests of women—if only within marriage. The American perception of sexuality shifted from an activity whose justification is the creation of new life to one that is pleasurable in its own right: from an emphasis on procreation to an emphasis on recreation. Gone, or going, were some of the emotional inhibitions that constrained female sexuality in the past. The 1960s would most resemble the 1920s in terms of closing the gap between male and female sexual behaviors, although a "double standard" of evaluation remains even in the 1990s.

Another important trend over the years has been the age at first marriage, which reached an historical low in the 1950s and then began a steady climb upward. In 1955, half of all American women were married by age twenty; by 1980, that figure was slightly over twenty-two years; and today the age at which half are married is twenty-four years. This increase reflects several other trends: higher rates of college-going, enhanced ability to support oneself outside of marriage, and lowered risk of unintended pregnancy.

It is important to distinguish between sexual freedom and gender equality. In many ways, the new permissiveness toward sexual activity renders women more vulnerable to exploitation than in the past; without genuine equality in the other spheres of social life, women cannot exercise freedom of choice in their sexual relationships. Thus, sexuality has become a major feminist issue.

Fertility.   Control over fertility is as important as labor force participation in the liberation of women. Most obviously, being freed from a constant cycle of pregnancy and breast feeding has clear health and energy benefits; having fewer offspring reduces the time required to raise a family; but, most importantly, being able to exercise choice in this most intimate area enhances a sense of power over one's own life.

With the exception of the years between 1947 and 1963, the long-term trend in our society has been toward lower birth rates (number of children per 1,000 population) and fertility (average number of children to women in the childbearing years). In part, lowered fertility reflects the high probability that each infant will survive birth and childhood, so that a woman need bear only as many offspring as desired. In the past, high rates of infant mortality meant that a woman might give birth to seven or eight children in the hope that three or four would live to adulthood. Declining birth rates are also characteristic of modern industrial societies in general; as people move off the land to towns and cities, the economic value of children changes from an asset to a financial burden.

There is also a strong link between a woman's employment expectations and her fertility behavior, although the direction of cause and effect probably runs both ways. That is, women are able to enter the labor force because they have few children, and a commitment to work reduces both the desire and the need to have many children. Clearly, married women who work outside the home, especially those oriented toward careers, do have fewer offspring than the nonemployed. Variations in fertility are also associated with educational attainment: the higher the level of education, the fewer the offspring, and we have already documented the expanding educational horizons of women currently in their childbearing years.

From 1965 to the present, the fertility rates and expectations of American women have moved toward smaller families. As women complete college and delay marriage, the median age at birth of a first child has also risen. Today, the daughters of the baby boom are in their prime childbearing years, and while most expect to have at least one child, a large number are deferring childbearing until after age thirty. But even women who begin childbearing in their twenties have low fertility expectations, with only three in ten anticipating more than two offspring (O'Connell 1991).

When low fertility goes hand in hand with increasing life expectancy—close to eighty years on average for American women born today—childbearing and child rearing will absorb only a small fraction of a woman's life. When linked to higher educational attainment and the relative fragility of contemporary marriages, such demographic realities enhance the likelihood that a woman will enter the paid labor force and remain there more continuously than in the past. Thus, a majority of American women will have the opportunity to develop a sense of self outside the traditional role of wife-mother, as well as to experience the obstacles and discrimination still prevalent in the workplace.

Women with few child-care obligations and those working outside the home (whether for pay or not) are "structurally available" for social movement recruitment, simply by virtue of not being isolated within the home. Nonemployed women with few offspring will also have time and energy to devote to movement activities; while those who are both employed and mothers have a doubly marginal position that enables them to take a critical stance toward both employment and motherhood as social institutions.

Housewives and Housework. What of the women who heeded the call to renounce work outside the home in favor of devoting themselves to the "labor of love" within the household? The 1950s are generally perceived as an era of domestic bliss in the United States, in which the fertility rate almost doubled that of the Depression years. The newly built suburbs drew millions of middle-class families from the cities; husbands, as members of the small birth cohorts of the Depression years, experienced unprecedented opportunities for upward mobility with the dramatic expansion of white-collar jobs (Oppenheimer 1982). Wives found themselves isolated in these new communities, continually encouraged by the media to reach ever-higher levels of consumership and cleanliness. In these circumstances the majority of suburban women devoted themselves to caring for their achieving husbands and their three or four offspring.

Despite the introduction of "labor-saving" devices such as freezers, clothes washers and dryers, and dishwashing machines, there was little change in the time spent on homemaking tasks between the 1920s and 1960s—nonemployed homemakers spent an average of 51 hours a week in 1924, and 55 hours four decades later (Vanek 1974). The time once spent in food preparation was used to shop for it; and the laundry that middle-class households once sent out was being done by wives in the home (Strasser 1982).

At the same time, many tasks once performed within the household were given to experts outside the home: most notably, the education of children, food preparation, and a variety of social services to family members. As Ryan (1979) puts it, as this type of work left the home, so finally did the women themselves, to perform outside what they had done inside: school teaching, nursing, social work, and food preparation and handling.

During this period, also, child-care tasks expanded, not so much because women were having more children but because they made a greater parental investment in the well-being of each child. Childcare became a more socioemotional task, as the middle-class family attempted to transmit a general level of school-tested competence, thus emphasizing the educational role of the mother, while the working-class family attempted to defend against breakup and downward mobility, thus casting the mother in the moral role of stabilizer (Ryan 1981).

For wives and mothers who steadfastly remained in the home, true happiness often proved elusive. Ultimately, as we know from events of the 1960s, a creeping sense of isolation in a daytime ghetto, of exclusion from the "real world" of power and prestige, led to vague feelings of discontent. Obliged to perform tasks once done by servants but now upgraded and mechanized, the suburban woman became a housewife in a more complete way than ever before. Many women began to perceive the restrictions of their lives, but until the emergence of the new feminism they lacked a frame of reference in which to interpret their discontent.

We must also remember that not all segments of the population shared in the prosperity of the 1950s. Many studies of working-class white families and communities during that decade found that interests and activities remained sharply divided by sex, in contrast to the new norm of "togetherness" that characterized middle-class family life. But as primary consumers of family advice columns in newspapers and magazines, women of all classes developed expectations of mutuality and partnership that men of that era did not necessarily share (Komarovsky 1962). The desire to change their husband and restructure their marriage along more companionate lines made many working-class women receptive to feminism.

African-American families also did not share the general prosperity of the 1950s. As with wives and mothers of the white working-class, women of color combined paid employment with their own housework, family caregiving, and personal strivings for autonomy but found little recognition or support for their double burden—from either their husbands or the wider society. Unlike their working-class white counterparts, African-American women remained largely confined to domestic labor in both their paid and unpaid work. Although it is often assumed that the ultimate ambition of African-American women is to become full-time housewives, dependent on stable wage-earning husbands, their daily struggle for survival and the many varieties of discrimination they have experienced (including social reforms aimed at bolstering the position of minority males) have brought many women of color into the embrace of the new feminism (hooks 1989; Collins 1990).

Women without Husbands.   Poverty is a powerful predictor of family instability and breakdown through desertion, divorce, and separation. Although divorce today is not uncommon at any social class level, there is more of it among the poor. One of the latent consequences of the companionate marriage ideal is that there are few compelling reasons to remain in a relationship that fails to provide affection or is clearly destructive. Thus, modern marriage systems are also characterized by high rates of divorce. Today, the probability of a newly formed marriage remaining intact for thirty years or more is roughly 50 percent. Because most divorced people remarry, at any given moment the great majority of American adults are in a marriage relationship. But for a number of years many women will be heads of single-parent households.

Most divorced women must earn enough to care for themselves and their children. In 1990, fewer than half of the 57 percent of divorced women who were awarded child support received the full amount due, and even fewer received any alimony payments (Bureau of the Census 1991d). Overall, payment from an ex-husband account-ed for less than one-fourth of the total income of these women. Since 1975, there have been approximately one million divorces a year, forc-ing large numbers of women with children onto the welfare rolls or into the labor force, typically in low-skill, low-paying employment (Okin 1991). In both their family and their work lives, then, millions of American women will have experienced the less beneficial aspects of being female.

African-American women are particularly likely to be raising chil-dren without the financial or emotional support of a husband. Because women's wages are typically too low to support dependents without assistance, and because the wages of minority women are especially low, African-American mothers supporting children have had to devel-op ways of sharing income and childcare. Families composed of sever-al generations of female kin are one alternative that not only makes financial survival possible but encourages female solidarity and an appreciation for both paid work and housework as essential contribu-tions to family well-being, a combination that can become a powerful impetus to feminism. Women of any race or ethnicity who must raise children without the support of a husband tend also to appreciate the importance of female independence and self-sufficiency, as well as family cooperation and solidarity that goes beyond the limits of the conventional nuclear family.

Another group of potential recruits to feminism were the growing numbers of "displaced homemakers"—older women who through divorce or widowhood have been left without financial support. Their children are too old to qualify them for family welfare programs, yet they themselves are too young to receive Social Security benefits. Thrust into the labor market with few skills, and subject to the general cultural devaluation of older women, many have been attracted to self-help groups and organizations concerned with their special needs.

These women have been victimized by the double standards of both aging and gender, but they also lack many of the resources needed to fight actively for change (Jacobs 1991).

These various changes in the institution of marriage and family life—in sexual mores, marriage ideals, fertility, and marital stability— constitute the reality of the lives of most women. As with the trends in employment and education described earlier in this chapter, changes both empowered women and confronted them with new obstacles. The home was no refuge.

The period between 1920 and 1960 was thus a very different environment from that which nurtured the earlier phase of American feminism. Historian William Chafe suggests that the earlier movement failed to survive because "the day-to-day structure of most women's lives reinforced the existing distribution of sex roles. . . . The real problem was a social milieu which proved inhospitable to more far-reaching change" (1977:119). The New Feminist Movement, on the other hand, has grown out of prevailing social trends and is thus grounded in the actual experiences of women—at work and at home—that have reinforced the perceptions both of inequality and unfairness, *and* of change and new opportunities, some of which brought women into direct competition with men (Rosenfeld and Ward 1991). The earlier movement went as far as the challenge to male supremacy could go at that historical moment. It required four decades of basic social change to create the conditions for the emergence of the third wave. Moreover, the early twentieth-century movement itself contributed to the rise of its daughter movement (Giele 1995; Rupp and Taylor 1987).

Political Trends

The Coalition after Suffrage. Having achieved their primary goal of bringing women into the political process, at least at the level of the right to vote, the various partners in the suffrage movement went their separate ways. The coalition could not have held together much longer in any event, given the deep divisions within its ranks. Some suffragists saw the movement as an opportunity to extend a basic American right to deserving segments of the female population. Angry that "drunken male immigrant layabouts" could vote while educated ladies could not, they held a longstanding elitist position, marked by explicit racism and anti-immigrant sentiment.

Other suffragists perceived the vote as a means of influencing legislation to protect the less fortunate, particularly impoverished and exploited immigrant and African-American girls and women, a long-standing anti-elitist position that united women across lines of social class (Tax 1980). Such alliances had been successful in organizing women workers and in providing community and neighborhood supports for housewives and mothers in the years before suffrage. These activists wanted newly enfranchised women to use their votes to transform society, to protect the weak (most often women and children), and to increase social equality—goals that were considered generally progressive and humane rather than distinctly feminist (Gordon 1989).

Only a minority of movement "radicals" viewed the vote as the first step toward full equality for all women. They were not very successful in promoting this vision among other members of the coalition, or in enlisting the support of the new generation of young women coming of age in the Roaring Twenties with its promise of sexual freedom, so often confused with liberation from gender role restrictions. The more the radicals insisted on the importance of organizing women to fight for their own special interests, the more they were ridiculed as "old fashioned" (Hacker 1951; Rupp and Taylor 1987).

As a result, with the exception of Alice Paul's National Women's Party (NWP), few women's organizations in the decades between 1920 and 1960 embraced explicitly feminist goals, and even the NWP had only one plank in its platform—passage of an equal rights amendment (Rupp and Taylor 1987). Rather, women's concerns were folded into the programs of many different organizations and groups. Many women shifted their attention to other social movements: for example, temperance, with its aim of restoring family security among the working class; settlement houses, concerned with improving the lot of the poor and immigrant population: birth control and family planning; or union organizing (then illegal) for better working conditions among all wage earners.

In addition, there were formal organizations such as the National Federation of Business and Professional Women's Clubs (BPW), the League of Women Voters (LWV) and the American Association of University Women (AAUW), whose members were very much aware of issues relating to the health and welfare of women and children, and who could be counted on to exert political pressure over particular pieces of legislation. And there were many such pieces of legislation over the next few decades for which the support of women's groups was essential: child protection laws, workplace safety rules, consumer rights, and public health programs.

Still, it was difficult to pinpoint a "women's vote" in the same sense that politicians spoke of other voting blocs such as farmers, Catholics, Jews, or southerners. Indeed, women's voting rates remained lower than men's throughout the next five decades, most likely as a lingering effect of domestic values among those born before World War I. Women also failed to rally around female candidates. On issues that did not have an obvious "women's" component, voters—both male and female—were influenced by their many other social identities: race, religion, ethnicity, region of the country, rural/urban residence, and the like (Buechler 1990). Although they had achieved the right to vote, its effect was less than they had hoped.

Yet it can also be argued that women needed experience in organizations they themselves controlled before they could gain the assurance and skills required to compete in male-dominated institutions (Freedman 1979). In this view, the Women's Christian Temperance Union, League of Women Voters, the National Federation of Business and Professional Women's Clubs, and even local women's organizations and PTAs served the crucial function of bringing women together and heightening their consciousness of being female and relatively powerless. Far from being a diversion, participation in organizations run by women was an essential precondition of the new feminism, especially when it allowed members to maintain a "women's culture" through separate institutions (Cott 1987; Rupp and Taylor 1987). Many feminists today see such a culture as an important source of support and esteem, which also encourages women to move on to the larger political scene.

Women in Electoral Politics. Moving into the world of politics has been a slow process for women. Between 1920 and 1970, few women ran for office, and even fewer were elected. On rare occasions, a widow entered Congress "over the dead body" of her husband, selected by a state governor to fill her husband's remaining term of office. Although the few women who filled a "widow's term" were typically politically active and able women, it was not expected that they would subsequently be nominated in their own right. This pattern was broken by Margaret Chase Smith of Maine who not only completed her husband's term but was reelected four times to the House of

Representatives before serving four additional six-year terms in the Senate. Later, both Maureen Neuberger of Oregon and Lindy Boggs of Louisiana were nominated and elected to Congress at the conclusion of their widow's term. Smith was the only woman senator throughout her two decades of office, and after she died, there were no others until 1978. As late as 1984, there were only two women senators out of 100, and nineteen women among the 435 members of the House of Representatives.

The first woman governor also entered over her husband's body (he was impeached in 1917): "Ma" Ferguson of Texas, who served two terms in the 1920s. It was not until 1974 that a nonwidowed woman (Ella Grasso of Connecticut) was elected governor on her own political record, and even then she faced hostility, as in the campaign slogan "Connecticut needs a governor not a governess."

Up to the 1970s, most women interested in politics were found in the lower ranks of campaign organizations—they were the envelope-stuffers and stamp-lickers without whom many a male candidate could not have won. Politically active women were able to make careers out of party organizational work, but unlike men of similar experience, they lacked an independent constituency to give them leverage within the party and were rarely supported for elective office. After suffrage, both the Republican and Democratic parties established state and national female cochairmanships of the party organization. Despite their titles and responsibilities, these women had little independent power; male party leaders chose loyal subordinates, not competitors (Freeman 1987).

Other highly political feminists who remained active after suffrage found a home in the National Woman's Party, the International League for Peace and Freedom, or the many union and socialist organizations of the 1930s, and in nonelective government offices. In general, however, political women faced the same dilemma as those interested in careers or higher education: the spirit was there but the support system was lacking. There was little encouragement in the culture or the social structure, or even in their interpersonal networks, for combining marriage, child rearing, and demanding responsibilities outside the home.

Yet many did remain in the political arena, although the 1920s offered little in the way of opportunity or recognition. The possibility of political power and influence came a decade later, with Franklin Roosevelt and the New Deal. By this time, many activist women had won a degree of recognition within the Democratic party and the labor movement—not leadership roles, but reputations for hard work and dedication. Some, such as Mary Anderson, head of the Women's Bureau of the Department of Labor, had been in place during previous administrations, but the New Deal brought increased responsibility to her department. Others, such as Frances Perkins, entered the Roosevelt cabinet at the top (as Secretary of Labor from 1933 to 1945), and still others moved into decision-making jobs at lower levels of the bureaucracy. While many of these women had received their political training in the suffrage movement, they entered government not as feminists first but social activists for many causes. In advancing the goals of their departments and bureaus—largely charged with social welfare programs—they also protected and extended the rights of women. The historian Susan Ware (1981) describes the network of personal and professional interests that bound together twenty-eight high-ranking women in the New Deal. These women were able to work together out of an overriding commitment to the cause of improved health, security, and welfare for all Americans. They wished to become role models of competence and dedication for other women, yet at no time did they openly confront the basic sources of discrimination against women or attack the ideals of patriarchy. The influence they exercised in the 1930s gradually declined as the New Deal itself drew back from major program initiatives, and as the war in Europe absorbed Roosevelt's attention.

It took another two decades for women's political influence once more to reach the level of the early days of the New Deal. With the exception of Margaret Chase Smith and Eleanor Roosevelt, few women's voices—much less, staunchly feminist ones—reached the public. Nonetheless, an important precedent had been set: women could handle the rigors of public office, administer a cabinet department, and represent a politically powerful constituency. Eleanor Roosevelt became an internationally recognized symbol of America's humanitarian concerns, most especially where the well-being of women and children was at stake. Because of her high symbolic value, she was selected by President John F. Kennedy to chair a special commission on the status of women in the United States that he had promised to create during his successful 1960 campaign, partly in response to continued lobbying by the NWP.

By this time, several dozen talented women had risen to positions of influence in both the Democratic and Republican parties, but it was the Kennedy staff that most clearly saw the potential appeal of women's issues. Emphasizing the traditional association of the Democratic party with social welfare programs most beneficial to women, and also embracing the newer demands for equal treatment although not an equal rights amendment, the Kennedy campaign brought women's issues back into the political forum.

By 1960, there were many female—and feminist—bureaucrats who had worked their way up through the system from the days of Roosevelt and Truman. They constituted a critical mass in the "woodwork" of the administration in Washington and various state capitals. Relatively invisible, but capable and well-connected, these women entered government in administrative posts largely concerned with health, education, and welfare programs. Having mastered the tasks of managing programs and dealing with legislatures, they were now in positions of influence, and available for recruitment to the new feminism. In chapter 3 we shall see just how crucial to the movement these women would soon be.

Conclusions

Thus the stage is set for the emergence of the powerful social movements of the 1960s. The four decades under review in this chapter were characterized by numerous shifts in values, attitudes, and beliefs concerning the proper roles of men and women in the workplace and in the home. Changes in access to crucial opportunities and resources gave women greater control than in the past over their productive and reproductive labor (Brenner and Laslett 1991). The old structures of thought and behavior could scarcely accommodate these changes. Traditional assumptions of inferiority and subordination were undermined, but as we will see in the next chapter, these changes needed to be analyzed and interpreted to create a social movement that would directly challenge male authority and power.

It is the function of a movement organization to provide such a frame of reference—an ideology that gives meaning and shape to these everyday experiences, and an agenda for action to bring about desired change and to mobilize a resource base of potential members, funds, access to media, and so forth (Snow and Benford 1988). This organization is linked to an external environment; that is, there will be historical moments in which certain actions are likely to be more (or less) successful, and historical conditions under which changes can endure or be turned back. Each of these elements seemed to fall into place in the early 1960s. All that was needed was the script, the set of ideas that could initiate action and structure events. The ideas, ideals, and ideology of the New Feminist Movement are the subject of the next chapter.

The Miss America Pageant protest of 1968 gave rise to the image of feminists as "bra burners." In fact, no undergarments were burned, but bras, girdles, curlers, makeup, and spiked heels were put into a "freedom trashcan" to symbolize rejection of cultural ideals of femininity that confine and distort women's bodies. *Photograph by Miriam Bokser.*

Chapter 2

Ideas, Ideals, and Ideology

If there is anything on which students of social movements agree, it is that a series of social, economic, and even cultural changes, no matter how dramatic, does not by itself give rise to a social movement. The considerable changes in the status and opportunities of American women described in the previous chapter were nonetheless important. They produced the conditions that made it difficult, if not impossible, to sustain a women's movement after suffrage, but at the same time created conditions that by the 1960s made it impossible to ignore women's second-class status. But social movements, which are organized efforts to change social arrangements, are different from broad currents of social change that take place without the intention of producing a specific outcome.

In this chapter we discuss the general problem of bringing a social movement into existence, the ideas people use to define the kind of change worth striving for, and the strategies adopted for accomplishing their goals. These ideological elements, in conjunction with available resources, generate the organizational forms that permit people to act collectively.

The Basis of Social Movements

Social movements do not emerge only because there is a problem in society. Problems always exist, but only certain conditions are protested and not even these at all times. It is obvious, for example, that American women faced a great many barriers in the 1930s and

1950s but did not then organize to fight for their rights. What does it take to construct a social movement that credibly represents the demands and aspirations of a group? Four factors are typically identified: grievances, collective identity, organization, and opportunity.

Grievances.   One way to explain the lack of protest over intolerable situations is to assume that many people are not bothered by terrible conditions. That is, individuals become reconciled to poverty and so protest only when they suffer further impoverishment; again, women may become accustomed to the idea that their husbands will beat them and so get angry only when the assaults increase. This line of reasoning explains protest as a result of changes in "grievance level": if people are not complaining, then they must not be unhappy. The idea that women who join the women's movement are more unhappy than other women and that those who do not join are satisfied with their situation is an example of this type of thinking. Actually, many people in extremely miserable conditions will never join any social movement because their situation seems so hopeless or because they have no energy left from the struggle for survival. Moreover, many people are joiners rather than leaders and will only be activated if there is an appropriate organization for them to join.

Relative Deprivation.   Although the grievance level alone cannot explain why protest emerges when it does, the translation of objective problems into subjectively experienced grievances is an important factor. Social comparison can help to establish a sense of what is fair or unfair, and to make people angry rather than simply unhappy. Problems often become protestable grievances when individuals see themselves as members of a group that is not doing well relative to some comparison group (Runciman 1966; Vanneman and Pettigrew 1972). Freeman argues that middle-class women in the 1960s became candidates for a protest movement as the gap in education between women and men closed, while differences in "qualitative and quantitative occupational rewards" widened, so that women saw themselves as relatively disadvantaged (1975, 31–32).

Perceived Costs and Benefits.   Another grievance-based explanation focuses on the expected costs and benefits of change. A generalized sense of trust supports social order by creating the perception that the government works for the long-run good of all (Gamson 1968; Paige 1971). When the government or the social system is seen as legitimate, people tend to interpret problems as individual failings or as unfortunate side effects of necessary policies (Kluegel and Smith 1982; Pettigrew 1979). By eroding this generalized trust, the other social movements of the 1960s made change seem more acceptable and protest actions more necessary.

However, even in times of change, participation in a social movement involves risks. People with grievances may not protest because of perceived costs—a broken marriage, a lost job, the ridicule of friends. Women demanding change on behalf of women risk the relationships with men that ensure certain privileges, and perhaps even their survival. Repression effectively increases the costs of involvement with a social movement. Yet once a social movement appears successful, other kinds of change seem more probable and less risky. Thus the naive assumption in early women's liberation articles that "The [New Left] Revolution" was just around the corner (e.g., Dunbar 1970) made feminist participation seem easier and more rewarding.

Collective Identity. A second factor in the emergence of a social movement is the sense of identification with a group that is able to act collectively, particularly among people with the resources to spare for movement activities. A group of individuals only becomes a collective actor when there is (1) a sense of identification with the fortunes of the group as a whole, and (2) a desire to change society on behalf of the collectivity (Melucci 1989). Neither of these aspects of collective identity is automatically present just because people share a social designation (such as "woman" or "Latino"). Identity emerges in the process of struggle.

Group Consciousness. Identification with a demographically defined category is always difficult, but particularly so for a group's relatively privileged members, who tend to disassociate themselves from the less fortunate in order to avoid sharing the latter's social stigma (Tilly 1978). In addition to this general tendency, women have special problems of group consciousness.

Describing women's lack of "minority group consciousness" in the 1940s, Hacker (1951) noted that unlike many racial and ethnic minorities, women were not socially segregated but were attached to men who provided protection and a limited amount of social power. Marriage as an economic contract and segregation on the job also meant that women competed with other women but rarely with men. As Jo Freeman, a founding feminist, describes herself in premovement days, "[I was] one of many girls who had internalized an individualistic version of what Betty Friedan was to call the 'three sex theory': there's men, there's women, and there's me. Thus, it was quite possible for me to share the socially accepted prejudices against women without ever drawing the appropriate conclusions about my own inferiority" (1975, viii). It was not uncommon for achieving women in the period between the 1930s and 1960s to feel that they had to choose between basing their identity on being a professional or on being a woman (Cott 1987).

Because identification with "a group called women" is necessary for collective action, it must be developed and nurtured (Cassell 1977). Social networks play a crucial role. People in the same social networks interact, exchange information, and, when they share a worldview, also develop a strong sense of attachment and common purpose (Mueller 1992). Those networks that have developed a common basis for sympathy with the goals of a social movement are said to be co-optable (Freeman 1973). While not explicitly feminist, co-optable submerged networks of women activists in such diverse locations as government offices, labor unions, and the civil rights movement were a precondition for the emergence of a sense of collective identity as women. This shared identity became the framework for interpreting their common experiences in a new light (Freeman 1973; Melucci 1989). Co-optable networks included formal organizations (e.g., the YWCA), other social movements (e.g., the New Left), and informal links (e.g., the office grapevine).

Empowerment. The feeling of "we-ness" allows people to frame problems as collective rather than individual and thus changes the way they seek solutions. The perception of gender solidarity offers a new way for women to interpret their life. This "click" experience, as *Ms.* magazine dubbed it, involves not simply a personal reaction but a new *feeling* — one of connection with other women with whom one has power to act collectively. This sense of empowerment opens the door to organizing for change by making people believe that things could be different. Successful organizational experiences, in turn, enhance the perception of collective strength that can reach across issues and other allegiances (Bookman and Morgan 1988). In this sense, many of the social changes and challenges of the 1950s and 1960s were empowering for the women who participated in them (Barnett 1994).

Representation. Collective identity is interactional—not simply a state of mind but a way of acting and being reacted to as a member of a group. Becoming a collective actor is thus an accomplishment, an identity that the individual has actively created in concert with others. Understanding oneself as acting on behalf of a larger group requires a definition of what that constituency represents, a claim to know, for example, what "women" want. During the 1940s and 1950s, those groups that called themselves "the women's movement" received little social validation, because even activist women tended to share the general belief that feminism was old-fashioned or a "dead" issue in postwar America (Chafe 1991; Rupp and Taylor 1987). This meant that reclaiming a positive collective identity for women in the society at large would be an essential condition for reviving the women's movement in the 1960s (Mueller 1988).

Organization. A third factor in the emergence of a social movement is organization. Both informal networks and formal associations provide the material resources required by the movement. "Resource mobilization" models of social movements place particular emphasis on the enabling characteristics of organizations rather than on the grievances or collective identities of participants (McCarthy and Zald 1977). When organizations devote resources to sustaining members' commitment, they are engaged in maintenance activity; group effectiveness involves directly using resources to produce a specific outcome. Resource mobilization theories focus on strategies and tactics directed at effective political change (Gamson 1975).

Yet because collective identity is an important factor in creating an effective social movement, the line between maintenance and goal-directed activities becomes blurred. "Working-class culture," for example, is partly a product of socialist organizing in the nineteenth century, but to the extent that it does exist, it reinforces the impression of the "working class" as an entity worthy of political representation (Thompson 1963). Similarly, creating and using a "women's culture" was a strategic choice open to the New Feminist Movement. Ironically, the very women's organizations and culture that were widely perceived as politically irrelevant in the 1950s and early 1960s nonetheless provided resources crucial to the emergence of a revived women's movement. For this reason, feminist theorists have expanded the concept of the "political" precisely to include such community and cultural organizations (Christiansen-Ruffman 1994; Ng 1988). Each wave of American feminism appears to have left a legacy of organizations that served as resources to later mobilizers (Mueller 1988).

Resources. The rise and fall of protest activities and thus of public recognition of the movement's existence depends to a large extent on the resources available to the group. *Social ties* are an important resource because people who are already participants in formal or informal networks are easier to recruit than are isolated individuals (McAdam 1988). Active participation, especially if it involves personal risk, requires a "push" as well as the "pull" of value agreement. The push could be the invitation or encouragement of friends or colleagues, or even the fear of appearing to be a coward in their eyes.

Time, money, and space are important generalized resources that make collective action possible, even such simple acts as printing an advertisement or distributing a leaflet. There are also more specific resources required for effective mobilization. Leadership—as innovative action, not hierarchical command—can convert potential into actual contributions from others. Media coverage is necessary to reach the public at large and activate additional resources. Access to decision-makers in other areas not only broadens the base of mobilization but can often neutralize potential opposition.

When social networks and material resources come together, the odds for effective mobilization are greatly increased. For example, labor union women who participated in the various state commissions on the status of women in the early 1960s used the phone banks and mimeograph machines of their unions to help launch the National Organization for Women (NOW).

Opportunity. A fourth factor contributing to the emergence of a movement is the amount and kind of opportunities for change to be found within the targeted social structures. On the one hand, existing belief systems provide ideological elements that can be creatively combined to promote change. These shared beliefs can be invoked to generate support for movement goals, as when Civil Rights groups called upon religious leaders to support their call for justice. On the other hand, even widely held beliefs about the need for change will not encourage mobilization if no mechanism for change can be identified. Both general goals and specific tactics are important aspects of the movement's relationship to its environment.

Frames. To convince others of the importance of certain social goals, the issues must be framed in the context of shared ideals and assumptions about reality (Snow and Benford 1988). Even within broad movements such as feminism, specific organizations will find that public support will vary dramatically depending on how they frame the issue of equality: Is it a problem of women of a certain race or class gaining the same rights as their male peers, or is it an issue of creating equal opportunity for all women and men?

Movements typically gain support when their proposals are framed so that they address widespread concerns and connect with widely held values. In some cases, this means that a movement's radical claims must be presented in modest language (Spalter-Roth and Schreiber, 1994). In other cases, the rhetoric of conflict may appear to be about a single issue, such as abortion, yet invoke wider frames of values about rights, religion, and motherhood (Luker 1984; Condit 1990.)

Cycles. In most societies, protest comes in waves, with mobilization around any given issue touching off unrest among other social groups. Authorities' responses to movement actions tends to co-opt some participants and to radicalize others, leading to different tactics at different points in a protest cycle (Tarrow 1990). The outcome of one wave of protest then provides the baseline of expectations and resources with which the next wave mobilizes. Opportunities for new advantages, such as a change in government or the entry of new constituencies into the system, provide openings that movements may be more or less able to exploit, depending on the first three factors: the nature of grievances; the presence of collective actors; and the availability of resources. Historically, the women's movement has benefited from cycles of protest led by African-Americans in which issues of justice, equality, and rights become salient.

In chapter 1, we outlined the problems and possibilities that confronted women in the 1960s. Women had very real grievances in the areas of work, sexuality, and family life. They had also acquired greater resources in education, income, and time than were available to women during the Depression, World War II, and the postwar decades of domesticity and fertility. They had experienced empowerment as members of women-led organizations and in the struggle for social justice that began with the Civil Rights movement of the 1950s. New ideas about achievement, equality, and intimacy had created an audience for a revived and revised feminism. In the next section of this chapter, we examine the ideological framework of the movement, the traditions upon which it drew, and the contributions of the creative thinkers who framed this message in language that resonated to the experiences and needs of many American women.

The Ideological Framework of Feminism

To understand the feminist critique and agenda for change, it is first necessary to define the concept of "feminism." Because of the diversity of feminist groups and feminist issues, confusion over the meaning of the term is common. No person or group in or outside the women's movement, including ourselves, is in a position to offer an authoritative definition, but there are elements that, taken together, characterize a feminist worldview.

Feminist Principles.   The first and most basic claim of feminism is that women are a special category of people with certain characteristics in common, whether owing to biology (e.g., the ability to give birth) or experience (e.g., the responsibility for feeding and nurturing children), whether fixed (e.g., being mothers) or historically and culturally variable (e.g., being housewives).

The second premise is that only women should define what is feminine. It is for women to say what women are like, what women want, what women enjoy, what women can do. This means both that each individual woman must be the judge of what is right for her, and that women can, by pooling experiences and sharing insights, arrive at a collective understanding of what it is to be a woman.

The third basic principle of feminism is a recognition of and dissatisfaction with living in a "man's world," where men define a "good" woman as one who meets their expectations, who serves and pleases them, who follows the rules they have created. Feminists are acutely aware that men have the power, but not the right, to do this.

Consequently, the fourth basic claim that feminism makes is for radical (root) change: to end men's unjust power, and claim for women what is rightfully theirs. For feminists, the crucial question in seeking change is what is good for women. In this view, making the world meet women's needs is not a means to some other goal, such as peace, socialism, or individual freedom, but an end in itself. Although placed fourth, in some ways this claim is the most essential character- istic of the feminist perspective. Many women accept the first three premises but do not go on from there to imagine the possibility of a different world. They say, "It's a man's world. . . . Boys will be boys. . . . What else could you expect from a man? . . . Women's work is never done. . . . "; this is how it has always been, and women will have to make the best of it. In contrast, feminism rejects the idea that women's subordination is natural and inevitable, the price paid for being born female. Change is possible, but it requires struggle; there- fore, women must take control of their own destiny.

Despite agreement on these fundamental principles, there is great diversity in ideas for realizing social change, stemming from the differ- ent ideological roots from which feminism has grown.

The Historical Roots of Feminism. Although the 1960s mark the emergence of a second major American feminist movement, femi- nism itself is much older. Even though there have always been individ- ual women who struggled to define themselves on their own terms, feminism as a system of ideas with widespread appeal dates from the mid-eighteenth century, when the industrial revolution had dissolved traditional social relationships and vastly accelerated the pace of change so that the issue of women's place became a topic of concern. In the flux of changing institutional patterns and values, new possibili- ties for personal freedom and individual achievement emerged. These options had to be opened or closed to women; they could not be ignored. For middle-class men, it was a matter of balancing their own freedom from traditional authority against the potential loss of their power over women. For working-class men, the extreme poverty of early capitalism seemed the result rather than the cause of women's growing independence. For both, a "place" had to be found for women that would not challenge male control. As men debated what women's place and women's nature should be, early feminists such as Mary Wollstonecraft asserted their right to determine this for themselves, not in terms of what would please men, but on the basis of what was good for women.

Many of the beliefs about women's nature and role in society that are called "traditional" are thus in actuality no older than feminist ideas; both developed a few centuries ago. But it was the men's definitions that prevailed and were subsequently transformed into actual new social relationships (e.g., the devotion of women's energies to full-time mothering of a limited number of children). These patterns have now acquired a taken-for-granted quality that makes them difficult to challenge. The status quo is thus perceived as representing some timeless "traditional" view of women, rather than as the outcome of a history of struggle in which feminists also won some battles. The idea of women as more moral than men, for example, was seen as shockingly feminist before the nineteenth century. Coeducation is another battle feminists won, although it remains a hollow victory when boys are given support that their female classmates do not receive.

Three Feminist Traditions.   Three intellectual traditions have nourished feminism, each imparting its own particular character and learnings. Olive Banks (1981) speaks of these as the three "faces" of feminism, each pointing in a different direction. These three traditions—moral reform, liberalism, and socialism—share certain concerns but also diverge in ways that greatly affect feminist thinking.

Moral Reform.   Moral reformers often draw their conclusions from religious premises, such as a belief that social justice is God's work. The moral reform tradition of advocacy for the oppressed and for world peace is a particularly strong element in reform Judaism, liberal Christianity, and Unitarianism and Quakerism. Moral reformers have a strong sense of identification with the poor, an aversion to violence (hence the commitment to nonviolent direct action), a vision of human relationships that affirms the dignity and value of each person, and a commitment to social and economic arrangements that would make such interpersonal relationships possible. This tradition influenced feminists to stress the link between the personal and the political, as integrity requires attention to how one acts in "little things" as well as in major decisions. Moreover, moral reformers condemn economic relationships that distort and corrupt our yearnings for human affection and self-realization.

In the nineteenth century, moral reform feminists fought against slavery and prostitution ("white slavery"), as well as the double standard in sexual relations. They tried to establish temperance in the use of alcohol and to provide social supports for immigrants. Most of these goals would improve the status of women (who were then, as now, overrepresented among the poor and exploited) as well as express the moral values that reformers thought women possessed in greater measure than did men. The moral reform tradition can be seen in the contemporary feminist concern with nonexploitive sexuality, in the demand for consistency in personal and political life, in the outrage over male violence, in the belief that women are "natural" pacifists or bearers of a distinctive ethic of care, and in efforts to provide support and protection to women who are victims of physical abuse and/or economic exploitation. The moral reform tradition is often most evident in what are called radical feminist groups today.

Liberalism. The liberal tradition of individualism and equal rights is based on the Enlightenment belief in the power of reason and personal development, as well as on the ideals of the French and American revolutions. Liberals see individuals as shaped by their experiences, particularly by their formal and informal education, which should develop each person's particular talents and prepare her/him for responsible citizenship. Classical liberalism affirms merit based on individual achievement (rather than status ascribed by birth), equality of rights as citizens (rather than a distinction between rulers and subjects), a social order based on contract (rather than divine law), and a minimum of social restraint on individual action (rather than a prescribed set of social obligations).

Not all liberals intended these principles to be applied to everyone; the "Founding Fathers" consciously excluded both women and blacks, appealing to "natural subordination" to deny women the right to vote, to be educated, to enter into contracts, to support themselves, or to live independently. Arguing that there were no fundamental differences in the nature of women and men that would legitimate this exclusion, liberal feminists—whether Mary Wollstonecraft in the eighteenth century or Betty Friedan in the twentieth—have stressed the importance for women of being, in Virginia Woolf's words, "independent of mind and of means." The liberal tradition can be seen in the contemporary feminist emphasis on a woman's need for her own income, on access to any and all occupations and to the responsibilities and privileges of citizenship, on the right to control her own body, and on the importance of education.

Socialism. The socialist tradition includes Marx and Engels but has an even longer history. Although Marxists distinguish their "scientific" socialism from "utopian" socialism, this distinction has more to do with the means of achieving socialism than with their vision of socialist society. Socialist principles affirm a society based on mutual support and the recognition of human needs, on collective decision-making and pooled resources, and on the value of work as a human activity. Socialism condemns the profit motive and individual rivalry, believing that greed and competition must be actively restrained for a caring community to emerge. In the caring community, many of the functions of the traditional family would be assumed by society as a whole—physical care of children, the elderly, and the ill; economic support for those unable to work; decisions about allocation of labor, and so forth.

In extending special benefits to mothers and underwriting many of the costs of childbearing, socialist governments in Eastern and Western Europe realized certain elements of this care-taking community. But socialist governments replicated the negative elements of the patriarchal family as well: reliance on the uncertain benevolence of the male-dominated state and men's definitions of what was good for women. Abuses of power by the "guardian" state, especially in Eastern Europe, and its failure to challenge the gender division of labor made it clear that socialism did not live up to its promise to liberate women. Socialist feminists critiqued its ideal of a heroic male worker, freed from child rearing by the paid and unpaid labor of women, and vainly sought a complete revaluation of women's work. The socialist tradition in feminism is particularly evident in attempts to develop communal alternatives to the nuclear family, in efforts to eliminate inhumane working conditions and to recognize and reward housework as labor, and in the emphasis on egalitarianism and collective decision-making.

To summarize, feminism is not a single point of view but a set of principles for interpreting the status of women and demanding change. The particular nature of the interpretation and demands depends on the broader ideological perspective from which the world is seen. The three traditions of moral reform, liberalism, and socialism have historically provided such frameworks, so individuals and organizations that share these traditions will be part of co-optable networks for the reemergence and growth of feminism. The feminism generated in each tradition will have its own distinctive characteristics but will also share concerns with other feminists as well as with nonfeminists of the same tradition.

The Race Analogy. American feminism has long been associated with efforts to end racism and the oppression of black people, efforts that have had their roots in all three of the traditions described above. Among the earliest active feminists were Frances Wright and the Grimké sisters. Fanny Wright (1975–1852) campaigned for free public education for both boys and girls, for an end to slavery, and for the establishment of racially integrated communities. She was a socialist who predated Marx and, like many of the socialists of her time, she attempted to demonstrate her principles by establishing a "utopian" interracial community called Nashoba in Tennessee in 1825. The commune lasted only four years, but Wright continued to the end of her life to give well-attended lectures on the virtues of education, the corruption of slavery, and the dignity of the working class.

Sarah (1792–1873) and Angelina (1805–79) Grimké were antislavery activists in the moral reform tradition who fought for women's right to participate directly in the abolition movement and not merely as fund-raisers for men's projects. The Grimké sisters gave public lectures against slavery and for the right of women even to give public lectures. The link between feminism and black rights in the liberal tradition had been apparent even before the abolition movement. When Abigail Adams wrote to her husband, John, to "remember the ladies" in the new Declaration of Independence since "all men would be tyrants if they could," he wrote back that "I cannot but laugh. We have been told that our Struggle has loosened the bands of Government every where . . . that Indians slighted their Guardians and Negroes grew insolent to their Masters. But your letter was the first intimation that another tribe more numerous and powerfull than all the rest were grown discontented" (quoted in Rossi 1973, 11).

Black women, like Sojourner Truth (1795–1883) and Ida B. Wells (1862–1931), also fought actively on both fronts. Sojourner Truth was an ex-slave and active public speaker for abolition who also made impassioned and effective speeches for women's rights. She reminded both movements that they were ignoring African-American women for whom both race and sex were real oppressions. Wells was a journalist whose primary cause was the abolition of lynching. Since black men were often lynched on the pretext of a supposed sexual assault on "white womanhood," she worked not only to organize black women but also to mobilize white women's organizations to reject this vicious form of sexual politics (Davis 1981). Both Wells and Truth felt that the rights of women and blacks were inseparable in practice as well as in theory. Sojourner Truth made the connection clear in a speech in 1867 that could as easily have been delivered in 1967:

There is a great stir about colored men getting their rights, but not a word about colored women; and if colored men get their rights and not colored women theirs, you see the colored men will be masters over the women, and it will be just as bad as it was before. So I am for keeping the thing going while things are stirring; because if we wait again till it is still, it will take a great while to get it going again (quoted in Stimpson 1971, 636).

As a result not merely of these beginnings but of the ongoing association of women's rights with black rights both in principle and in practice, American feminists tend to frame women as a "minority" group.

The analogy of sex and race, common to all three major traditions, can be both helpful and troubling. It is helpful when it clarifies the extent to which disabilities facing both white women and African-Americans arise from their previous common status as property rather than persons, or when it illustrates the common stereotypes that are developed for subordinated people: neither intelligent nor ambitious, but childish and unreliable: happy with monotonous work and hard labor, but in need of "protection" in their nonwork lives. This analogy, prevalent in the nineteenth-century feminist movement, was reexamined in Gunnar Myrdal's famous study of racism, *An American Dilemma,* published in 1944 and widely read by black rights activists in the 1950s and 1960s. The appendix, entitled "A Parallel with the Negro Problem," gave a shock of recognition to many women students and Civil Rights workers. Feminists coined the term "sexism," on the model of racism, to describe a condition based on more than stereotyping and prejudice, an exclusion built into the very institutional framework of our society.

The link between sexism and racism becomes problematic when it is asserted that the processes of exploitation and liberation will necessarily be the same for both groups. One of the earliest claims made by women who were rediscovering feminism was that women were "the niggers of the world"; that is, that they were exploited in just the same fashion as blacks, but even more pervasively (Willis 1970, 56). Implicitly, however, claims about women's exploitation "as women" also obscured the variety of these experiences and established middle-class white women as a norm. As Spelman points out, the feminist belief that African-American, Asian-American, or Latin-American women could separate their "women's voice" from their racial or ethnic voice rested on a double standard: "while on the one hand there is a seamless web of whiteness and womanness, on the other hand, Blackness and womanness, say, or Indianness or womanness, are discrete and separable elements of identify.... In other words, the womanness underneath the Black woman's skin is a white woman's" (1988, 12).

The analogy "male is to female as white is to black" encouraged feminists to stress that women would have to organize separately from men. Marge Piercy, for example, argued: "We are oppressed, and we will achieve our liberation by fighting for it the same as any other oppressed group.... I once thought all that was necessary was to make men understand that they would achieve their own liberation, too, by joining in the struggle for women's liberation; but it has come to seem a little too much like the chickens trying to educate the chicken farmer. I think of myself as a house nigger who is a slow learner besides" (1970, 429).

Integration raised the danger of co-optation, of receiving too many advantages from the "master" to risk demanding change, so that even relationships with men that women found rewarding were seen as undesirable. Concepts such as imperialism and colonialism that describe the relations between countries were first extended to encompass "Third World people" within "first world" countries (e.g., racial minorities in the United States) and then by analogy to women, so that some feminists spoke of male control of women's bodies as "colonization." In this framework the solution is independence for women as a group rather than as discrete individuals. But this analogy hardly helps to clarify what collective independence would mean.

Separatism also builds on the minority group analogy in more positive ways, by acknowledging the value of a separate culture, first, as a source of social support for individuals whose own worth can be affirmed there as nowhere else in society and, second, as a practical contribution to resistance. Social movements depend heavily on the co-optable networks and group consciousness that a subculture can provide. Black churches, colleges, and communities contributed significantly to an African-American protest tradition. To what extent could women find or create a "woman's culture"? The danger in self-segregation as a strategy for change is that such isolation from the powerful can actually decrease access to resources and perpetuate powerlessness.

The minority group analogy is positively misleading, moreover, in its implication that women and blacks are distinct groups, ignoring black women entirely, that is, assuming that "all the women are white, all the blacks are men" (Hull, Scott, and Smith 1982) and that these "minority groups" are in competition with each other. In fact, black men, black women, and white women have each been taken advantage of in different ways, and thus now occupy different social and economic positions. Little is gained by comparing these positions and trying to decide who is worst off. As Stimpson notes: "Behind the competition for the unpleasant title of Most Oppressed Group in America lay a serious moral and political question. If history, which is so miserly about justice, is to help only one of several suffering groups, what standards can we possibly use to choose that group?" (1971, 638).

Effective coalitions can replace invidious distinctions only by recognizing "common differences" (Joseph and Lewis 1981). Race and sex are both used to oppress people, but they are differently institutionalized forms of inequality. White women can secure certain privileges within the system but also pay for them with personal subservience; black men are given license to exercise male privileges but only within the confines of the black community, and at great cost to black women; black women have more independence from the patriarchal family but are subject to extreme economic exploitation and poverty. Collins (1990) uses African-American women's experiences and critiques of the social order to formulate a vision of inclusive justice that she calls "black feminist thought."

Parallels between racism and sexism, therefore, must always be treated with caution. In some respects, the nature of oppression is illuminated; in other respects, essential differences are obscured (Spelman 1988). However, for contemporary feminists, including many women of color, this analogy was a steppingstone to their own increasingly sophisticated analyses of "woman's place."

Feminist Issues and Authors

For the generation of women who came of age in the 1940s and 1950s, feminism as an intellectual tradition was virtually invisible. The few authors who raised feminist concerns in those years went unread until they were rediscovered in the 1960s. The popular wisdom was expressed in Freudianism and functionalism, two approaches to social behavior that assumed gender differences were given by nature even while advising men and women to make constant efforts to adjust and conform to "nature." These beliefs were among the first targets of feminist critics, who claimed that the social sciences were being used not to understand reality but to construct it, and thus to control individual behavior (Friedan 1963; Weisstein 1970; Millett 1970). As a consequence, the nature of sex differences in reality and in ideology became a crucial issue in the development of feminist theory.

Sex Role Stereotyping and the Limitation of Human Potential. The recognition that many of the observed differences between men and women were created and maintained by arbitrary beliefs and social arrangements was greatly helped by the republication in 1963 of Margaret Mead's classic study of preliterate societies in which the "natural" roles of each sex were reversed or obscured (1935). Yet, regardless of ascribed temperament or division of labor, women's roles were everywhere subordinate and more limited than those of men. The different evaluation of male and female roles was explored in *The Second Sex* (1953) by Simone de Beauvoir, a French existentialist and socialist. She showed that women are not treated as the subjects of their own experiences but are instead described as objects of men's wishes and anxieties. Although existentialists see self-awareness and conscious action as crucial to genuinely human existence, de Beauvoir noted that women were assumed to lack these capacities. Further, women's position in society undermines their chances of coming to awareness, as women are cast in the role of "the Other," less able to experience themselves as full human beings than as persons different from, and existing in relation to, male humanity.

Perhaps the single most influential critique of women's position in contemporary society was Betty Friedan's ten-year follow-up study of her Smith College graduating class, *The Feminine Mystique* (1963). Friedan documented a widespread unhappiness that she called "the problem that had no name." Unwilling to blame this unhappiness on a woman's "failure to adjust" to life as a housewife. Friedan argued that the problem lay, first, with the nature of housework as a full-time occupation for women who had been trained to be able to do more, and second, with the culture that presented housework as the only acceptable career for "normal" women. She showed how the mass media promoted the belief that the only truly happy woman was the housewife—as those who worked outside the home came to a bad end. Further, even colleges failed female students by teaching conformity rather than personal growth, and by encouraging husband hunting rather than self-sufficiency. Friedan also criticized the American psychological establishment for accusing achieving women of "unresolved oedipal conflict" and "masculinity striving."

The Feminine Mystique struck a responsive chord. It was an immediate best-seller, excerpted or discussed in all the leading women's magazines. Friedan herself became an instant celebrity, although distorted by the media who interpreted her thesis as an attack on the hallowed American housewife, whereas her basic point was precisely that the fault lay in the system and not in individual women. But her readers understood her message—that their personal problems were not unique or owing to their own inadequacies. Yet Friedan's solutions were limited—return to school, find a challenging job—leaving other, more basic issues unresolved.

Because feminist thinking has grown and developed enormously since 1963, it is now possible to recognize some of the limitations of Friedan's analysis. One issue she never raised, for example, was the question of why women alone should be held responsible for housework and child care. Friedan argues only that women should be allowed *additional* spheres of activity for self-development. Nor were issues of class or race considered; it was simply assumed that any women who wanted to could get a decent education and pursue a fulfilling career. Since there have never been enough high-status jobs to go around, the hard question of how the workplace could be restructured to make fulfilling work possible for all who want it must also be addressed. Friedan thought the "problem that had no name" was limited to college-educated, middle-class women, but thirty years later it is possible to see that it is more widespread. Even women with little formal education find that raising a few children is not a lifetime occupation, and that the isolation of full-time childcare can be oppressive. Finally, Friedan's assumption that heterosexual, monogamous, genitally focused intercourse was necessary for a woman's sexual satisfaction is a claim that has been increasingly questioned.

Power and Sexuality: The Longest War. Unlike their nineteenth-century counterparts, women in the 1960s believed that they were entitled to a fulfilling sexual life, but it had become clear that most women, regardless of their level of sexual activity, were not satisfied with their sexual experiences. Under the influence of Freudian psychology, they had interpreted their dissatisfaction as a personal failing: they refused to "accept their femininity." In a group context, however, such individual problems could be recognized as collective in nature and as a legitimate grievance. These realizations were brought to widespread attention with the publication of Kate Millett's *Sexual Politics* (1970).

Written at the height of the Vietnam War (1969–70), *Sexual Politics* drew an analogy between contemporary American culture and that of "primitive" societies characterized by a "men's house" and initiation rituals for boys coming to manhood. In both, the penis is viewed as a weapon, and masculinity is equated with killing, violence, and militarism. This was encouraged by "bonding" with other men, and by rejecting and despising everything "feminine" in themselves or others. As Millett presents it, patriarchy (the rule of men) is a universal form of social organization related to all that is violent and abusive in society, but most particularly to violence against women, as exemplified in the act of rape. Millett presented rape not as an expression of sexual desire, but of "aggression, hatred, contempt and the desire to break or violate personality" and argued that "masculine hostility (psychological or physical) in specifically sexual contexts" functions "to provide a means of control over a subordinate group" (44–47).

International politics and interpersonal relations display the same underlying dynamic—men trying to prove their "masculinity." Inherent in this process is contempt not only for all women but for "unmanly" men; homosexuals are patriarchy's "failures." In her analysis of misogyny (the hatred of women), Millett established a framework for seeing "the personal as political," so that even women's experiences in bed are part of the larger pattern of male dominance. The link between sex and violence, therefore, is not deviant but a central aspect of our society's view of ordinary sexuality that views women as "sex objects" and accords status to men on the basis of their "conquests" of women.

Other feminists were also examining women's sexual experiences in patriarchal culture. Ann Koedt (1970) refuted the accepted Freudian view that "mature," passive women had a deeper and better ("vaginal") orgasm and showed that "frigidity" was more a product of passivity and ignorance than of "poor adjustment" to the female role. The prevalence of rape and the way in which the victim is punished were examined in detail by Brownmiller (1975) and Russell (1975), whose analyses suggested that rapists were "normal" in that they were acting out a culturally approved pattern rather than a personal psychological disturbance. Heterosexual relationships under patriarchy were presented as fundamentally exploitative, unsatisfying, and potentially dangerous for women—and patriarchy seemed a virtually universal principle of social organization. The "sexual revolution" of the 1960s, as manifested in the increased availability of pornography and in the assumption that buying a woman dinner entitles a man to sex, made women more, not less, vulnerable to sexual exploitation.

Feminists insist that mutually satisfying sexuality requires relationships of equality, where both partners can freely express their desires (Shulman 1980; Diamond 1980). But as long as women are socially and economically unequal and dependent on the support of men, how can women be free to enter into or reject sexual relationships? As Shulman put the problem, "The heart of our sexual dissatisfaction with men was that without power women were forced to sell [sex] or forgo it, and we were still powerless" (1980, 620). For some women, the search for egalitarian and mutually satisfying sexual relationships led to adoption of a lesbian identity; a few argued for celibacy; and many tried to restructure their heterosexual relationships to eliminate the effects of social inequality.

The Lesbian Alternative. The choice of a lesbian identity was based not only on a view of male sexuality as invariably violent and woman-hating (Dworkin 1974), but also on the positive value given to female sexuality and female identity. Such an evaluation is difficult to achieve in a society characterized by a male definition of sexuality that tends "to lump the female and sex together as if the whole burden of the onus and stigma it attaches to sex were the fault of the female alone" (Millett 1970, 51). To value both the female body and oneself as a woman and person is clearly related to the ability to love oneself and to love other women, whether in a platonic or a sexual sense. Advocates of the lesbian alternative present this as part of a continuum of female solidarity, with the most highly "woman-identified woman" expressing her commitment in a physically loving relationship (Rich 1980).

Some feminists took this concept to the extreme of claiming that "feminism is the theory, lesbianism the practice," as if any relationship with a man were at best hypocritical and at worst self-destructive, thus defining a lesbian as a better feminist than a hetero- or bisexual woman. Most feminists, however, refused to reduce politics to sexuality, even while continuing to see sexuality as part of political reality (Shulman 1980). As we will see in later chapters, the role of lesbians and lesbianism in the New Feminist Movement remains a lively issue, but the idea that a woman could break free from the constraints of patriarchy by changing sexual partners, or erotic identity, or even by forgoing sex altogether, is now widely acknowledged to be simplistic. Concentrating on sexuality as a source of identity and a means of self-expression, Millett and others struck some common themes but too quickly jumped to the conclusion that these were universal. For example, the evidence for women's "essential" pacifism is just as mixed as the evidence for women's "natural passivity." Although Millett herself argued that male violence and hostility toward women were products of culture rather than of nature, her emphasis on the universality of patriarchy led others to conclude that male aggression was somehow innate, and that women were therefore morally superior (e.g., Daly 1978). This claim was central to the moral reform tradition of feminism in previous generations, but now as then, by emphasizing innate qualities, this claim minimizes the potential for change. Moreover, those who propose an essential difference in nature between men and women too often stereotype and dehumanize "the Other." It is possible, however, that the real radicalism of a feminist revolution will arise from its refusal to dehumanize anyone, even those men who have hated and physically abused women.

Motherhood and Autonomy.   While Millett offered an introduction to a feminist analysis of power and sexuality, Shulamith Firestone took the first step in reexamining the old Freudian argument that "biology is destiny." In *The Dialectic of Sex* (1970), she combined Freudian with Marxist analysis. Suggesting that Freud was basically correct that women envied men, she argued that it was not the penis itself but the social power that goes with it that is the object of envy. Because a mother's position in the family remains subordinate, the psychological dynamics continue to unfold as Freud described them. Rather than seeing patriarchy as based on attitudes and ideas alone, she sought the roots of men's social power in concrete facts, especially in the facts of reproduction. Because she did not see any way for mothers to avoid subordination, she concluded that the only way for women to be free was to renounce motherhood. *The Dialectic of Sex* ends with a vision of the future in which childbearing would be taken over by technology; not only test-tube conception but gestation as well. Although most readers, including most feminists, found Firestone's conclusions distasteful, they were prodded to think about how women could be mothers without being oppressed by the experience.

Freedom for mothers, the emerging feminist analysis argued, will exist only when women can freely choose to have children or not (Petchesky 1980). Compulsory motherhood, whether due to the absence of birth control or of any other meaningful life's work, is not acceptable. A woman's right to make that decision herself, unimpeded by government policy or by social pressure for *or* against childbearing is crucial to the freedom of all women. As feminists noted, even the experience of giving birth had become an exercise in powerlessness, as male doctors and hospital administrators assumed control over the birth process. Mothers themselves had little to say about the timing, the setting, or the techniques of childbirth (Rothman 1982). In addition to control over the decision to give birth, therefore, women need to repossess the entire process through such choices as home births, midwives, limited anesthesia, and active participation of self and other family members in the birth. The developing feminist analysis of mothering as a source of power taken from and turned against women has generated both controversy and constructive strategies for change (Rossi 1977; Rich 1976; Ruddick 1980).

The distinction between motherhood as the biological experience of giving birth and mothering as the social experience of caring for children remains a crucial element in feminist analysis. As a biological experience, the critical problem is increasing women's control over motherhood; as a social role, the issue of control is combined with the issue of sharing childcare with men. Some theorists (Chodorow 1978; Dinnerstein 1976) propose that children raised exclusively by women develop psychological traits (such as the desire to mother in women, and hostility to women in men) that inevitably reproduce the gender-based differences in personality and behavior evident in present society. From this point of view, the continued oppression of women rests on the material base of the division of labor in child rearing rather than on either simple prejudice or "natural" differences between the sexes. Some feminists argue that men are and will continue to be largely excluded from intense involvement in childcare because the structure of the economy penalizes child rearing so severely—few families can afford the total or partial loss of a "man-sized" paycheck. Thus, to change the division of child-rearing labor in any significant way will necessitate substantial changes in the structure of other types of work (hooks 1984).

Most feminists agree on the need to relieve mothers of some of the burden of child rearing by provision of childcare outside the home: many also argue that increased participation by fathers is equally essential to women's freedom. Additionally, some are beginning to question whether the view of children as a burden and impediment to women's autonomy does justice to the meaning of children in women's lives; if women were not forced to give up so much when they have children, perhaps the role of childcare in teaching adults spontaneity and generosity would be more valued. Others note that psychodynamic theories assume that most children will be living in the same households as their biological parents, or at the very least, in nuclear families, yet the question of shared parenting could involve a larger and perhaps more voluntary family (Collins 1990).

Equality and Difference. Raising questions about pregnancy and motherhood also evoked basic beliefs about the meaning of equality and difference in relations between men and women. Did equality mean "equal to men," and if so, did that imply taking men's values and experiences as a standard for all? Could women be treated differently from men without reinforcing stereotypes and perpetuating subordination (Hall 1986; Rothman 1989)? Whenever American courts had invoked the concept of natural gender differences, their decisions had disadvantaged women, as in the case of protective labor rules. Could a recognition of the special needs or distinctive strengths of women be compatible with equal treatment (Vogel 1993)? The basic question of whether or not women were special or distinctive in any way became so controversial among feminists that some scholars today divide feminists into two opposing camps: "equality feminists," or "minimalists," who tend to downplay sex differences, urging equality of treatment in most or all circumstances; and "difference feminists," or "maximalists," who claim that women's historical responsibilities for nurturing children has led to the development of distinctive personality traits and values that the society should affirm and accommodate.

Although the initially "radical" position among feminists was to deny all differences that were socially ascribed to men and women, the minimalist claim soon came to be seen as encouraging too much accommodation to a male-defined world. Carol Gilligan's influential study of moral choices (1982) became the rallying point for scholars who felt that an "ethic of care" and a sense of responsibility for others in the context of relationships was not only "women's way" but superior to the abstract rules, formal rights, and isolated individualism of "men's way." The belief that women embodied a different, more relational approach to politics has also been used to justify separate feminist peace and ecology movements (McAllister 1982; Diamond and Orenstein 1990).

Other feminist theorists point out that because the opposite of equality is not difference but *inequality,* sameness need not be a prerequisite for equality. In fact, equality may be impossible without recognizing certain differences, such as the effects of pregnancy and infant care. Several scholars argue that moral equality demands respect for the many differences among individuals and groups (Scott 1988; Vogel 1993). Particularly from the perspective of women of color, the recognition of diversity is critical. When the argument is reduced to a singular difference on the basis of gender rather than plural "differences" among both men and women, there is a danger of essentializing women-ness as something distinct from the actual embodied experiences of real women, in which gender is not experienced in the abstract but in interaction with race, class, age, and other aspects of the self. Spelman (1988), for example, critiques the tendency to treat gender as a "pop-bead" in a strand of separable and additive identities.

Collins (1990) offers a different vision of feminism, grounded in the life of African-American women. She argues for integrating gender with race and class, for a circle of multiple perceivers as a means of finding truths. Other "standpoint" theorists (Smith 1987; Harding 1991) also emphasize the need to recognize diversity as a source of knowledge, since individuals are necessarily limited in their understanding by the particular circumstances of their life. Pooling knowledge and testing it against the perceptions of others who are differently situated becomes a preferred strategy for doing social science, on the one hand, and an expression of a genuine egalitarian politics, on the other.

Theoretical Diversity in the New Feminist Movement Today.   At this time there are some interpretations of feminist principles that seem to cluster together and other ideas on which feminists frequently disagree. One controversial question concerns the limits of individualism, both as means and as end of social change. Is the whole purpose of feminism to produce free and unfettered individuals or to create a new form of community? Is feminism to be realized through individual transformation (and consequent sociopolitical change) or through a sociopolitical struggle that creates the conditions for individual transformation? All social movements are points of intersection between personal and social change, but the tension between the individual and the social dimensions seems especially pronounced in the New Feminist Movement.

Indeed, present-day feminists combine personal and social change in virtually all possible ways in developing an agenda for the movement. If we look at both the *means* (personal transformation or sociopolitical change) and the *ends* (an individual freed from social restraint or a new and stronger community) of social change advocated by feminists, the following typology emerges:

FIGURE 2.1

Varieties of Modern Feminism

		MEANS	
		Personal Transformation	*Sociopolitical Change*
	Free Individuals	Career	Liberal
ENDS			
	New Communities	Radical	Socialist

The particular terms used in this table describe different emphases and are not necessarily in opposition. An individual feminist may move from one orientation to another as the conditions of her life change, or she may seek a balance by simultaneously joining groups with different emphases. The point of this typology is that these differences do not reflect a tension between better or worse feminisms, but between different styles and strategies, each of which may be appropriate for certain situations or at certain times.

Career feminism emphasizes the need for individual women to take their lives into their own hands and dare to be what they can become, to fight back if men try to stop or limit them, and to help other women. For many, this orientation centers on women's right to any sort of job in society, even those that have been traditionally defined as male. If women stick together and refuse to let men dictate to them, they will discover that they have the power to accomplish their goals. But first, women must discover their own potential and learn to act assertively. Creating support networks and achieving personal goals are key ideas in this approach. Even some critics of the women's movement endorse this vision of personal empowerment and see themselves as feminists in this vein (e.g. Roiphe 1993).

Radical feminists also emphasize the power that women already have in themselves and the need for mental transformation that would free women to act powerfully. This power, however, is not to be used to enter and achieve in the male world, but rather to reject that world and its values. Women's ties to one another are crucial, not as a defense or a lever to power, but as a source of joy in themselves. Women who define and care for themselves create a community that does not need men to function or to be important. While this leaves the "rest" of the world under male control, a radical feminist community provides an image of female freedom and possibility that is healing and transforming for women. By offering women an alternative to male control, radical feminists plant a seed of doubt about the naturalness or inevitability of current social patterns and encourage resistance to these arrangements. Many, but not all, radical feminists would also call themselves lesbian feminists; others would use the term separatists.

Liberal feminism is most typically expressed in demands for social and political change that would eliminate the unjust advantages of men and guarantee equal rights. Throughout its long history, liberal feminism has stressed the importance and the autonomy of the individual. In contrast to the traditional liberal's exclusion of women, the liberal feminist claims that women and men are equally entitled to be treated as individual people. Unlike career feminists, liberal feminists see social policy as an important force in establishing access to economic opportunity and civil rights. Liberal feminists fought hard for the Equal Rights Amendment as an important affirmation of women's individualism and personhood. They are also strongly "pro-choice" on issues of reproductive rights. In addition to such political struggles, liberal feminists stress changing the division of labor in individual households and eliminating stereotypes in child rearing. This is the most common interpretation of feminism in the United States.

Socialist feminism focuses on the importance of changing the basic structural arrangements of society, a goal shared with liberal feminists. Socialist feminists, however, consider the liberal concept of isolated individuals with abstract rights and choices a harmful myth that perpetuates inequalities. In contrast, both men and women are seen as social beings, imbedded in a network of concrete social and economic relationships. Capitalist relationships force people to compete with each other in order to survive, restricting and distorting human nature, both male and female. Socialists seek an end to these competitive relationships, and to the exploitation of the weak by the strong. In contrast to traditional socialists, socialist feminists see patriarchy as another force that distorts and limits human possibilities. They argue that all social structures permitting one group (men, capitalists, whites) to control and benefit from another (women, workers, blacks) must be eliminated. Despite controversies about which form of exploitation, if any, is more fundamental than the rest, socialist feminists share a vision of a new community that, as a community, recognizes and develops the human potential of every person. Globally, the socialist perspective is much more common than it is in the United States.

Conclusions

As social movement theorists have pointed out, movements need not only material resources but also ideologies that frame grievances, support collective identity, and offer perspectives for desired change. The diversity of feminist traditions developed over the past century and a half provided a basis for developing a spectrum of feminist ideology that combines concern with individual and collective transformation in a variety of productive ways. Important as these ideas are, however, movements also demand organizational resources and political opportunities. It is to these factors that we turn in the next chapter.

I'M PROUD to be a FEMINIST

From the very beginning of the most recent mobilization of the women's movement, there have been efforts to discredit the label "feminist." Despite widespread opposition, women such as this delegate to the NOW Conference in Houston in 1974 have continued to affirm the power of a feminist identity to transform one's life. *Photograph ©* *Bettye-Lane*

Chapter 3

Reemergence of a Feminist Movement, 1963–72

In the preceding chapters we have traced the demographic and ideological foundations upon which a social movement could be established. By the early 1960s there were hundreds of thousands of women "structurally available" for recruitment; that is, they had actually experienced discrimination and recognized the gap between their talents, skills, and expectations on the one hand, and the reality of their position in the home, schools, and workplace, on the other. Ideas about the causes of their lower status became personally relevant, and authors who addressed this issue found—finally—a ready readership. But resources and ideas must be mobilized in order to create a social movement organization. In this chapter we describe the reemergence of an organized feminist movement and follow its early history, beginning with the link between feminism and Civil Rights activism in the 1950s and 1960s.

Feminism and the Civil Rights Movement

The history of the New Feminist Movement is intricately interwoven with that of the other dominant social movement of our times—the Civil Rights movement (Blumberg 1984). In this respect, contemporary feminism resembles the earlier movement for women's rights that was linked to the cause of abolishing slavery in the United States (Giele 1995). The abolition and Civil Rights movement provided models of moral protest and effective change that inspired women to seek full equality for themselves. In addition, in both eras the active involvement of African-American and white women prepared them for their later activism on behalf of feminist goals.

From their work in the Civil Rights movement, women acquired a number of valuable resources. First and most important was a sense of personal power, of taking on a difficult task and making things happen (Barnett 1994). Secondly, women became skilled in organizing people and events, and in using effective tactics for implementing change and manipulating the media: civil disobedience, mass demonstrations, passive resistance, community organizing, law suits, and the mimeograph machine and press release. They also learned another crucial lesson: that if they were to pursue feminist goals, it would have to be in a movement of their own. This realization came slowly, to many different groups of women as they participated in the other social movement of the 1960s.

The Civil Rights movement that came to public notice in the mid-1950s was actually the continuation of a century-long struggle for equality and justice waged by African Americans in the South (Morris 1984). The American public was galvanized by media images of acts of civil disobedience—a tired working woman refusing to move to the back of the bus; college students staging a sit-in at a department store lunch counter—that provoked violent reactions from local officials, thus transforming the movement into a moral crusade. This appeal to religious values had an immediate impact on many southern whites, especially younger women who recognized the inherent conflict between southern culture and Christian ideals (Evans 1979). The white women who joined the Civil Rights crusade were also deeply influenced by the strength and courage of the African-American women engaged in community organizing, who presented an ideal very different from their own tradition of southern womanhood. Both black and white women in the movement became increasingly aware of the link between racism and sexism.

Yet when they attempted to articulate their own concerns within Civil Rights organizations, women were told that their issues were of minor importance compared to the overwhelming need for racial justice, a scenario all too reminiscent of the earlier abolition movement. And in both historical periods, believing that the two social movements were competing rather than complementary agents of change, many women deferred feminist goals to what they perceived as the greater struggle (Wallace 1982). The existence of cycles of protest, however, means that diverse social movements have a mutually rein-forcing effect, leading to eras of remarkable change along a variety of fronts. Conversely, periods of political repression and normative rigidi-ty, as in the America of the 1980s, are inhospitable to all social move-ments, regardless of the issues or constituencies. Thus, activists typically have more to gain than to lose from the existence of other movements for change. But for male participants, threatened by women's demands for sharing leadership and setting priorities, the advantages of cooperation were obscured by the challenge to their authority.

Women's own grievances would not be deferred indefinitely. In both the abolition and Civil Rights movements, women saw that some of the same men who spoke so eloquently of freedom and justice openly showed their contempt for women and shared the attitudes of most men of their era (McAdam 1988). Women were sexual con-quests, support workers behind the scenes, effective organizers on a local level; only in these secondary roles were they welcome in the movement. When women questioned their limited power within the movement and society at large, they were ridiculed, abused, and excluded—reactions that have persisted to this day.

The tension between the Civil Rights movement and the emergent women's movement was not merely a matter of competition for resources or of internal power struggles but also reflected a conflict in goals. Much of the African-American male leadership, and virtually all of their white male sympathizers, believed that the costs of racism were borne primarily by black men, "emasculated" by their lack of economic power. They claimed that without the power that comes from earnings, black men "lost" control over their families, and with-out the ability to dominate their wives and children they lost their self-respect. The ideal that men should be sole providers for their families was accepted uncritically, so that poverty was seen as a blow to the male ego, the only ego that counted.

In this view, female-centered families were equated with female power or matriarchy and considered psychologically damaging (par-ticularly to male children) as well as socially destructive (Moynihan 1965). Black women who did not subordinate themselves to their "nat-ural" superiors were accused of being "castrating," further contribut-ing to the inability of black men to become stable breadwinners. The relative strength and independence of black women was considered less an asset to the black community than a symptom, if not the cause, of its distress. As long as leaders in the Civil Rights movement accepted the norm of male authority in the family and community as the ideal toward which they were striving, women's challenges to that authority would create a fundamental conflict.

Thus, while the Civil Rights movement offered a model of analysis and organizing experience for women who became active in the New Feminist Movement, there were areas of potential discord between the two movements. Yet decades of protest and growing public support for the principle of equal rights under law had created a climate of opinion in which the feminist message appeared less exotic or unreasonable than it might have if the women's movement had been the first to surface. But male authority, in both theory and practice, in the Civil Rights movement was in direct contradiction to feminist goals.

Organizational Styles of the New Feminism

As we have noted, there is no single entity that can be labeled "the" new feminist movement. Rather, several different organizational forms and theoretical emphases developed out of divergent sets of experience. The contemporary women's movement is a collection of formal organizations, occupational caucuses, friendship circles, collectives, and interest groups. Nonetheless, it is possible to identify historical moments when important elements in this mix emerged as self-conscious units, committed to social change on behalf of women.

It is first necessary to distinguish two major strands in the early development of this new feminist movement. Some analysts (e.g., Cassell 1977) use the terms "women's rights" and "women's liberation" to refer to these different types of groups. *Women's rights* groups were those formal, structured organizations established to pursue equality through legislation, the courts, and lobbying; that is, to fight a political battle on political turf. *Women's liberation* groups were the relatively informal, loosely structured networks of women in the community, struggling for feminist goals outside of the conventional political system, through consciousness-raising (CR) and support groups, self-help projects, media-directed actions, and efforts to construct more egalitarian relationships in their personal lives. They were often inspired by the vision of participatory democracy and mutual empowerment that Ella Baker had brought to the Civil Rights movement (Payne 1989; Mueller 1990).

Other students of the movement, following Freeman (1973, 1975) prefer to speak of "two branches," an older one and a younger one, that differ in age, structure, and style. Both branches were concerned with rights and liberation, and the distinction between them is not simply that of reform versus revolution. Rather, each branch emerged from a unique set of historical circumstances involving a particular age cohort. In the decade 1963–73 younger and older women faced different problems and responded in different ways. Within each age group, a branch of feminism developed independently of the other branch, recruiting members from the co-optable networks available to it. Only in the early 1970s, as the mass media brought awareness of feminism to the general public, did the two branches begin to develop overlapping memberships and complementary strategies, a process that accelerated in the 1980s.

It is, therefore, more accurate to refer to "strands" rather than branches, since branches grow apart and remain separate; whereas strands typically intertwine to produce a particular fabric. Following the distinction proposed by Rothschild-Whitt (1979) we shall speak of a "bureaucratic" strand and a "collectivist" strand of feminism taking shape in the period between 1963 and 1972, characterized by two different organizational modes, reflecting the history and needs of their members.

Bureaucratic and Collectivist Modes of Organization. The terms "bureaucratic" and "collectivist" describe more than variation in organizational structure: there are also marked differences in recruitment, activities, and the actualization of values. Most fundamentally, bureaucratic organizations are concerned with achieving concrete goals, while for collectivist organizations the means are as important, if not more so, than the ends of action. A comparison of these basic differences can be seen in Table 3.1.

The bureaucratic organization, in terms of Max Weber's (1922) ideal type, is characterized by a formal division of labor, written rules, universal standards of performance, hierarchical offices, impersonal relationships, technical expertise, and individualistic achievement norms. In contrast, the ideal type of collectivist organization is a community of like-minded persons, with minimal division of labor, rules, or differential rewards. Interaction among staff is wholistic, personalized, informal, and designed to achieve consensus, as embodied in the food cooperative, storefront health clinic, or alternative newspaper characteristic of the youth counterculture of the 1960s.

It is not difficult to see that bureaucratic organizations would appeal to women who have already achieved some personal success within that type of organization. They know how the game is played and are confident of their ability to make such systems work. In addition, their time is limited by family and work obligations, so that engaging in collectivist activities or in day-long consensus-seeking meetings would seem an intolerable waste of time. Whereas members of collectivist organizations take pride in "doing the right thing" (i.e., actualizing values); the bureaucratic mode is designed for "effectiveness" (i.e., realizing goals). For this reason, bureaucratic organizations attract women confronting specific obstacles and seeking concrete changes. The bureaucratic mode also separates work from other activities, to the benefit of women already balancing competing demands.

Collectivist organizations, on the other hand, appealed to the anti-authoritarian principles of youthful veterans of the 1960s community organizing campaigns and student resistance movements. The job rotation characteristic of such groups also provided skill training in various fields. The time-consuming decision-making process meant that only those without demanding family and career commitments could fully participate. Value realization and solidarity were especially compelling incentives to people with weak family ties but strong moral commitments. Friendship and peer relationships in general were more crucial to younger than to older women. The communal, expressive, egalitarian nature of collectivist work organizations required a degree of personal attention and nurturance that younger women without children could better afford.

As the following brief history suggests, the women in feminist collectives differed in many respects from those who were the founders and the leaders of bureaucratic organizations. Most obviously, they were younger in age and came from the counterculture rather than from the establishment. Whereas the older women had mastered the techniques formal organization, the younger ones were fiercely antielitist and antihierarchy. The older women had careers that gave them access to the system, but that also made them vulnerable to retaliation. Students and young housewives in the younger branch enjoyed more flexible hours and fewer scheduled commitments, so they could throw themselves into full-time "careers" in the women's movement. Both strands were effective in using the media, but the events they placed before the cameras were very different.

Nonetheless, their actual policy positions differed less than the styles with which their ideas were advanced (Ryan 1989).

This old/young distinction also reflects a difference in cohort membership. A cohort refers to a group of individuals who enter a given system at the same time and age together through a particular slice of history. The women who founded NOW and other bureaucratic strand organizations were members of the very small birth cohorts of the Great Depression, strongly influenced by the social activism of the New Deal, often daughters or granddaughters of earlier feminists who took their own career commitment as self-evident. Because of the small number of college-educated women in their birth cohorts, they felt themselves part of an elite. They emphasized women's autonomy and individuality, and because of their personal success, they saw existing restraints as holdovers from a less enlightened era, and they advocated working through the system to correct remaining limitations.

Collectivist strand women, in contrast, were the first of the baby boom cohorts to enter a greatly expanded educational system: they had grown up in the comfort of the relatively affluent 1950s and were encouraged to achieve more as a matter of course than as a mark of distinction. Unlike the older women, they were reluctant to define achievement in purely material terms. The Civil Rights movement and the New Left provided a focus for their idealism, although neither movement fully recognized or used their talents. The New Left also offered an alternative education in critical social theory and the dynamics of political oppression that they would later use to analyze their own situation.

Thus it was that feminists of the 1960s arrived at their organizational niches from two very different histories and traditions. In the remainder of this chapter we shall describe the development of these two strands of feminist activism.

The Bureaucratic Strand

The President's Commission on the Status of Women. Presidential candidate John F. Kennedy vowed, in 1960, that if elected he would establish a national commission to study the status of women in the United States. He won, and he did. The driving force behind both the promise and the commission was Esther Peterson, a long-time activist in the trade union movement, educational organiza-

Controversy and Coalition

TABLE 3.1.

Comparison of Two Ideal Types of Organization*

	Bureaucratic	*Collectivist*
1. **Authority**	Resides in individuals by virtue of the offices they hold	Resides in collectivity as a whole, although may be temporarily delegated
	Hierarchical structure	Compliance to consensus
	Compliance to fixed rules	fluid and subject to negotiation
2. **Rules**	Fixed and impartial	Ad hoc, situational
3. **Social Control**	Supervision, formal sanctions	Personalized appeals, and shared values
4. **Social Relations**	Impersonal, role based, segmented, instrumental	Communal, wholistic, personal, expressive
5. **Recruitment and Advancement**	On basis of skill, specialized training, and formal certification	Network contacts, values, personality factors
	Employment as career, with advancement by seniority or achievement	Career and advancement not meaningful
		No hierarchy of positions
6. **Incentives**	Money and power	Solidarity and value realization
7. **Social Stratification**	Differential rewards by office; inequality	Egalitarian; limited differentials in rewards
8. **Differentiation**	High degree of division of labor	Minimal division of labor
	Difference between mental and manual work, and between administrative and performance tasks	Administration combined with performance tasks
	Specialization of function, segmental roles	Generalization of jobs and functions
		Wholistic roles
	Ideal of specialist, expert	Ideal of amateur, jack-of-all-trades

*Adapted from Rothschild-Whitt 1979, 519.

tions, and the Democratic party. In 1961, Kennedy appointed Peterson to head the Woman's Bureau in the Department of Labor, a traditional source of political influence for women in the federal government. She was also named to the post of vice-chairman [*sic*] of the President's Commission on the Status of Women, with Eleanor Roosevelt as honorary chairman. From her wide experience, Peterson was able to draw upon the pool of women described in chapter 1 as feminists in the "woodwork" of national politics—those who had singly and quietly risen to relatively high positions in the federal bureaucracy, political party hierarchies, and established women's organizations (Freeman 1987).

The composition of the commission was carefully drawn to represent a variety of interest groups and officials, including a large number of men. After almost two years of fact-finding, the commission's report—*American Women* (1963)—was presented to the president at a White House ceremony on 11 October 1963 (Eleanor Roosevelt's birthday). The report documented widespread discrimination against women and made specific recommendations for guaranteeing equal treatment, including a cabinet post to monitor compliance, as well as an executive order requiring equal opportunity for women in private firms that received federal funds. The remaining proposals leaned strongly on the existing legal system, urging women to use the courts to test their grievances (Harrison 1988).

The Equal Rights Amendment had been a polarizing issue for women's organizations ever since it was introduced in 1923, and commission members had been selected to ensure a strong majority against the ERA. Nonetheless, the commission was more critical of using gender as a justification for unequal treatment than many had anticipated. It argued that equality was already embodied in the "equal protection" clause of the Fourteenth Amendment to the U.S. Constitution, and it expressed the belief that legal challenges would soon lead the Supreme Court to affirm this interpretation, as it has. In sum, the commission's report presented a critical but optimistic view that once the facts of women's disadvantage were known, the situation would be remedied.

Legislation: 1963–64.   To a limited extent, this optimism was rewarded. A presidential order was signed, although no Cabinet-level official was appointed. The Equal Pay Act of 1963 embodied the princi-

One of the largest and most impressive demonstrations of the 1970s took place in Washington, D.C., as over one hundred thousand feminists gathered to press for extension of the deadline for ratification of the Equal Rights Amendment. Marchers dressed in white and displayed the colors—purple, green, and gold—of the earlier movement for women's suffrage, linking past and present. *Photograph © Bettye -Lane.*

ple of equal pay for men and women doing the same work but did not mandate equal access to jobs. In this respect, the legislation reflected union concern that employers not hire women at a lower rate of pay in order to replace men or to drive down male wages.

In 1964, the pending Civil Rights Act was broadened to include "sex" as well as race in the section (Title VII) concerning equal employment opportunity, largely through the efforts of Representative Martha Griffiths of Michigan, with the unwitting help of a very conservative southern colleague (Howard Smith, D–Va.) who thought that including women in a Civil Rights Act would allow legislators to vote against it on grounds other than racism. The act, as amended, was finally passed in July 1964 and signed into law by Lyndon Johnson at a ceremony with no women present, and with no mention made of equal rights for women (Robinson 1979). The word "sex" would probably not have remained in the act had not a small group actively lobbied for it, including all but one of the few women in Congress (Davis 1991).

Favorable legislation is one thing; ensuring that it is enforced is quite another. The Civil Rights Act of 1964 provided for an Equal Employment Opportunity Commission (EEOC) to handle complaints brought under Title VII. From the beginning, a high proportion of the complaints pouring into EEOC offices were charges of sex discrimination. Yet even such an enforcement mechanism was no guarantee that women's rights would be taken seriously. It would take another decade to bring sex discrimination into the center of EEOC concern (Robinson 1979). Nonetheless, Congress had acted, and there was a potential federal presence for ensuring equal treatment in employment. It is doubtful that either would have occurred without the groundwork done by the president's commission and a growing network of feminist activists in government.

State Commissions on the Status of Women.   Perhaps the most important legacy of the Commission on the Status of Women was not in the area of legislation at all, but in the mandate to convene commissions on the status of women at the state level. Eventually, every state in the union would have such a body, although in some instances (e.g., New Hampshire) the governor would appoint active antifeminists. Most of the state commissions on the status of women were created at the urging of women already active in state politics, and in many cases this became a simple way for political leaders of both parties to pay off a debt to women who had worked in their campaigns

(Freeman 1973). More importantly, the state commissions were almost entirely composed of women who had risen to the leadership of organizations representing various racial, religious, occupational, and ethnic constituencies.

The state commissions served a number of functions. Officially, they were charged with gathering data on the roles and resources of women and with documenting areas of discrimination in the laws and practices of the individual states. In doing so, many latent (unanticipated and unintended) consequences followed. First, the members of the commissions and their staffs (often also predominately female) came to know one another and to share a common concern with women in general. The data they gathered was often eye-opening, since many commission members had little awareness of the cumulative impact of discrimination on women. Additionally, in the process of data gathering, many other groups were drawn into the activities of the commissions and began to identify their interests with those of other women. Publicity in the form of hearings, news releases, reports, and media interviews brought the work of the commissions to public attention.

As with the presidential commission, the emphasis was on legal remedies and legislative action, but the state units were likely to be—or become—more radical than the federal commission, pushing for state Equal Rights Amendments. The state commissions also created a "climate of expectations that something would be done" (Freeman 1973, 798). Moreover, the state commissions were linked through a Federal Interdepartmental Committee and a Citizens Advisory Council that became clearinghouses for information. In sum, a national network of activists was created, consisting of the commissioners, their staffs, the groups that these individuals represented, other constituencies activated during investigations and hearings, and political and community leaders.

The particular events that led to the formation of a social movement organization occurred in June 1966, when representatives of state commissions were meeting in Washington, D.C., for their third annual conference. During the same month, Representative Griffiths charged that the EEOC had failed to take its mandate seriously. EEOC's lack of interest in sex discrimination was well known; its commissioners made open jokes about the topic; and in any event, EEOC had little enforcement power (Robinson 1979). When delegates to the conference of state commissions on the status of women presented a resolution demanding that EEOC enforce the sex clause of Title VII, conference officials refused to allow it to come to the floor for a vote. Several angry women agreed that the time had come to organize a group that could lobby for women in the same way that the National Association for the Advancement of Colored People (NAACP) worked on behalf of African-Americans. Thus was the National Organization for Women (NOW) formed, by two dozen delegates to the conference and a woman who was gathering material for her second book—Betty Friedan.

NOW and Other Bureaucratic Organizations. As described in chapter 2, Friedan's first book brought feminist ideas into public discourse. It also gave her personal visibility, ready access to the media, and credibility with the public, especially after she was invited to the White House. Friedan had also maintained contact with the network of state commissions, whose members were increasingly convinced that their goals could not be achieved solely through government channels. Although the EEOC would ultimately become receptive to feminist influence, and be granted limited enforcement powers, Friedan and others felt that a new organization independent of government and both political parties was needed to create pressure for a shift in public policy and practices.

By the time of NOW's first organizing meeting in October 1966, the two dozen founding members had grown to several hundred women and men. The name—National Organization *for* Women—expressed a commitment to recruit both men and women who shared a belief in gender equality. The early cohort of members was primarily drawn from the ranks of the educational and occupational elite—articulate achievers with little movement experience but good media presence and government contacts—so news of the movement traveled far in advance of NOW's ability to organize followers (Freeman 1973).

The new organization drew heavily on the resources of that elite, not only for the specialized skills these women had developed, but also for access to the resources of their organizations, that is, facilities for printing, mailing, and the maintenance of membership lists that had to be kept secret for fear of retaliation by employers.

NOW's first target was the EEOC, in support of a sex discrimination suit brought by flight attendants (then called "stewardesses") against the airlines' policy of forcing them to retire upon marriage or at age thirty or thirty-five. NOW also challenged an EEOC decision that sex-segregated employment advertising in newspapers did not constitute discrimination. Television networks were invited to cover a few small demonstrations that embarrassed the commission into holding hearings on both issues. When the EEOC ruled in favor of NOW's position in both cases, President Lyndon Johnson issued an executive order barring discrimination by all federal contractors (Davis 1991).

Yet when NOW applied for membership in the Leadership Conference on Civil Rights, its application was refused on the grounds that women's needs were not an authentic civil rights issue. Thus, rather than one umbrella movement seeking equality for all Americans, there would henceforth be separate movements on the basis of race and gender, which presented a particular dilemma for those women of color who were also feminist activists (Brown 1986).

Almost as soon as NOW was created, its leaders were confronted with one of the most basic and persistent challenges of American feminism: defining the ultimate goals of the movement. Was NOW's mission to improve women's opportunities within the existing systems of family, education, and employment, or should it embrace the broader and more controversial goal of confronting and eliminating sexism throughout the society? This question of direction was immediately raised in the context of both the ERA and reproductive rights; namely, should NOW challenge the laws that made abortion illegal? When the 1967 NOW Convention passed an agenda supporting the ERA and also advocating repeal of antiabortion statutes, a number of members resigned from the organization; labor union women left because they saw the ERA as undercutting legislation protecting women workers, and others left because they felt that reproductive freedom was too radical an issue for the American public to accept.

This latter group of feminists then founded the Women's Equity Action League (WEAL), described by its founders as a "conservative NOW" with the goal of achieving equality through conventional means, primarily lobbying and lawsuits (Costain and Costain 1987). Over time, however, WEAL's leaders found that their moderate stance gained them little respect or influence in Washington or the state capitols, so by 1972, WEAL was also advocating reproductive choice and other relatively controversial positions. During an important period in the formative stage of the movement, however, WEAL's moderation and emphasis on litigation left NOW free to experiment with more radical forms of confrontation: protest events, strikes, and mass demonstrations.

Another addition to the bureaucratic strand in 1971 was the

National Women's Political Caucus (NWPC) a bipartisan association with the goals of lobbying for women's issues within the two national political parties and encouraging more women to enter politics. Although its membership is largely Democratic, leadership posts in NWPC are carefully divided between Republican and Democratic activists. In practice, NWPC's ability to affect party platforms has been minimal, especially at Republican conventions over the past twenty years (Freeman 1993). The organization has enjoyed greater, though still limited, success in recruiting and supporting women candidates, but two decades after its founding, NWPC leaders acknowledged that their early optimism had given way to frustration over the slow pace of progress toward political equality (Berke 1991).

All three organizations began as small cadres of highly placed activists coordinating their activities at the national level, and only gradually expanded into mass-membership associations with state and local units. Media attention to the emerging movement in the 1970s attracted the attention of large numbers of women looking for something to join. In many cities, autonomous groups formed, recruiting members through informal networks and generating their own programs of action. Eventually, NOW evolved a structure that included local and state units, although it took several more years of confusion before lines of communication and responsibility would be regularized. A compromise was reached that allowed for substantial local autonomy, but at the cost of increased bureaucratization of the organization as a whole. State-level committees were formed to coordinate local activities, and national priorities were established at annual conventions.

These early, tentative efforts to form a broad-based women's movement proved more successful than anyone had dared to dream. In the five years between 1968 and 1973, NOW, WEAL, and NWPC were joined by dozens of other formal associations centered on specific issues or constituencies—for example, women in government, female athletes, older women, union women, members of racial and ethnic minority groups, and students and faculty in academic institutions or intellectual fields (see Wandersee 1988 for a detailed history of organizations in this period). Together, these organizations form the backbone of the New Feminist Movement. As in the human backbone, the separate elements remain discrete and flexible yet firmly linked to one another, thus lending to the whole a strength greater than that of a single rigid structure.

There is, however, a sense in which the bureaucratic strand is only the visible tip of the movement, the surface manifestation of deeper changes that have been taking place within the society and in the consciousness of men as well as women. To grasp fully the breadth and depth of the women's movement requires an examination of the other major strand of contemporary feminism in the United States.

The Collectivist Strand

The second strand of feminist activism originated in the southern Civil Rights Movement (CRM) of the late 1950s and in the student-led New Left Movement (NLM) of the 1960s. In both causes, idealistic young white women rejected the privileges of race and class, engaged with women of color and other local activists, and experienced the strength of creating change through community organizing. However, especially in the NLM, they found themselves treated less as colleagues than as trophies by the men (Piercy 1970). For African-American women also, their sense of independence, integrity, and power repeatedly conflicted with their treatment by their male peers.

Women in the Civil Rights Movement. As noted earlier, many black men had attitudes toward women very similar to those of white males. The aggressively sexist ("macho") style of the young black men who suddenly found themselves in positions of power in student-led organizations appalled their black female colleagues, who were the first to raise the issue of sexism in the student Civil Rights organizations. But it was more difficult for black women to break away from primary involvement in the Civil Rights movement than it was for their white sisters, not only because of their deep personal commitment but because of the hostility directed at them. African-American feminists were called traitors to the greater cause of civil rights (Wallace 1982). Black women and white women often found a common cause in confronting the sexism of movement men, even though that sexism also drove a wedge between them.

The African-American women who were leaders in organizing their communities often found that they were ignored in favor of the male ministers who were more visible spokesmen for the movement (Crawford, Rouse, and Woods 1990; Robinson 1987), however personally empowering their leadership roles had been (Barnett 1994).

White women also found their work in black communities personally transforming, even when they were assigned "safe" and stereotypical jobs in the Freedom Schools (McAdam 1988). White women often accepted sexist behavior from white and African-American men that their black sisters would not tolerate, and African-American women, in turn, often resented the rivalry and the white women who "won" this demeaning sexual competition. White standards of beauty and male definitions of leadership were both turned to the double disadvantage of African-American women. Neither black nor white women, however, found their humanity and skills affirmed by the male leadership that defined them as "support staff" or sexual trophies, and they began to discuss their common oppression as women.

Women in the New Left.   The "New Left" is a term used to describe the loosely linked groups of predominately white college-aged men and women engaged in challenging the basic values and institutions of American society in the 1960s. Among their many targets were the universities, the military, racism, materialism, the entire political process, and economic imperialism in the Third World— almost every aspect of the status quo except sexism. QUESTION AUTHOR- ITY was the bumper sticker of choice. These groups' critique was essentially "leftist" in being anticapitalist, echoing many themes of the 1930s' "Old Left": brotherhood, equality, anticolonialism, and a fairer distribution of societal resources. As the decade wore on and American military intervention in Vietnam expanded, the New Left found a broad and growing constituency.

But the New Left differed from the Old Left in many important ways (Trimberger 1979). Whereas the older movement was authoritarian and doctrinaire, the newer one emphasized spontaneity, personal freedom, and direct democracy. The Old Left subordinated personal needs to the broader goal of collective well-being; whereas the New Left raised individual freedom to the highest good. And in contrast to the Old Left's ideological commitment to equality for women, the New Left was silent.

Not only was the New Left silent on sexism, but as the movement became increasingly militant, its male leadership "found it an excellent arena for competitive displays of virility, toughness, and physical courage" (Flacks 1971, 118). Having enlisted in the cause of freedom, New Left women were galled by their own lack of power or their treatment as mindless sex objects. Thus the personal became political, and many women gradually turned away from the New Left, becoming structurally and ideologically available for a movement of their own.

At first, small groups of women met to discuss their grievances within the NLM, composing resolutions demanding that movement men recognize how they were oppressing their female colleagues. But when the women sought to place their issues on the agenda, they were frequently laughed off the stage and told that such concerns were insignificant in comparison to matters of war and peace, draft resistance, and justice for Native Americans.

But there was a limit to the ridicule that women of the New Left would endure. They had already shed their "good girl" image to become "radicals." In city after city, individually or in caucuses, they decided to split with male-run New Left groups and began to extend their analysis of sexism from the movement to the society as a whole. The year 1970 marked the end of a phase in which the collectivist strand of new feminism had operated as the women's auxilliary of the student left, and the beginning of an autonomous feminist movement at the "grass roots."

The anger of these women was liberating and invigorating. Out of their experiences in both the CRM and the NLM came not only profound self-awareness but insightful criticisms of the broader society. Breines (1979) summarizes the scene as follows:

In the midst of sexist movements, women were having experiences that transformed their consciousness and changed their lives. . . . [D]emocratic and egalitarian values inspired women and offered them an alternative vision of society. . . . When women acquired the experience and skills that enabled them to feel strong enough to move out on their own, it was with political ideas that they had inherited from the sixties. (504–505)

Unlike bureaucratic organizations, the small, self-contained women's groups of the collectivist strand could take root anywhere and everywhere and were accessible to a wide spectrum of women. Autonomous "liberation" units could experiment with attention-getting "zap" actions such as picketing the Miss America Pageant to protest the sexual objectification of women, or conduct sit-ins at bars that served men only. It is difficult to imagine the women of the older branch holding "abortion raps" at a time when the procedure was illegal, or forming groups with such names as Radicalesbians, or WITCH (Women's International Terrorist Conspiracy from Hell).

While such groups added energy and zest to the movement in its early years, as well as serious intellectual content to the emerging debates within American feminism, their influence soon diminished. Internal disputes and personality conflicts were commonplace, draining members' energy (Echols 1989; Sealander and Smith 1986). Radical groups in general were stymied in their efforts to develop effective tactics as the cycle of protests in the 1960s made Americans increasingly nervous and hostile to "extremists" (Tarrow 1989). Only the relatively few women who had self-identified as radicals were prepared to risk ridicule and rejection (Ryan 1989). By 1980, grassroots organizing had been greatly curtailed, and many collectives had disbanded (Strobel 1994; Sealander and Smith 1986).

Nonetheless, collectivist feminists left a legacy of vitality and ideals that filtered into the broader movement. Perhaps the event that marked both the high point and the beginning of the end of a distinctive collectivist presence was the remarkable Women's Strike for Equality demonstration in New York City on August 26, 1970, the anniversary of the passage of the suffrage amendment, when tens of thousands of women and men, old and young, reformist and radical, joined in a jubilant march down Fifth Avenue.

In addition, collectivists, left a more complex legacy in their concepts of consciousness-raising and of sisterhood, terms that have come to seem almost synonymous with feminism. The impulse toward community, common to the Civil Rights movement and the New Left, characterized the collectivist strand of early feminism, as well. It was this desire to create a new community that became embodied in the technique and structure of the consciousness-raising (CR) group and in the ideology of "sisterhood."

Consciousness-Raising.   Even before they broke away from the New Left, women would meet in small groups to discuss sexism in the movement and to reassure one another that their experiences were valid and their concerns worthy of attention. In ideal form, the CR process was essentially a four-step discussion. The first stage involved self-revelation as each women spoke about her feelings while other participants engaged in "active listening." In the second and third stages, group members brought their individual experiences into a larger discussion, relating them to societal forces rather than to personal factors. Finally, group members tried to link their analysis to other theories of oppression (Bunch-Weeks 1970, 1990).

This process stood conventional New Left practice on its head; rather than starting with theory, as in Freudian or Marxist analysis, and then trying to fit contemporary patterns into the theoretical model, New Left women began with lived experience and then developed an explanatory framework. Recognizing the oppression in their life as part of the systemwide practice of male dominance rather than as a result of some failure on their own part as women (or as revolutionaries) not only was personally liberating but also fostered deep commitment to the goals of the New Feminist Movement—a conversion experience of quasi-religious intensity.

The process of self-discovery and the creation of new forms of community did not proceed without difficulty. CR groups had varying life spans; much depended on the particular chemistry of participants and their other commitments. Although the demand for CR groups was very heavy in the early 1970s, their popularity soon peaked, and as the recognition of gender inequality became part of the general culture, women increasingly skipped over the stages of self-discovery and theory-building and moved directly into participation in feminist activities. Some analysts see this loss of intensive political socialization as the source of a narrowing of the feminist vision (Echols 1989); others look to more institutionalized organizations as settings for political socialization today.

Sisterhood and Power. The popularity of CR groups was also limited by a feature of New Left ideology that ultimately drained the emotional resources of many members: a commitment to nonhierarchical structures and relationships, that is, those without formal positions of power and subordination. For collectivist feminists, "hierarchy" carried the additional negative meaning of a distinctly male principle of organization in contrast to a female model of "sisterhood," a relationship of equality (Ferguson 1984). Rejecting hierarchy and expertise may have been crucial for the intimacy of CR groups, but they encountered problems when their work began to move from analysis to action.

Without mechanisms for conflict resolution, CR groups wrangled endlessly over goals and tactics, and when informal leaders emerged, they were often accused of being power-hungry and subjected to a form of character assassination known as "trashing" (Freeman 1976a). As one analyst put it, "sisterhood is powerful; it kills sisters" (Echols 1989). The radical vision of equality in which each member of a group dedicates her talents to the collectives, often produced paralysis, as no one member dared to appear to be an achiever or to seek public recognition. The tendency to mistrust expertise and to trash individual achievement soon blended into anti-intellectualism, causing many talented women to cut ties to the collectives, although not to the goals of the new feminism.

It is perhaps understandable that in the emotionally charged small-group setting, women newly energized by personal awareness and revolutionary images should find themselves making the political personal; that is, reducing the big issues to personality problems (and, in the process, turning their own ideology upside down). Much the same pattern was evident among American socialists in the 1930s. Powerlessness makes it difficult to confront those who actually wield power and easier to displace anger horizontally. Existing on the radical fringe of social movements appears to produce a "siege mentality" that frequently leads to both personal and ideological attacks on comrades-in-arms. Although suspicions that getting ahead meant selling out were not always unfounded, holding women down to the lowest common level as a means of ensuring "equality" could in the long run only perpetuate powerlessness, breed resentment, and create divisions within the movement (Remington 1991). In any event, personal trashing diminished as women became integrated into other social institutions, including a larger and more diverse feminist movement (Taylor 1989a), and as local groups shifted from self-exploration to self-help and finally to providing community services (see chapter 5).

Legacies of the Early Strands

Thus, by the early 1970s two very different age groups of women had produced two very different organizational modes based on divergent visions of appropriate goals and methods. Although it might seem that such a division would diffuse the energies and commitment of feminists, this structural diversity was a source of strength, allowing various women to find a place for themselves within the broader movement. Moreover, the two modes of activity provide a counterpoint, or "dialectic," in which each feeds and corrects the other. That is, the collectivist impulse ensures that humanistic concerns and nonhierarchical styles remain visible, not only as ultimate feminist goals but as a means of transformation now. However, collectivists have difficulty dealing with bureaucracies, and since most American institutions are bureaucratically structured, the possibilities for influencing these are limited. Bureaucratically structured organizations in the women's movement, conversely, can conduct the type of nationwide money-raising and lobbying activities that bring pressure to bear on other bureaucracies, including legislative and administrative bodies. Collectives are created in order to change institutional patterns directly, by providing alternative ways of meeting members' needs. Bureaucratic activists focus on indirect change, through lawsuits, political pressure, or "moral suasion" (mobilizing public opinion), and changing the ways existing bureaucracies function.

What we have been describing are "ideal types": polar opposites and pure examples. More often, the lines between the types blurred as groups originally based on collectivist principles were transformed into local units of a broad-based movement organization, or as local chapters of national organizations served the functions of a primary group. One such pattern can be found in the academic community, where women across a variety of departments first came together in informal support networks to explore women's lives from a woman's perspective, before becoming part of a nationally organized women's caucus in their discipline, with the broader goals of bringing a new perspective to that field of study and of working collaboratively to establish interdisciplinary Women's Studies programs and departments. This development will be examined again in later chapters as we see how feminist organizations transcended conflicts between expressive and instrumental goals, successfully blending the personal and the political.

Still, the importance of collectivist groups in the New Feminist Movement declined in the early 1970s as all feminist organizations became increasingly goal-oriented, and the two strands grew closer together in both structure and style. One factor in this development was, quite simply, the time element involved in consensual decision making, often to the exclusion of accomplishing concrete tasks. Another factor was the immediate need for women to organize effectively to achieve certain political goals: the Equal Rights Amendment and the protection of reproductive rights. The tendency toward bureaucratic domination, however, is not total. The movement then and now embraces a spectrum of organizational modes, with the national mass-membership organization (often asking only for money in their direct mailings) at one pole, and community-based women's centers, health or music collectives at the other. In between, one can find thousands of separate groups of women engaged in the work of the movement, in one form or another, for any or all of the stated goals of contemporary feminism. This diversity and creativity gave the emergent movement a strength and resilience that attracted an outpouring of support in the early 1970s. The feminist boast that "we are everywhere" could no longer be taken lightly.

The number and diversity of feminist publication, as illustrated in this collage, are unequaled by another contemporary social movement. The New Feminist Movement has attempted to address both the range of women's experiences and their common interests. *Photograph by Myra Marx Ferree.*

Chapter 4

Dilemmas of Growth: The Promise of Diversity

The rapid rate of growth of the New Feminist Movement in its first decade also brought new challenges. As with other social movements, it originated in the activities of a small nucleus of people who shared similar backgrounds and experiences. To become an effective agent of change, the movement had to expand this base, adapting its ideologies and structures to take into account the situations of others. As the movement reached out, its own publications and the mass media spread the word beyond the range of interpersonal contacts. This growth demanded new resources and new organizational forms.

As described in the previous chapter, the New Feminist Movement developed from two very different groups of activists, leading to the creation of two organizational strands: the bureaucratic and the collectivist. From the beginning, both types of organizations attempted to reach a broader audience, in order to influence public opinion and attract new members. In this chapter, we examine these outreach efforts, their successes, and the dilemmas that these successes posed for the movement. Our first focus is on how word of the movement spread from the initial networks of interpersonal influence to the public at large, and, second, on public response in the form of changing opinions on women and the feminist movement. As rising proportions of the public supported change in women's status, a constituency was created that could be mobilized for more specific demands.

But even in a favorable climate of opinion, not all sympathizers are equally willing or able to become activists. In the second half of this chapter, we look at the processes of mobilization that lead people to become personally involved in movement activities, whether for a single demonstration or in an ongoing group context. In the New Feminist Movement, as in all social organizations and movements, these processes of mobilization are biased in certain predictable ways. Some people stand a much greater chance than others of becoming active, and in the last section of this chapter we examine these biases and their meaning for contemporary feminism.

Publicizing the Movement

Feminist Publications.   Most movements for social change, precisely because they are outside established networks of influence and communication, must find inexpensive and effective means of reaching and maintaining contact with potential followers. In common with members of other social movements of the 1960s, feminists first kept in touch through mimeographed newsletters, photocopied articles, and flyers to announce important events. Already in 1971, there were over a hundred women's liberation journals and newspapers in circulation (Hole and Levine 1971), a few of which are still being published (e.g., *off our backs*).

By the end of the decade, several radical feminist groups were publishing newspapers and magazines; the national office of NOW was printing an organizational periodical (*Do It NOW*); local NOW chapters were producing monthly newsletters; and, for a short period, feminist newspapers appeared in several American cities such as Milwaukee, Wisconsin (*Amazon* 1972) and Cleveland, Ohio (*What She Wants* 1973).

These early efforts were quickly augmented by a veritable explosion of feminist publishing in the 1970s. Each interest group established its own journal, newsletter, or monthly report: women in the arts, Jewish women, women of color, older women, women in professions and various academic disciplines, working women, neighborhood women, and lesbian feminists. Within a few years, over five hundred explicitly feminist periodicals, newsletters, and magazines were being produced in the United States alone (Farrell 1994). Although each had a limited circulation, cumulatively they provided a vast network of common reference, demonstrating that experiences were indeed shared.

New ground was broken with the introduction of *Ms.: A Magazine for Women* in 1972, a risky attempt to reach a mass-circulation market with what founding editor Gloria Steinem called a "how-to magazine for the liberated human female—not how to make jelly, but how to seize control of your life" (Farrell 1994). Available on newsstands in a glossy, commercial format, the initial run of 300,000 copies sold out within a week. An early *Ms.* article introduced the term "click" to describe the sudden recognition that sexism was the explanation for a particular experience; it soon became a movement byword. For two decades, *Ms.* tried to be a "feminist tool" in a capitalist workplace, as its editors struggled to reconcile readers' demand for a unique forum with advertisers' demands for a compatible environment in which to sell their products, and with their own desire to attract advertising for "big ticket" items not typically marketed to women (Farrell 1994).

Over time, the magazine lost its cutting edge under pressure from all sides. Rising publication costs led to increased reliance on advertisers, subscriptions to schools and libraries were challenged by conservative censors, and the magazine's feminist perspective was partially co-opted by other women's magazines that cut into its circulation. *Ms.*'s financial position left it at the mercy of advertisers, who had discovered the appeal of "consumer feminism," that is, selling products such as cigarettes, alcohol, and fast foods as surrogates for liberation. Eventually, advertiser pressure made *Ms.* almost indistinguishable from other commercial periodicals targeted at women. Although the editors continued to see their mission as potentially radical, whenever this vision resulted in critical articles and cover stories, advertising revenue dried up. Finally, at the end of 1989, the magazine folded as a commercial venture, to reemerge the following year as the "new" *Ms.,* without advertising but with much of its "old" radical spirit. Dependent now upon subscribers, the magazine is no longer as widely or as cheaply available as before (Farrell 1994). Yet by mid-1992, the press run for the new publication was approximately 200,000.

The second most widely circulated feminist publication was a tabloid-format newspaper called *New Directions for Women.* Begun in a kitchen in 1972 as a mimeographed newsletter for New Jersey feminists with a press run of two thousand, the newsletter was hand-delivered to libraries and other public places. *New Directions,* with a peak national circulation of fifty-five thousand, grew steadily both more radical and more professional, but paid subscriptions lagged behind production and distribution costs, a combination that had effectively silenced many other early publications, and ultimately *New Directions* itself in 1993.

The Washington-based news monthly, *off our backs,* with a circulation of twenty-five thousand has survived since 1970. Even periodicals that have ceased publication, such as *Women: A Journal of Liberation,* left a lasting mark on their participants and readers (Blanchard 1992). Despite such obstacles, at least two hundred openly feminist publications (excluding directories and regional newsletters) are listed in the 1993 edition of the *Standard Periodical Directory.*

Feminist publishing has particularly flourished in academe. The mid-1970s saw the inauguration of several periodicals of high-intellectual quality and cross-disciplinary interest, most notably *Feminist Studies* (1972), *Women's Studies Quarterly* (1972), and *Signs: Journal of Women in Culture and Society* (1975). In the following decade, specialized journals appeared in various academic fields, including publications such as *Sex Roles* and the *Psychology of Woman Quarterly, Affilia* (social work), *Hypatia* (philosophy), *Gender & Society* (sociology), *Gender and History, Women and Politics,* and even *Minerva: Quarterly Report on Women and the Military.* New journals continue to emerge; in 1988, the National Women's Studies Association launched *NWSA Journal.*

The development of an audience for feminist perspectives in the 1970s encouraged the founding of women-owned and operated publishing firms and collectives, such as The Feminist Press. Today, there are over fifty such enterprises in North America, mostly with very small and specialized lists. Many of the earliest volumes were republications of out-of-print works by women authors, especially first-wave feminists. The more recent emphasis, however, is on original works of fiction and poetry, including the emerging genre of feminist mystery novels, and even feminist children's books.

Finding an outlet for the earlier publications was another difficult hurdle, as independent bookstores were losing ground to national chain branches that reserve shelf space for mass-market books. Throughout the decade, women responded by establishing bookstores that also served as meeting places for local feminists, primarily in college towns and large cities. By 1980, there were more than seventy women's bookstores in over thirty states. Despite rising rents and growing competition from the chains, many feminist bookstores have survived into the 1990s.

Commercial publishers also sensed an opportunity in this boom and brought out anthologies making feminist articles that originally appeared in the alternative press available in mass-market paperbacks. These collections and other works, such as Kate Millett's *Sexual Politics* and Germaine Greer's *The Female Eunuch,* became best-sellers. Consequently, major publishing houses have expanded their "women's list" and continue to bring out important feminist books and anthologies. However, there is also a large market for antifeminist publications by women authors.

Nonetheless, a bookstore browser today will find several shelves devoted to women's issues; whereas in 1970, the category did not even exist. Furthermore, as women's studies programs and courses multiplied, every major academic publisher scrambled for part of this rapidly expanding market. In sum, what had been esoteric in the late 1960s was widely available in the mid-1970s and is today a well-established subfield in American commercial and university publishing.

While books, magazines, and newsletters are important elements in spreading the word during the early stages of a social movement, they typically reach only those already in a co-optable network. To inform and involve a wider audience, modern social movements are dependent on the mass media.

Mass Media Coverage of the Movement.   As attention shifted from the Civil Rights movement to the ghetto riots of the late 1960s, and as the student movement and New Left dissolved under the guns of the National Guard and in factionalism over "revolutionary violence," the media discovered the New Feminist Movement. In large part, this was intentional. Women in the bureaucratic strand were both media-wise and media-conscious; some were from the communications industries, others had extensive contacts in publishing and news services. The younger women, despite an antimedia ideology, had also learned how to catch public interest for New Left activities through media events such as protest marches, mass demonstrations, and "street theater."

Although there was much to report on the emergent movement in the 1960s, there was very little media coverage until the end of the decade, when the media treated the New Feminist Movement as a new discovery. Mentions in the national press increased tenfold between May 1969 and March 1970 (Morris 1973), and television coverage nearly tripled (Cancian and Ross 1981). Not only did the number of stories increase, but there was a distinct change in tone, from faintly amused or bewildered to something approaching serious consideration, even though most newspaper articles still appeared in the "life-style" pages rather than the news sections.

And because many feminist leaders, mindful of their dismissive treatment in the New Left movement, refused to deal with male reporters, the press was forced to send female correspondents to cover demonstrations and news conferences. This raised consciousness within media organizations, as many editors suddenly "found" the well-qualified women who had been toiling in the backrooms for many years.

Although some of the newly authorized women reporters may have been selected in hopes that they, too, would trivialize the movement (the *New York Times* assigned the wife of a senior editor), many newswomen found themselves personally affected and transformed by their contact with feminists and feminism. Not only did they file sympathetic reports, but they began to organize for changes in their own workplaces—more women in responsible positions, greater control over editorial content, and increased attention to topics of feminist concern in the news sections as well as the social or "women's" pages (Tuchman 1978).

A sex discrimination case filed in 1978 against the *New York Times* and eventually settled out of court not only greatly enhanced the status of women at that newspaper but had spillover effects on other journalistic settings (Robertson 1992). Women became more visible as news anchors and reporters on television and gained influence behind the scenes in production roles. Their presence led to changes in both entertainment programming and news coverage, which became more sympathetic to women's issues than in the past. Certainly *Murphy Brown* presents a far more powerful image of a woman journalist than did *The Mary Tyler Moore Show*.

Staff writers on traditional women's magazines also struggled to raise the awareness level of publishers and the public. They demonstrated and lobbied for articles on working women, the New Feminist Movement, nonsexist child rearing, violence against women, the women's health movement, and the Equal Rights Amendment. Feminist-inspired social science research began to be reported in their articles and editorials. In this fashion, 1969–70 marked a turning point not only in quantity but quality of media coverage. Ideas that had previously circulated only by word-of-mouth or among the small number of subscribers to "alternative" publications now appeared in mass circulation newspapers and magazines, reaching millions of women without personal links to the tiny feminist groups that existed in major cities.

This media coverage was essential to the success of the new feminism. For any social movement to expand its base and to develop latent support from the public at large, the initial network of activists must be able to communicate to a potentially sympathetic public. The movement ideology must be widely broadcast, so that individuals throughout the society can see that what they thought were personal problems are not at all unique. These effects are reflected in actual patterns of recruitment. One study of movement members found that all who joined before 1969 had heard about the movement from personal contacts; while among joiners in or after 1969, about one in four had been activated solely on the basis of media reports (Carden 1974).

In addition, as more books are published and reviewed, as more magazine articles appear, as more mention is made on radio and television, as newspaper coverage expands, the movement itself becomes "institutionalized"; that is, it becomes a "normal" part of the social landscape. In this way, media attention creates reality, validating the existence of whatever it covers. Even though it had been a growing force for several years, the New Feminist Movement became "real" as soon as the reporters and cameras focused on it (just as, a decade later, the movement lost much of its "thereness" when the cameras and reporters turned away).

The reality created by the media was, in many ways, a different one from that experienced by members. Indeed, the most memorable media image was of an event that never actually occurred: the "bra burning" during a protest against the Miss America contest in Atlantic City in 1968. And what an image! Here is the distillation of resentment over the status of women as sex objects, over the need to contort one's natural shape to fit a culturally defined ideal; and, yet, how easily ridiculed and trivialized the movement can be made to appear through such images. The glare of publicity exaggerates both the strengths and weaknesses of a social movement and its membership. In these early years of the new feminism, media attention undoubtedly served to spread the word and activate constituencies, making the movement appear more powerful than the actual numbers of committed feminists would suggest, an impression that probably accounted for many early legislative gains, but that also awakened countermovement forces.

Indeed, as organized antifeminist forces emerged and gained

legitimacy, especially during the Reagan and Bush administrations, the tone of media treatment changed once more. This shift took advantage of the typical biases in media routines for creating stories. First, in the interests of "journalistic balance," in which every story has two and only two sides, favorable coverage must be coupled with critical commentary, increasingly supplied by well-funded conservative think tanks. The new wisdom became the claim that all reasonable efforts had been made to redress past grievances, and if the system still seemed unfair to minorities and women, this was evidence that some differences by race and sex cannot be overcome by "social engineering."

A second built-in bias of the media's coverage is their interest as gatekeepers in selecting provocative stories, even when they have few independent means of evaluating information. Thus, as documented by Susan Faludi (1991), reporters have exaggerated and oversimplified "research data" that warn women about the harmful effects of attempting to achieve equality—the shortage of marriage partners, the trauma of latchkey children, the dramatic loss of income with divorce, role overload, burnout and other disorders of the mind and body— blaming these conditions on feminism rather than on the persistent inequality that the movement seeks to overcome.

Third, the media are attracted to novelty, so as the women's movement became widely known, it ceased to be "newsworthy." Coverage declined even as the movement grew dramatically in numbers and influence, leaving many Americans with the mistaken conclusion that its invisibility meant that the movement was "dead" and that a new "postfeminist era" was at hand. These impressions were encouraged by media, which had already declared the movement dead by the early 1970s. For the general public, the media's definitions of the identity, goals, and prospects of a social movement "easily attain the status of objective and factual truth" (Van Zoonen 1992: 434). Despite stories that present feminism as foolish, harmful, or even old-fashioned, the media also offer a forum for feminists to make known their existence, especially through *media events* such as mass demonstrations.

Demonstrations and the Media.   Media attention can spread the message, letting potential recruits know they are not alone, but there must be something to join—a local organization or CR group—before the feeling of solidarity can be translated into active support. Here is where local groups or chapters of national organizations assume critical importance. They are rallying places of activated commitment and visible symbols of a movement's vitality. Demonstrations also serve this function, while at the same time contributing to the "newsworthy" quality of the movement, attracting even more media attention.

A demonstration operates at several levels. In addition to the obvious appeal to those who watch it on television or read about the event in magazines and newspapers, there is also the effect on participants. Marching together creates a sense of solidarity, deepening protesters' commitment to the movement; if the situation has an element of danger, there is the additional exhilaration of risk taking on behalf of the cause. Just being with others who feel as they do helps to legitimize their feelings; the shared ideals can become an important part of their identity.

The New Feminist Movement has orchestrated a number of demonstrations serving the dual functions of broadcasting a message and reinforcing the commitment of participants. The first mass demonstration in New York City in 1970, for example, exceeded the expectations of its organizers when twenty thousand marchers took over Fifth Avenue to the general amazement of onlookers and the police.

Other notable mobilizations include three mass rallies in Washington, D.C., at crucial moments in the struggle for reproductive rights and for the Equal Rights Amendment. Each enormous turnout raised the crowd number needed for the next rally to be defined as successful, and each in turn became the largest demonstration in the Capitol's history. In April 1992, over 500,000 women, men, and children joined a March for Women's Lives as the Supreme Court was deliberating the consitutionality of state limits on access to abortion services, a powerful indication of the movement's growth since 1970.

As effective as mass rallies are in focusing media attention and reinforcing the allegiance of marchers, one cannot go to the well too often. Demonstrations are expensive and time-consuming productions, requiring advance planning from publicizing the event to renting portable toilets. Demonstrators also make an investment of time and money, and they cannot be expected to take a day out of their life with great frequency. Thus feminist organizations have begun to question the effectiveness of mass demonstrations in swaying legislators or public opinion (Spalter-Roth and Schreiber 1994; Staggenborg 1991). Yet without a mass forum for displaying and revitalizing commitment, younger generations of feminists may have no direct link to activism, or a personal basis for refuting claims that the movement is dead and/or irrelevant. Nonetheless, the vast majority of Americans who think of themselves as feminists have probably never attended a meeting or taken part in a demonstration. Their commitment is largely expressed in their willingness to provide support to specific movement causes. These men and women constitute a latent force that can be mobilized periodically on behalf of a particular candidate or piece of legislation. This constituency is kept abreast of the movement primarily through the media. Therefore, keeping the movement in the news is an essential element in retaining this base of support, provided, of course, that the news being reported does not ridicule or trivialize the movement.

In other words, the audience for many media events may not be the announced targets as much as bystander populations outside the arena of action, such as politicians, employers, "closet feminists," potential sympathizers, and media executives who need to be convinced that the movement is still alive and well and living in towns and cities across the nation.

Sympathizers and Activists: Problems of Mobilization

Public Attitudes toward Women and Women's Issues.   By the early 1970s, through their own publications and the attention of the mass media, "women's liberation" had become a household word. While some of this attention was negative if not outrightly hostile, as in the use of such terms as "women's lib" and "libbers," much of the response to the New Feminist Movement was astonishingly positive. No one was more surprised than the feminist organizers and activists themselves when hundreds showed up at events where only a few dozen had been expected, and thousands appeared where hundreds had been anticipated. Public lectures, women's studies courses, and CR groups were all overflowing. Even so, those who came out were but a small fraction of the movement's potential constituency: the 51 percent of all Americans who are female, plus a sizable proportion of male sympathizers. The general population was certainly aware of feminism after the media explosion of 1969–70; how did they respond to this information?

Public opinion data available from this period indicate a basically favorable response. It is difficult to tell how much these attitudes differed from those held before 1970, since questions on feminist issues were not asked in the 1950s or 1960s. As feminist activities and media interest mushroomed, so too did the monitoring of attitudes by national opinion polling organizations. There are a few studies that include data from the 1960s. Mason, Czajka, and Arber (1976) were able to assemble a set of questions about women's roles in the labor force and the family that had been asked of women in special surveys in 1964, 1970, and 1973–74, suggesting significant attitude change in virtually every subpopulation of women questioned. For example, disagreement with the statement "a man can make long-range plans for his life, but a woman has to take things as they come," increased by over 30 percentage points among college-educated women between 1964 and 1970. The attitudes of non-college-educated women changed little between 1964 and 1970 but in subsequent years kept pace with changes among college-educated women.

Another extended time series of opinion data comes from Detroit women, initially interviewed in 1962 and contacted again in 1977 (Thornton and Freedman 1979). Four questions were asked: about male authority in the family, men doing housework, women's activities outside the home, and sex-segregated roles in general. In 1962, the proportions giving "nontraditional" responses to these questions ranged from 32 percent to 56 percent. By 1977, no item received less than 60 percent egalitarian response. Attitude change was most marked among younger and better-educated respondents, and least among fundamentalist Protestants, but all subgroups showed increased support for feminist goals. These same women were reinterviewed in 1980 along with the children born to them in 1962, who were, therefore, eighteen years old (Thornton, Alwin, and Camburn 1983). The researchers found no signs of backlash: changes in mothers' attitudes between 1977 and 1980 continued at the same rate as between 1962 and 1977. In addition, egalitarian mothers tended to have egalitarian children. Sons were more traditional than daughters, but both were less traditional than their mothers had been in 1962.

Another time series is available on respondents' willingness to vote for a woman as president of the United States (or unwillingness to admit otherwise). Up to 1969, only 55 percent said that they might vote for a "qualified" woman, a proportion virtually unchanged since 1958. In 1972 this figure jumped to 70 percent among both men and women and was more closely associated with acceptance of a black nominee, suggesting that public attitudes had been influenced by the analogy between race and sex (Ferree 1974). Support for a woman candidate grew steadily over the next two decades, reaching 87 percent in 1991 (Schreiber 1978; Cherlin 1982; General Social Survey 1991). Such an abstract question, however, may only be tapping reluctance to express prejudice against women. When the issue is framed more concretely, in terms of a particular candidate such as Geraldine Ferraro, a double standard of judgment appears, with women voters somewhat more likely to support the female candidate, but men less likely to do so, primarily white southern men (Clymer 1984). Surveys in the late 1980s suggest that although 10 percent of respondents would vote for a female over a male candidate, 25 percent would favor the man over the woman (Associated Press 1988; Roper Organization 1990). However, a survey conducted in 1992 suggested that women now held a slight edge (37 percent would prefer a woman, 25 percent a man, all else being equal [ABC/WP 1992]).

Questions about whether a woman described herself as "feminist" first appeared in national surveys in the mid-1980s, and affirmative answers have hovered around 30–40 percent, with one in ten describing herself as "strongly feminist" (Yankelovich, Clancy, and Shulman 1989; Gallup 1987; Voter Research and Surveys 1990). In addition, close to one-fourth of all women under age forty-five said that they had become *more* feminist as they grew older, compared to only 9 percent who had become less sympathetic (Gallup 1986). And although it is often pointed out that college women in the 1980s were more likely to endorse feminist issues than to take on the "feminist" label per se (Renzetti 1987), this was also the case in the 1970s (Jacobson and Koch 1978).

Attitudes toward the feminist movement itself have become steadily more positive: from 40 percent of women in favor of "most efforts to strengthen and change women's status in society" in 1970 to 64 percent in 1980, and 77 percent in 1990 (Roper Organization 1990). In one 1989 survey, 89 percent agreed that the feminist movement had given women more control over their lives, and 82 percent thought that the movement "was still improving the lives of women," although opinion was more divided on whether or not the movement "accurately reflects the views of most women," with 53 percent answering yes and 42 percent no (Yankelovich, Clancy, and Shulman 1989).

Thus, despite the recent media claims of a popular antifeminist backlash, often described as "postfeminism," general survey data continue to show high levels of support for the movement and concern over such issues as violence toward women, job opportunities, equal pay, and balancing work and family responsibilities (e.g., *New York Times* 1989). Indeed, it could be said that the backlash appears to be largely within the media itself (Faludi 1991). Rather than highlighting the positive numbers, columnists and editors tend to draw attention to the nonfeminist responses. For example, commenting on a 1992 *Time*/CNN poll, *Time*'s editors suggested that "what readers may be looking for is an explanation for why . . . 63 percent of American women do not consider themselves feminists" (Gibbs 1992, 50–51). Yet what is truly impressive in these data is the close to one-third who do identify themselves as feminists—about the same percentage as consider themselves Republicans or Democrats! And even though the numbers appear overwhelmingly favorable, as when 65 percent of all respondents agreed that NOW is "in touch with the average American woman," *Time* used a single interview to assert that the organization is generally dismissed as out of touch (Wallis 1989, 81). To be sure, the *Time*/CCN survey did find negative views, but these are clearly minority opinions, as when 35 percent believe that the feminist movement "looks down on women who do not have jobs" or is "antifamily" (24 percent) or "antimale" (23 percent).

Another myth that has received much media attention and that is not supported by the data is the belief that feminism appeals only to middle-class white women. In fact, African-American women have always held more favorable views toward the movement than have their white sisters: 60 percent versus 37 percent in 1970; 77 percent versus 65 percent in 1980 (Roper 1980); and 85 percent versus 64 percent in 1989 (Sapiro 1991). In comparison with white women, African-American women's attitudes to feminism were less affected by their paid employment, while single parenting emerged as more strongly associated with their critical attitudes toward gender norms (Dugger 1988). Yet although African-American women are more feminist than are white women, the same is not true for African-American men, so conflicts on gender-related issues may be greater among African-Americans than among their nonblack counterparts (Ransford and Miller 1983).

Women's attitudes toward feminism do *not* appear to be influenced by their husband's income or his status as a blue- or white-collar worker (Mason and Bumpass 1975; Burris 1983) or by their own occupational status (Thornton, Alwin, and Camburn 1983). Feminist attitudes *are* positively influenced by a woman's level of education and labor force participation, and negatively by age and church attendance

(Cook 1989; Sapiro 1991). Over time, however, differences by education level have narrowed, as support for feminist issues increased across all age/sex/education categories (Mason and Lu 1988).

Remaining subgroup differences in attitudes can be explained in part by differential access to social networks. For example, employed women with many workplace friendships are more feminist than are other employed women, and full-time housewives with home-based friendship networks are less feminist than are other housewives (Ferree 1980). Simply being in the labor force—regardless of occupational status or income—or even being in a nontraditional job, tends to raise feminist consciousness (Mason and Lu 1988; Rinehart 1992; Cook 1989; Gurin 1985). Among a sample of homemakers in 1973, those who subsequently entered the labor force soon matched other employed women in positive attitudes toward feminist issues; whereas those remaining at home became even less supportive (Sapiro 1991).

Regarding attitude differences between men and women, not surprisingly women are more likely (55 compared to 39 percent) to agree that "most men are willing to let women get ahead, but only if women still do all the work at home" (Sapiro 1991). Also, by 67 to 51 percent, women are more likely than men to agree that "the United States continues to need a strong women's movement to push for changes that benefit women" (Dionne 1989). Sex differences are less extreme on such issues as preference for an egalitarian marriage (57 compared to 50 percent), although both women and men also believe that his career takes precedence and his economic position determines the family's status (Simon and Landis 1989). Yet on such central issues as reproductive choice and the Equal Rights Amendment, men have been as supportive as women (Davis and Smith 1990).

Survey data indicate not only that there has been a rise in favorable opinions toward feminist issues, but also that respondents are increasingly linking their attitudes across a range of issues. For both feminists and antifeminists, positions on a range of issues have tended toward internal coherence, so that a distinct set of attitudes characterizes each constituency, making it easier for people to choose sides consistently. These "issue packages" have also become increasingly identified with political party preference, with feminists supporting Democratic candidates, and antifeminists favoring Republicans (Freeman 1993). In the 1990 election, only 8 percent of Republican women voters identified themselves as "strong feminists" in comparison with 18 percent of Independent or Democratic women voters (*American Enterprise* 1991, 93).

Despite this trend toward internal consistency, attitudes toward abortion remained relatively unconnected to other opinions about women's rights, being primarily influenced by church attendance and feelings about adolescent sexuality (Hall and Ferree 1986). Indeed, abortion remained something of a "single issue" throughout the 1970s, only gradually becoming linked to other positions (Mueller 1983a). Among those for whom this issue remains unconnected are African-American women, who, although strongly supportive of feminist positions, are less likely than white women to support the right to abortion (Combs and Welch 1982; Hall and Ferree 1986). Deeply religious respondents also have difficulty integrating their views on various aspects of women's rights, although they did not become more antifeminist in the 1970s (Mueller 1983a). Among American Catholic laypersons, despite increasingly vocal opposition from the religious hierarchy, support for abortion rights increased from 67 to 79 percent between 1975 and 1983 and remained high throughout the 1980s (National Opinion Research Center 1991; Harris 1991).

Overall, there has been strikingly little change in public attitudes toward abortion following *Roe* v. *Wade* in 1973, despite the high level of mobilization by activists on both sides over the past two decades. Support for legal abortion increased throughout the 1960s, reaching 80 percent (for cases in which a woman's life was in danger) by 1972, before *Wade* (Condit 1990). In the 1970s and 1980s, both men and women overwhelmingly supported a woman's right to abortion when her health or life was at risk (80–90 percent in most polls).

However, opinions on legal abortion were more ambivalent for other than health-risk conditions. In 1991, 92 percent of Americans felt that a pregnant woman should be able to obtain a legal abortion if her health was endangered; 86 percent were in favor if the pregnancy was the result of rape; and 83 percent supported the right to an abortion if there was a strong chance that the fetus was seriously deformed. These percentages are all higher than when similar questions were asked in 1965. However, only 48 percent approved the right to an abortion when the primary reason was low family income; 45 percent were in favor when a nonmarried woman did not want to marry or when a married woman did not want more children. Overall, in 1989 and 1991 43 percent said that a woman should be able to obtain a legal abortion for any reason, compared to the 37 percent who held a similar opinion in 1978 (National Opinion Research Center 1991; Yankelovich, Clancy, and Shulman 1989). Conversely, a consistent 12 percent of respondents have held that abortion should be illegal under all circumstances. The salience of this issue is reflected in the fact that three out of four women in a recent survey selected abortion as one of the "very important issues for women today" (Yankelovich, Clancy, and Shulman 1992).

In summary, the feminist activism of the early 1970s initiated sharp and sweeping changes in the public perception of women, of the feminist movement, and of many of its specific goals. All the books and pamphlets, meetings and demonstrations, and the media coverage discussed in this chapter had a major consciousness-raising effect on the general public. Shifts toward feminist positions continued and consolidated over the following decades, both as individuals changed their opinions and as new generations with different attitudes entered adulthood. Media backlash appears to have had little success in undermining public acceptance of the movement and its goals, which continued to gain support in the face of a hostile federal government and an organized antifeminist countermovement (to be discussed in chapter 6). The attention paid to feminism produced heightened debate over women's roles, so that attitudes became more internally consistent and more closely linked to partisan politics in the 1980s. This polarization, especially sharp on the issue of abortion rights, tends to stabilize opinions, anchoring them in networks of social relations and general political positions.

It seems safe to conclude that feminist ideas have spread well beyond the ranks of movement activists and have become part of the taken-for-granted world of most Americans. This is a remarkable achievement in itself and provides the backdrop against which both strands of the organized movement reached out to new constituencies and dealt with the inevitable strains and stresses of growth in this period.

Biases in Mobilization.   Members of the two original strands were recruited through existing social networks; that is, by word of mouth among women already organized for other purposes. These existing co-optable networks were essential to the early growth and survival of the movement, but they were also narrow bases of recruitment. In the early years, many women were "left out" of the movement because they were not linked to either the bureaucratic organizations or the collectivist groups of the 1960s. As a result, recruits for both strands were disproportionately drawn from the ranks of urban, educated women, with older ones located in the bureaucratic-legal structures that gave birth to NOW and similar organizations, and younger ones in the student/intellectual milieu of radical politics. In either case, few working-class women—old or young, black or white—were available for mobilization via these interpersonal influences.

Although the movement is often described as being "white and middle class," women of color were always represented among its leadership in these early years; most notably, Pauli Murray, a black writer, attorney, and ordained Episcopal priest; Aileen Hernandez, an attorney and president of NOW; and Florynce Kennedy, also an attorney. These women, and other black and Hispanic professionals, were already integrated into the network of bureaucratic activists. Non–middle-class activists were much rarer. The New Feminist Movement, like most social movements, depended on an affluent and educated elite to provide organizing skills and to publicize the cause. People involved in a struggle for daily existence can only rarely afford the time and energy required for organizing; they are also more vulnerable to the risks entailed in movement activity.

Not only do middle-class women have the resources, but they are also encouraged to have high aspirations. Educating people for positions and responsibilities that they are not permitted to assume generates grievances that feed into social movement activism. In addition, middle-class women have acquired the organizational experiences and the ability to articulate movement goals. Even when working-class women have such skills, they are rarely recognized or encouraged (Bookman and Morgen 1988).

All social and political organizations therefore find it easiest to mobilize their middle-class sympathizers (Verba and Nie 1972). Critics of the New Feminist Movement invariably refer to this recruitment bias in order to discredit the entire movement, claiming that it cannot speak for all women, and most especially for the doubly oppressed: women of color and of the working class. Curiously, although this charge is most often leveled against the bureaucratic feminist organizations, it was the collectivist groups that displayed greater homogeneity in membership. This is so, according to Rothschild-Whitt (1979), because value agreement and normative consensus are essential to the success of collectives; whereas in hierarchal organization, order can be imposed from above by impersonal rules despite individual differences. One can be more confident that others share one's values when they are similar in social background characteristics. In addition, friendship networks rather than organizational memberships were the primary recruitment channels for the collectivist strand and were also more segregated.

It would be a mistake, however, to continue to perceive feminism in the United States today as a middle-class phenomenon. The 1970s were a period in which many other constituencies saw themselves as beneficiaries of movement goals: women of color (African-American, Native-American, Asian-American, and Hispanic women) and working-class women. From their earlier position of hostility, many labor unions have endorsed feminist positions and working-class women have begun to organize on their own behalf. As a result, the racial, ethnic, and class composition of feminist activists has become broader and more varied.

In addition, white feminists, confronted with a legacy of racism within their movement, have begun the long process of rethinking feminism from a more inclusive, multicultural perspective. This effort requires more than simply recruiting racial/ethnic minority women to a movement whose goals and priorities have been set by middle-class white women. Authentic inclusion demands that attention be paid to the perspectives and needs of all women, particularly the most disadvantaged.

Participation by Women of Color and Ethnic Women. For Asian, Latina, and African-American women, participation in the movement is often rendered problematic when the movement seems to place the demands of gender identification above those of race or ethnicity. Minority women's experience is not one of separable and distinct oppressions but of simultaneous subordinations and loss of particular identity. As women of color, they have a specific history and face unique problems that cannot be neatly or exclusively attributed to gender or race or ethnicity (Giddings 1984). One aspect of minority women's experience, unfortunately, is confronting the racism of white women in situations ranging from exploitative working conditions for domestic workers (Rollins 1985; Romero 1992) to the exclusion of African-Americans from "women's" organizations (Cott 1987; Barnett 1994).

Working for the liberation of women of color thus demands conscious and sustained efforts to eliminate racism within the movement as well as in society at large. For many women of color, this means working with those who share the experiences and awareness of racism that many white women still lack (hooks 1984). However, the impact of sexism can be obscured by an overwhelming concern for racial unity and pride and a desire to improve the life of men of color. In addition, cultural stereotypes of women's strength or submissiveness can be manipulated to discourage acknowledging sexism within the subculture (Giddings 1984; Garcia, 1989).

Despite such obstacles, feminist consciousness has expanded greatly among Latina (Garcia 1989), Asian-American (Chow 1987), and African-American (Collins 1990) women. In fact, their participation in collective efforts to end racial oppression has often led them to an awareness of sexist behavior and attitudes within their own community. But feminist consciousness does not automatically lead to activism. Participation takes time that might otherwise be devoted to survival: earning money and/or caring for children. One must also be in a position to be recruited—that is, in contact with other people willing and able to become active in a social movement. For these reasons, it is typically the more affluent and socially integrated women of color, rather than the most burdened and deprived, who become active in women's (or other) organizations.

Furthermore, because most social contacts in a segregated society remain within racial boundaries, white women have not always made the effort to extend their networks to involve more than a token number of minority women. This is one reason why separate African-American, Asian-American, and Latina feminist organizations are so important to the integration of the movement as a whole. Paradoxically, diversity can enhance unity.

Organizations specifically of and for racial/ethnic women were founded at the very outset of the movement. As early as 1971, Chicana feminists in California opened a center for working women; the National Conference of Puerto Rican Women first convened in 1972; and the Mexican-American Woman's Association was established in 1974. In 1982, Chicana academics formed Mujeres Activas en Letras y Cambio Social as a support network for research and activism (Garcia 1989). Many local projects, such as the Hispanic Women's Health Center in Hartford, Connecticut, or the East Los Angeles Rape Crisis Center address the needs of Latina women from a uniquely feminist perspective.

The first American Indian Women's Conference was held in 1975, providing an organizational base for the American Indian/Alaskan Native Caucus that emerged from the 1977 National Women's Conference in Houston, Texas. Radical women activists in the

American Indian Movement (AIM), recognizing common problems of sexism, also formed their own feminist organization, Women of All Red Nations (WARN).

Among African-American women, the National Council of Negro Women, a long-established leadership group, was an early endorser of the Equal Rights Amendment and other mainstream feminist goals, while the Third World Women's Alliance was one of the early collectivist groups taking part in the 1970 Women's Equality Day march. Black feminist involvement was also substantial in the early years of NOW, but the failure of many of NOW's significant white leaders to support Representative Shirley Chisholm's candidacy for the Democratic presidential nomination in 1972 fueled suspicion that white women wanted support but not leadership from African-American women. Other, explicitly feminist, African-American women's organizations began to emerge in the 1970s: the National Black Feminist Organization in 1973, the short-lived but influential black lesbian Combahee River Collective in 1974, the National Association of Black Professional Women in 1977, the National Coalition of 100 Black Women, and the Black Women's Health Network in 1981. Other political groups organized and led by African-American women focused on specific issues of immediate concern to poor and working-class women. One such was the National Welfare Rights Organization, which had enrolled 20,000 welfare recipients by 1968, before succumbing to internal and external pressures (Piven and Cloward 1977; Roach and Roach 1978).

Because of the great diversity among Asian-American women, it has been difficult for activists to generate a sense of shared fate that bridges specific ethnic communities (Lee 1971). Thus we find both women's caucuses within ethnic organizations (e.g., the Organization of Chinese American Women) and multiethnic coalitions of Asian-American feminists, primarily operating at the grassroots level, but sometimes growing into interregional and interethnic regional networks. Other groups have moved from a base in ethnic and women's studies programs to the provision of direct services (Chow 1987). More recently, broader alliances, such as the National Organization of Pan Asian Women and Asian American Women United, have emerged on the national scene.

The development of local and national organizations to deal with the interlocking issues of race, gender, and class oppression is a crucial thread in the tapestry of the New Feminist Movement. Separate organizations, however important, cannot substitute for change in the movement as a whole or in society. Women of color remain invisible despite their presence, as if "all the women are white, and all the blacks are men" (Hull, Scott, and Smith 1982). In addition, many minority women feel that they are being asked to make an impossible choice between naming their race or their gender as "the" locus of oppression (Mohanty, Russo, and Torres 1991). Women of color also feel that they alone carry the burden of repeatedly pointing out that the needs of white women cannot be equated with those of "women" in general, as if white women had no race or racial privilege (Auzaldua and Moraga 1981; Russo et al. 1991). Finally, inclusiveness requires attention to problems faced by poor and working-class women, dispro-portionately drawn from the ranks of racial and ethnic minorities (Garcia 1989; Bookman and Morgen 1988).

Participation by Poor and Working-Class Women. For many poor women, some of the stated objectives of the movement appear to be intrinsically narrow and class-bound—breaking through the "glass ceiling" on professional advancement, for example—and other goals are achieved in ways that primarily benefit middle-class women. The confinement to a suburban home and dependence on a husband's wage that was such a stifling experience for middle-class housewives in the 1950s was not only alien to the daily life of women factory work-ers but actively oppressive to the domestic workers hired by affluent women (Rollins 1985). When middle-class feminists call for enhanced work and educational opportunities, they are often not thinking of expanding the kinds of schooling and jobs available to poor women (Gittell and Naples 1982). Even though on a statistical basis the "body issues"—rape, abortion, and domestic violence—have at least as great an impact on the lives of working-class women as middle-class women, the political importance of these issues may be overshadowed by the need to secure economic justice. For many poor women, supporting and caring for the children they do have is the crucial family issue, and gender oppression within the family is a secondary to their oppression in the rest of society (Baca Zinn 1990). Middle-class efforts at promoting contraceptives (such as Norplant) or abortion rights have been interpreted, with good cause, as sometimes targeted at lim-iting fertility among the "lower classes," defining birth control as a right for the affluent, but a duty for the poor (Davis 1981).

Social class differences in focus are nicely illustrated in the contrast between two feminist organizations devoted to reproductive rights: the Committee for Abortion Rights and Against Sterilization Abuse (CARASA) and the National Abortion Rights Action League (NARAL). For CARASA, "reproductive rights" includes the right to *have* children, to be protected against involuntary sterilization (as still practiced in the South), and to *resist* pressures to have abortions. In contrast, NARAL, an organization heavily supported by middle-class feminists, was devoted to the single issue of legal abortion until changing its goals and name in 1994.

Working-class women have organized, even when little concern and attention was paid to their interests by mainstream feminist groups. Such organizations have characteristically existed in the community, as the many case studies in Bookman and Morgen (1988) illustrate, or in the workplace (e.g., Sacks 1988). Some of these organizations have been quite active in promoting women's interests and have a strongly politicized gender consciousness, even though they avoid the feminist label, feeling that this implies merely the middle-class version of feminism. For example, the National Congress of Neighborhood Women, organized in 1974, focuses specifically on women's empowerment and offers a variety of services from its Washington, D.C., office. For those in unionized workplaces, the Coalition of Labor Union Women (CLUW) was formed in 1974 at a convention attended by three thousand delegates from fifty-eight unions. This organization now has over fifteen thousand members and continues to be a pressure group working for greater representation of women's interests within the labor movement.

Organizing the unorganized was also a priority for working-class women. The National Union of Hospital and Health Care Employees was founded in the 1950s, and its New York affiliate, District 1199, worked with Civil Rights organizations in the late 1960s and early 1970s to win better wages and working conditions for the women of color who are the industry's primary work force. In addition, the Union responded to its members by developing a feminist analysis of their working conditions (Giddings 1984). Also beginning in 1973–74, women in various cities formed associations of office workers: Women Employed (Chicago), Women Office Workers (New York), and 9 to 5 (Boston). By 1979, many of these groups joined in forming Working Women: A National Association of Office Workers, renamed 9 to 5 and affiliated with the Service Employees International Union. At its tenth anniversary, 9 to 5 had a national membership of over twelve thousand (Burton 1987).

The struggle for inclusiveness has been a constant challenge to the New Feminist Movement. Awareness of the need to reach out to and take account of the many constituencies of women was present in the 1970s, and it is no less salient today. Some successes have been achieved; for example, among delegates to the National Women's Conference in Houston in 1977, white middle-class women were actually *under*represented and had to be added to several state delegations in order for the conference to achieve racial balance (Rossi 1982). Yet failures also abound; women of color and working-class women often feel patronized and tokenized by the middle-class white movement leaders who seek them as recruits but not as equal partners. Thus the goal of representing all American women remains an elusive vision.

Realizing the Promise of Diversity

Despite the barriers to participation experienced by women of color and working-class white women, the New Feminist Movement today encompasses dozens of organizations specifically devoted to their concerns. Moreover, their issues and perspectives are being brought increasingly into the mainstream of predominately white women's organizations through the scholarship and activism of women of color (Collins 1990). Constructive criticism of the middle-class assumptions underlying certain feminist demands has already had a visible impact on organizational goals and strategies—for example, by including sterilization abuse along with barriers to abortion as a denial of reproductive rights or by increasing attention to women's ability to enter apprenticeship programs as well as professional schools. But the movement is still far from achieving full integration.

Incorporating such a variety of perspectives will continue to broaden the vision of the New Feminist Movement as well as expand its base of participation. But diversity also brings conflict, fear, and anger. The phenomenal growth of feminism has been accompanied by considerable organizational stress and strain. As women joined the movement, they brought with them their deepest needs and dreams and spurred the movement to grow not only in numbers but in the breadth and inclusiveness of its vision. Both new issues and old tensions have generated organizational change, conflict, and growth. It is to these developments that we turn in the next chapter.

A "Take Back the Night" march in Washington, D.C., one of many around the country through which feminists have drawn attention to commonplace violence against women, an issue that crosses lines of race, class, and ethnicity. *Photograph courtesy of Joan E. Biren.*

Chapter 5

Feminist Organizations in Transition, 1973–1982

As the New Feminist Movement grew, its organizational life expanded and became more diverse. By 1973, the *New Women's Survival Catalog* listed hundreds of groups around the country. The next edition, in 1975, already called itself a "sourcebook" rather than a catalog, since it was no longer possible to list all the rape crisis centers, health clinics, art galleries, theatre groups, credit unions, child-care facilities, research libraries, bookstores, restaurants, self-defense studios, lobbying organizations, task forces, therapy collectives, retreat houses, record companies, women's studies programs, career counseling enterprises, and other business and services through which the movement established a local and national presence.

Not all of them survived the decade, and even those that did underwent substantial changes. In the first part of this chapter we look at the diversity of feminist organizations that emerged in the 1970s and at the conflicts and challenges they faced in the following decade. While the abundance and variety of feminist groups continues to defy efforts at cataloging, it is possible to identify three broad organizational strategies for challenging male domination: direct action/self-help groups, educational/political associations, and cultural/entrepreneurial organizations. Each of these forms has drawn on both the bureaucratic and the collectivist strands of feminism in shaping its internal structure and external policies, but each has blended them in different proportions and patterns. Because of this interweaving, by the end of

the decade, the distinction between collectivist and bureaucratic organizations could rarely be made in practice. Nonetheless, feminist organizations in this period did vary substantially in their goals and
approaches, and each of the three strategic forms made significant
contributions to the growth and success of the movement as a whole.
As the movement's base was broadened by the proliferation of organizations and activities in the 1970s, so also did contradictions and disputes emerge. In the second part of this chapter we examine some of
the most significant of these conflicts—over racism and anti-Semitism,
over lesbianism, and over pornography—and their effects on the
development of the New Feminist Movement.

Proliferation and Consolidation

In this section we look at the emergence of three distinctive organizational types—direct action groups, educational/political organizations, and cultural/entrepreneurial associations—but postpone to the
next chapter our consideration of those political organizations that
function as a significant feminist interest group on the national scene.
Such nationally organized groups are a type of educational/political
association, but the significance of their entry into the lobbying and
electoral process and the backlash mounted against them requires
special consideration. However, we should not lose sight of the fact
that the grassroots groups whose proliferation we describe below provide an important context of recruitment and support for these national lobbying associations, and that the broad-based nationally organized
groups have provided money and publicity that have sometimes been
crucial to sustaining the local or state efforts. Even in this section, as
we divide the groups into their characteristic types, it is important not
to lose sight of how the different forms of organization support each
other.

Direct Action/Self-Help.   Direct action groups represent a strategy of collective organization and self-help. Their message is that sisterhood is already powerful, that women can act together to create
immediate change in their lives. Self-help is a way for people who
think of themselves as powerless to realize that they do have options.
Direct action is an appealing strategy for both radical and socialist
feminists, because it offers partial realization of the ideal of a new femi-

nist community, although the ideal of socialist feminists is a relationship of equality between women and men; whereas radical feminists are primarily concerned with relationships among women, so their ideal community is often separatist.

Direct action groups often try, at least initially, to embrace the collectivist organizational form as a means of empowering all members, and then they struggle to maintain the most egalitarian structures possible under real-life conditions (Ferguson 1984). Rather than "pure" collectives, the direct action groups that survive are more likely to be "flattened hierarchies," in which some division of labor and authority structure are present, while power differences are minimized (Martin 1990). Direct action/self-help groups have been most effective in the fields of law and medicine, precisely where male domination of the system has generated widespread and recognized problems for women. Most of these groups began with an emphasis on immediate self-help and then expanded to other collectivist goals and activities.

Law. Deficiencies in the American law enforcement system were first recognized in cases of rape and sexual assault, because the prevailing tendency to blame the victim has forced the rape and assault victim who reports a crime to endure a second ordeal in which the police, lawyers, and judges could discredit her testimony on the basis of past sexual activity (real or implied) and her "failure" to defend herself successfully. As many feminists of this period pointed out, a woman's right to safety on the streets and in her home has never been taken seriously, although the criminal justice system vigorously pursues this right for men (Brownmiller 1975; Griffin 1971; Russell 1975). Throughout the 1970s, rape was still treated as a joke, a sexual turn-on, and even as a sign of male accomplishment, but rarely as a physical assault, a psychological trauma for the victim, or a major crime. To the extent that these perceptions have changed, credit is due to feminist antirape organizing (Martin 1993).

Two early forms of antirape action were self-defense training, especially karate, and hot lines that offered immediate advice and support to assault victims. Self-defense training, in addition to counteracting an attacker's typical height and weight advantage, allows a woman to protect herself without the assistance of a male "protector" (who may himself become an attacker). Perhaps this is why self-defense programs have never received as much support from law enforcement personnel as have the hot lines and other support services for those who have already been assaulted (Searles and Berger 1987).

Support services emerged when former victims of sexual assault began to speak out. These survivors refused to be made to feel "dirty" and guilty; instead they offered advice to other recent victims via hot lines and rape crisis centers and even accompanied victims to hospital emergency rooms. Such ad hoc former-victim volunteers were soon replaced by trained feminist counselor/advocates (still often former victims), and in many cities, such advocates have been added to the staff of hospitals and police departments.

Although such "mainstreaming" of services helps to reach more victims than in the past, feminist rape crisis centers continue to provide counseling and political advocacy for rape survivors in ways that challenge the system more than the police and hospital services do (Martin 1993; Matthews 1994). Feminist rape crisis centers spread the message that the problem is systematic male violence rather than individual male deviance, do more advocacy work for victims, and do more prevention education than do the mainstream service providers (Martin 1993). Acquiring funding from the criminal justice system made it possible for the explicitly feminist centers to survive and even to expand into low-income and ethnic minority communities, but feminist rape crisis centers receiving such funding also became less willing to direct blame for the mistreatment of victims at the system that was supporting their work (Matthews 1989 and 1994).

Direct action groups centered on rape also realized that providing services to victims and raising public awareness was not enough; institutional changes would have to be made to make rape cases easier to prosecute. Feminist organizing on the issue of rape led many states to change their laws to eliminate the demand for witnesses or evidence of struggle and to bar use of the victim's previous sexual history (so-called "rape shield laws"). Some states have removed the rule that exempts husbands from prosecution for sexual assault on their wives. Other local efforts have attacked the cultural supports for violence against women, such as media depictions of rape as sexually gratifying. Across the country, "Take Back the Night" demonstrations have focused public attention on the inability of women to enjoy the same freedom of movement that men take for granted.

Self-help groups have also been organized for victims of violence within the family. These efforts also began with hot lines and crisis centers, such as Casa de las Madres in San Francisco and Transition House in Cambridge, Massachusetts, where the provision of immediate shelter was combined with consciousness-raising on the roots of male violence, and where victims helped staff the shelters. The publication of feminist analyses, particularly Martin's *Battered Wives* (1976), brought the problem to widespread public attention, so that shelters and services for battered women multiplied, far exceeding the number that could have been provided by movement members. By 1978, the U.S. Commission on Civil Rights listed over three hundred shelters, hot lines, and groups acting as advocates for victims of family violence (Tierney 1982). Although fewer than half of such shelters were explicitly feminist in orientation, the presence of a feminist group in the community was one of the strongest predictors of the existence of a program for battered women (Johnson 1981; Tierney 1982).

As with rape crisis organizing, feminist direct action/self-help groups responding to the needs of battered women continue to exist along with more mainstream service providers. The feminist political analysis they offer has often penetrated the mainstream, and coalitions of advocates for battered women and state agencies now work together to provide services to victims as well as to increase prosecution of their batterers (Reinelt 1994; Arnold 1994). There has been a growing awareness of the need to change the laws on assault and self-defense to provide better protection for battered women, and to redouble efforts to do more than provide temporary shelter in acute crises. Feminist direct action groups have successfully pushed for mandatory arrest policies, woman-defined standards of what constitutes reasonable use of force in self-defense, and strong enforcement of restraining orders in many states and local communities.

Another legal area in which direct action through self-help has proliferated is that of family law in general. Collectives help women negotiate the legal system with or without a lawyer—for example, in filing a *pro se* divorce petition, thus avoiding legal fees. Other groups provide information and emotional support to those involved in custody disputes (especially lesbian mothers) and to women in prison. In some states, feminists have sought the decriminalization of prostitution, often defined as a crime that only women can commit, and a crime whose enforcement has exclusively focused on the provider rather than the purchaser of sexual services.

Feminist direct action groups have been instrumental in changing not only the legal context but also the cultural climate confronting women who are victims of violence. Rape, whether by a stranger or an intimate, became more widely understood as a crime of violence rather than just an expression of sexuality. Reports of rape increased, but successful prosecution remains problematic. Although the concept of marital rape may be difficult for some people to accept, wife battering is no longer a joke, even when cloaked in such gender-neutral terms as "domestic violence." In the struggle for change, feminists developed legal and political skills that were personally empowering and brought benefits to many women who may never recognize or acknowledge their debt to the movement.

Health. The second major area in which self-help has been an essential component of feminist strategy is that of physical and mental health. A number of important studies in the early 1970s (Broverman et al. 1970; Bart 1970; Chesler 1972) showed that mental health professionals perceived the characteristics of a "normal" woman as dependence, low self-esteem, anxiety, and insecurity. Women without these traits were subjected to "cures" for their "masculine protest" and inability to "adjust" to their natural roles. Feminist therapy clinics refused to accept this definition of mental health for women; they began with the assumption that the same qualities of assurance, independence, and self-esteem that were "mentally healthy" for men applied to all human beings. Feminist therapists help women take direction of their lives and make their own choices. At first, the expertise of mental health professionals was challenged by lay "facilitators" who simply encouraged women to stop blaming themselves, but over the decade, more and more feminists became accredited counselors, and "feminist therapy" became a recognized professional subspecialty (Burstow 1992).

In the field of physical health, resistance to male professional judgments was carried out on a range of issues, many related to sexuality and reproduction. For example, the process of childbirth was defined by the obstretrical establishment as an illness to be managed by drugging, restraint, isolation, and surgery. It was the doctor, typically male, who then "delivered" the baby to a grateful mother. The medicalization of childbirth had replaced the natural process of labor that employed the support and assistance of other women (Arms 1975; Rich 1976; Rothman 1982). Self-help groups promoted the advantages of home births, lay midwives, and breast-feeding and found allies among existing mainstream advocates of natural childbirth such as

Lamaze and La Leche League. Unlike their allies, feminists also note that this emphasis on breast feeding and natural childbirth can produce new standards of "true femininity" to which women can be pressured to conform.

In an era of declining fertility, hospitals and physicians became concerned about competition from midwives and home births. After making some concessions in the form of hospital birthing rooms, natural childbirth clinics, and nurse-midwives as labor attendants—all under the doctor's control—physicians were able to block further inroads to natural childbirth by refusing to provide crisis backup for home births, withdrawing hospital privileges for doctors who cooperated with midwives, and encouraging third-party insurers to impose prohibitively high premiums on clinics that permitted lay midwives to practice. By the end of the 1980s, most lay midwives had been driven out of business, and home birth was no longer a realistic alternative for most American women (Weitz and Sullivan 1986).

Self-help also meant self-examination. So mystified and medicalized had their sexual organs become, that few women had ever seen them for themselves, or even wished to do so. It was a daring act, therefore, in 1971 for one NOW member to insert a plastic speculum in her vagina and invite her friends to take a look. The idea spread rapidly. Women who had been socialized to think of the female body as unclean and to be ignorant of the most elementary physical facts became more knowledgeable and comfortable handling their own bodies. During this period, for example, use of the diaphragm, the female contraceptive with fewest side effects, increased substantially.

Actual health-care services provided by direct action groups had begun in the period before 1973 because of the need to provide medically safe abortions to women who could not afford to go abroad, or who might otherwise die or be mutilated by self-induced procedures or the work of illegal abortionists (Fruchter et al. 1977). In addition to providing an essential service, members of the collective gained a sense of personal competence and demystified medical skills for themselves and others (Schlesinger and Bart 1981). Even after the Supreme Court decision that legalized most abortions, many self-help clinics and women's health centers have continued to provide abortion services because local hospitals and physicians refuse to do so. Although the income from abortion services allowed many clinics to survive financially, such facilities have been under continual, escalating attacks from antiabortion forces, ranging from blockading entrances to arson and murder.

By 1973, over a thousand women's health projects in the United States were engaged in direct action strategies to challenge and change medical practice and/or to provide primary care. Over the next decade, these early projects provided the infrastructure for the establishment of several hundred women-controlled feminist health clinics stressing self-help, lay involvement in all aspects of care, and affordable, client-centered services (Ruzek 1978; Morgen 1994). The transformation of many women from passive patients to assertive consumers generated a need for accurate, easily understood information on women's bodies and existing medical procedures.

This gap was partially filled by the publication in 1972 of *Our Bodies, Ourselves* by the Boston Women's Health Collective. In 1976, the collective found a mainstream publisher and a wide audience, and they used the proceeds of the book to establish a clearinghouse for women's health information and to develop other publications and films that are now distributed worldwide. The clearinghouse, the National Women's Health Network, defines self-help as an activist approach to health care that encourages involvement in policy and research issues as well as in one's own individual care (Mellow 1989).

Feminist health groups have also been established in minority communities. The National Black Women's Health Project was founded by Byllye Avery in Atlanta, Georgia, in 1981, to address the specific concerns of African-Americans, such as endemic high blood pressure, and to provide health and sex education. Similar projects have been developed by Native American and Latina feminists (Mellow 1989). In addition, the women's health movement has gone international, with national networks in over twenty countries exchanging information and working together (Tudiver 1986). These consumer-oriented groups have found common ground with groups of activists in the health professions such as Cassandra, self-described as "the network of radical feminist nurses."

In sum, the emergence of legal and medical direct action/self-help groups reflects what Nancy Fraser (1990) calls the "politics of need interpretation"—that is, bringing women's perspective to bear on defining as well as meeting their own needs. In addition, their involvement in self-help groups led many women to acquire professional training. Whether their feminist politics can survive professional socialization remains an open question. The line between being a good nurse, therapist, physician, or lawyer and being a committed feminist has blurred as many of the perspectives and services pioneered by feminists have been partially absorbed into the systems the women have challenged. Even though empowerment through self-help rather than institutional change was the initial goal of direct action groups, many institutions were pushed and prodded into changing the way they dealt with issues of concern to women, from rape to childbirth. Yet despite important reforms in the criminal justice and health-care systems, ultimate control remained in the hands of the "experts" and "authorities," typically elite white males, who successfully prevented or co-opted the more radical attempts at institutional change (Morgen 1986) and limited the effectiveness of the new feminist professionals (Lorber 1989).

Few of the organizations that attempted to provide cooperative, nonhierarchical, women-controlled alternative settings for the direct provision of services have survived in their original form. To some extent, the visible differences between feminist and nonfeminist shelters and clinics have eroded, even though the former retain a greater emphasis on political advocacy and personal empowerment than do the more "mainstream" providers (Maxwell and Martin 1992). In a later section we examine the forces that made these organizations' survival as distinctive forms so problematic.

Educational/Political. Educational and political associations are the organizational expression of a strategy for change that focuses on placing pressure on existing institutions, from the federal government to universities to local employers. As such, they are particularly attractive to liberal and socialist feminists. One aspect of their approach is to educate decision-makers and the general public about how current practices affect women, thus generating a desire for change among a broad consituency and a recognition that collective rather than individual action is the key to success. An equally critical facet of this strategy, therefore, is to organize those who want change into a political and economic force. The most prominent feminist organization of this type was and is the National Organization for Women (NOW), often perceived by the media and the public as the sole representative of organized feminism.

In reality, this type of feminist organization is best represented by the women's policy network (discussed in chapter 6) formed in the early 1970s in Washington, where it rapidly expanded into a formida-

ble force (Gelb and Palley 1987; Spalter-Roth and Schreiber 1994). The
activities and transformation of the Washington-based network are the
main theme of the next chapter, for although not all of the early com-
ponents of the network survived (e.g., the Women's Equity Action
League, founded in 1968 and disbanded in 1989), a majority still actively pursue feminist issues in the political arena. These organizations
and their educational lobbying work have provided an opportunity for
women to pursue paid and unpaid careers in activism, including policy
research, public relations, and community organizing (Daniels 1991).

In addition to the women's policy network in Washington, feminist
educational and political organizations also multiplied rapidly within
occupational and academic settings. At times, such groups could offer
little more than professional networking, a key goal of career feminists, but many were also involved in raising the issue of sex discrimination and in pursuing actual cases. Class-action lawsuits, brought on
behalf of a group of similarly situated individuals rather than a single
person, were the strategy of choice in the 1970s, as this was the only
decade during which the Equal Employment Opportunity
Commission (EEOC) could be considered an ally.

Although founded in 1964, the EEOC was given significant enforcement powers only in 1972, as a result of successful lobbying by the
Washington-based network. In 1980, with the election of Ronald
Reagan, class-action suits were discouraged and the EEOC ceased to
be an effective watchdog agency. But for a period in the 1970s, the
commission was "a strong and successful proponent of women's
rights" (Meehan, in Gelb 1989, 102) and a source of support for
antidiscrimination organizing in the various caucuses and committees
that were being formed in virtually every occupation and profession in
the 1970s. Of special importance was the 1973 settlement of a class-
action suit against American Telephone and Telegraph (AT&T) that
provided millions of dollars in relief to the women plaintiffs. The
AT&T case sent a message to the business community that sex discrimination was a serious issue, and it encouraged women in other
companies to take legal action.

As one example of how occupational organizing emerged and
developed over the decade, women teaching in American colleges and
universities had, by 1971, already formed at least fifty organizations to
deal with the status of women in various fields of study and institutions
(Klotzberger 1973). Membership in these organizations continued to
expand even as women's caucuses were established in additional disci-

plines. In sociology, for example, Sociologists for Women in Society (SWS) grew from a few dozen founders in 1972 to a dues-paying membership of over twelve hundred women and men in 1993. SWS now publishes a highly regarded professional journal, *Gender & Society,* underwrites discrimination cases, and funds a graduate scholarship for women of color. In history, the Berkshire Conference on the History of Women was first held in 1973 with about 500 attendees and drew nearly 3000 to its 1993 meeting. In academe at large, the American Association of University Professors (AAUP), the leading professional organization of faculty, reactivated its Committee W (on the Status of Women) that had been "excused from further service" in 1928. Committee W publishes a *Salary Discrimination Evaluation Kit* that has helped female faculty to bargain for more equitable salaries. Although many more cases have been lost than won, class-action victories at major institutions such as the University of Minnesota have continued to encourage similar suits.

At a number of colleges and universities, pressure from female faculty led to the formation of committees on the status of women that subsequently documented inequities, demanded reforms, and precipitated change. In many universities, new coalitions of women crossed traditional boundaries between faculty, students, and staff, as well as departmental divisions, to demand day-care facilities, gynecological services, improved campus security, and scholarships and fringe benefits for part-time workers and students, the great majority of whom are women. On many campuses, women's centers were established to house and coordinate the dozens of services and activities that sprang up almost overnight. Most centers were collectively organized and oriented to self-help projects, and some offered noncredit courses in car repair, carpentry, and other nontraditional skills.

Throughout the 1970s, women's studies as an intellectual specialty was being transformed from a set of collectively run noncredit courses on the fringes of academe into fully institutionalized programs, with departmental status at some universities. The first accredited course in women's studies, "Evolution of Female Personality," was offered at Cornell University in 1969. By December of the following year, there were at least 110 women's studies courses in the catalogs of American colleges and universities, and by the end of 1971, more than six hundred such courses at almost two hundred institutions of higher education (Howe and Ahlum 1973). By 1989, the number of individual course offerings in women's studies was too numerous to count, and there were at least three hundred formally structured programs nationwide as well as many without a director or formal curriculum. And by 1992, the number of formal programs had doubled, with 140 institutions, including Harvard and Princeton, offering an undergraduate major in women's studies. In the 1980s graduate-level courses multiplied, as did graduate degree programs and research centers.

Increasingly, the directors of these programs found themselves playing university politics: lobbying for resources, for curricular reform, and for research funding and facilities; organizing conferences; and managing institutes and journals. Partially to keep track of these diverse organizations and programs, the National Women's Studies Association was founded in 1978. In addition, the National Council for Research on Women, founded in 1981, coordinates the work of institutes involved in feminist research and policy analysis.

The experience of women on college campuses is an example of the processes taking place in a variety of settings, as the movement's ideas spread through the society. The explosive growth of women's groups in 1970–71, the discovery of their common concerns, alliances with others of varied backgrounds, the rejuvenation of organizations, and the achievement of semi-institutionalization are all typical of the history of feminist political/educational organizations. The academic example illustrates again the blurring of distinctions between self-help collectives and the bureaucratically organized lobbying organizations, the original two strands of the New Feminist Movement. In recent years, mutual respect has grown as differences in style between the strands have diminished and as both types of groups increasingly combine organizing for institutional change with providing women-run alternatives.

The existence of thousands of occupational and other interest groups across the country gives the movement a diversity of focus and organizational flexibility that makes it unusually open to grassroots input. By the same token, problems of coordination are magnified; resources are increasingly diverted to maintenance activities such as sharing information among groups. This extensive network ensures the presence of the New Feminist Movement in every area of society but does not guarantee group effectiveness. Obstacles to success include competition between groups, co-optation by established institutions, and goal displacement, that is, a shift in goals from accomplishing concrete changes to maintaining the organization and enjoying the company of other members. Nonetheless, the existence of a feminist organizational structure capable of applying significant pressure for social and political change is an enormous and meaningful accomplishment.

Cultural/Entrepreneurial.   From the beginning, the New Feminist Movement has given birth to a wide variety of cultural and entrepreneurial groups more concerned with self-maintenance and sociability than with exerting pressure on existing institutions. Founders of these groups interpret their very existence as a key aspect of social change, as "alternative institutions" whereby women can provide service to other women. Rather than developing women's individual resources through collective action, as self-help groups do, these enterprises focus on developing the community through women's individual contributions. The basic argument is that as long as women patronize male-run banks, restaurants, or gas stations, the money does not recirculate among women, nor is it likely ultimately to be donated to feminist causes. In the same way as black or ethnic businesses serve local needs, prosper individually, and contribute to the financial stability and growth of the community as a whole, women-owned businesses are targeted to a particular clientele: the "feminist community." Because they provide an outlet for individuals to act on their commitment, they appeal particularly to career and radical feminists.

Among the first such specialized feminist businesses were bookstores that carried feminist material not available in mainstream shops and also provided a meeting place for poetry readings, rap sessions, and casual encounters. Other feminists opened restaurants and coffee houses where women could go alone without fear of harassment. The stated goal of one such restaurant, Full Cycle, in Minneapolis, was to "recycle feminist energy by serving nutritious food, providing women with employment and skills and returning any profits into other feminist projects" (Grimstad and Rennie 1975). Some restaurants are run as collectives, others are profit making, but all combine vegetarian food, feminist politics, and community service; some struggle to define the conditions under which men would be welcome as guests.

Later, feminists began to offer not only a place to eat, but a place to stay, such as the Retreat for Women in rural Connecticut. Short-term feminist gatherings—music festivals, worship services—were organized, some of which evolved into full-time institutions such as Olivia Records, a women-managed music distributing company, or the

Mother Thunder Mission, a feminist church in New York City. Theater groups, film collectives, and feminist art galleries can be found throughout the country (Solomon 1991). In Los Angeles, a number of activities can be found under one roof in the Women's Building.

Individual feminists have offered their services to the community, as tax consultants, car mechanics, therapists, midwives, and physicians. A recent issue of *Sojourner,* a Boston-based feminist newspaper, carried dozens of advertisements for women health-care professionals, building contractors, moving companies, feminist law firms, a typesetter, a clothes designer, a "performance space" for music, restaurants, auto repair shops, and inns/retreat houses. Nationally recognized musicians such as Sweet Honey in the Rock combine feminist themes and other political songs in concerts that bring feminists together and raise funds for national and local feminist causes.

Cultural activities also include organizations centered on women's spirituality. Some of these may be found within traditional religious denominations; while others attempt to discover and define a new spiritual direction for women, as in the revival of "pagan" rituals expressing closeness to and dependence upon nature. The emergence of explicitly feminist covens of witches reflects a desire to affirm women's history as healers and rebels, and to reclaim the old religion of "wicce," or witchcraft, persecuted and displaced by Christianity many centuries ago. While their reconstruction of history is not entirely accurate, the idea of creating rituals and structures that affirm women's bodily and spiritual needs and strengths is important (Adler 1979; Ruether 1983). Producing nonsexist liturgies and supporting individual women in the ministry are ways in which feminists have sought to realize these goals within traditional religious structures, but their initially modest critiques often spilled over into a more radical reexamination of religious structures (Katzenstein 1994). In the late 1980s, explicitly feminist forms of Christian spirituality were combined with self-examination to produce nonhierarchical "house churches" that functioned much like the consciousness-raising groups of the early 1970s (Ruether 1986).

These various cultural and entrepreneurial activities not only serve the feminist community but create it. By bringing women together to enjoy each other's company, and by providing services and support for one another, cultural/entrepreneurial feminist re-create a base of interaction and interdependence that had almost disappeared when women were confined in isolated nuclear households. These ties create bonds of experience and mutual reliance that could support direct action but are more commonly used to build a distinctive "feminist community." Such supportive communities focus members' energies on feminist issues and help to prevent burnout among activists (Taylor and Rupp 1993).

Feminist cultural and entrepreneurial groups have often been criticized for blunting the movement's radical edge by diverting energies into personal growth rather than political change that would benefit all women (Echols 1989). Members of such groups, however, see their efforts as producing change in a dimension that complements rather than competes with the direct action of other organizations. Through an ongoing system of consciousness-raising, they sustain "oppositional cultures that embody values, practices, and meanings derived from concrete struggle" (Taylor and Rupp 1993). In addition, by changing the language with which women name their experience, and by fostering social networks in which alternative definitions can be reaffirmed, cultural groups practice what Katzenstein (1994) calls "discursive politics." Although they run the risk of creating closed circles of like-minded members out of touch with the mainstream of American life, these groups do nurture a supportive community in which new words can be discovered that will eventually enter the common vocabulary, naming women's oppression in terms that help combat it, as for example, the concepts of date rape or sexual harassment.

Conclusion.   In sum, the proliferation of feminist groups in the early 1970s afforded expanded opportunities for mobilizing women. Feminists with broad concerns could be active in dozens of narrow-focus groups, creating dilemmas of priority and allocation of energy. By the end of the decade, a web of national, state, and local women's organizations was able to provide the coordination necessary for broad-based coalitions around single issues.

Carden (1981) notes that the proliferation of differentiated groups encourages a flexibility in ideas, activities, and organizational forms that reflects the movement's dual emphasis on autonomy and sisterhood, on cooperation and achievement. The range of such groups is impressive, and most have achieved at least some of their primary goals. Activists also realize "secondary gains" in enhanced feelings of competence, the development of skills, and the sheer pleasure of being with like-minded individuals and "fighting the good fight." Both the primary and secondary gains of movement involvement continue to attract a broad spectrum of support, mobilizing women of all ages and social backgrounds.

Tarrow argues that "the range and flexibility of its tactical repertory is often a good predictor of movement success" (1983, 8). In this respect, the New Feminist Movement laid a solid foundation in its first decades, upon which it has continued to build. Combining efforts to change institutional practices through direct action and lobbying with those designed to change consciousness, self-concept, and collective discourse, the movement has produced a spectrum of organizational modes that create new forms of leverage for women to reshape all social institutions. Such "institutionalized participation" in Tarrow's terms, enlarges the resource base for future mobilizations as well as for immediate, albeit often transitory, reforms.

The problems associated with proliferation, however, are not minor. Although loosely linked under the banner of women's rights, these groups and organizations do represent divergent ideologies and constituencies. Energies may be deflected from the larger struggle, and some members may become personally estranged, by dissent from within, by compromises made in the name of coalition, or by failure to agree on priorities. As Carden (1981) also concludes: the diversity, creativity, and enthusiasm associated with proliferation are crucial assets, but a great deal of energy can be siphoned off in trying to accomplish too many goals with too few resources. Proceeding in many directions at once, as the New Feminist Movement has attempted to do, helps bring the movement into contact with virtually every aspect of women's lives, but by the same token makes it difficult to point to any single accomplishment as the movement's primary achievement.

While the decade of the 1970s was a period in which the movement's base was broadened and its diverse goals and strategies defended in the name of "militant pluralism," internal dissent has periodically threatened its fragile unity. In the next section we examine some of these conflicts and their implications for the continued growth of the New Feminist Movement.

Internal Conflict in the Women's Movement

At various times in its brief history, the New Feminist Movement has been torn by internal disputes. Many early conflicts were related to structural factors, as in trashing described in chapter 3. Other conflicts reflect disagreement over priorities. We have selected three of these—lesbianism as a feminist issue, the politics of pornography, and the interplay of racism and anti-Semitism—as illustrative of the dynamics of conflict within the movement. Inevitably, in a movement as open and media-oriented as this one, each dispute has been aired in public. The ways in which conflict has been resolved have not always been ideal, yet in each case potentially destructive issues have been successfully managed. This is not to say that strains do not continue, but only that their negative impact has thus far been limited, and that the process of self-examination engendered by divisive issues has often strengthened the movement.

Lesbianism.   One of the earliest internal debates centered on the issue of lesbianism: namely, what degree of recognition was to be given to the double oppression of homosexual women? The locus of this debate was NOW as the most visible and broad-based feminist organization (even though, at that time, it had only a few thousand dues-paying members). The question was raised at NOW's 1971 national conference over the strong objections of representatives from the South and Midwest, and of Betty Friedan, a NOW founder and past president. Their argument against recognizing lesbian interests as a feminist issue was based on the fear of losing whatever legitimacy the fledgling organization had worked so hard to obtain. The "lavender menace," according to Friedan, threatened NOW's public image by evoking the great American fear of homosexuality. The argument *for* raising the issue was precisely that the fear of homosexuality (homophobia) and the hatred directed toward homosexuals has been used throughout our history to enforce conformity to "proper" feminine or masculine behavior. For example, parents continue to discourage boys playing with dolls and girls with trucks for fear that such atypical behavior will lead to homosexuality, even though family roles, job interests, and choice of sexual partner are actually quite separate preferences.

"Compulsory heterosexuality," or the belief that homosexuality is so abnormal as to be almost unthinkable, has particularly negative consequences for women. It not only means punishment for sex-inappropriate behavior but also reinforces the assumption that a woman without a man is necessarily incomplete, immature, sexually frustrated, and "fair game" for male attacks (Rich 1980). The male response to feminism, typified in statements such as "all she needs is a good fuck," increased many women's awareness that their claim to independence was already being interpreted in sexual terms. Feminists were thus placed in the position of either having continually to deny that they were lesbian (regardless of their actual sexual orientation), which could only affirm and perpetuate the idea that every woman needs a man, or having to attack head-on the definition of lesbianism as bad or sick.

Faced with these alternatives, a majority of delegates to NOW's 1971 convention passed resolutions approving "a woman's right to define and express her own sexuality and to choose her own lifestyle," recognizing "the oppression of lesbians as a legitimate concern of feminism," and supporting the child custody rights of lesbian mothers (Carden 1974, 113). The endorsement of these resolutions by NOW's national board was not followed by a wave of resignations, nor was the public response unexpectedly harsh. As Carden (1974) points out, the issue had already been resolved in local NOW chapters where gay and straight women engaged in dialogue and mutual exchange. Debate and discussion continue over questions raised by lesbian feminists: the value of separatism, the costs and benefits of loving women, and the privileges heterosexual women take for granted.

Although homophobia (the extreme fear of homosexuality) undoubtedly still exists within some segments of the movement, most of the objections to linking feminism with lesbianism are based on the political consequences of supporting gay rights in a homophobic society. In the 1977 Houston conference, for example, one speaker referred to support of lesbian civil rights as "an albatross around the neck of the movement" (van Gelder 1978)—a common response at the time, but one that has long since become a minority position. As a matter of principle, no movement claiming to represent "women" can turn away from those who are doubly oppressed for being female and loving women. Furthermore, lesbian activists have played a significant role in supporting the movement at many levels, so that participation far outweighs any negative effects their presence has had on public opinion. As Taylor and Rupp (1993) point out, the "women's community" at the local level is likely to be sustained by the interpersonal ties of lesbian feminist activists. Such ties connect activists across the many different organizations in which they are politically engaged, provide a base for community-affirming rituals (such as concerts or even demonstrations), and offer support for shared values. Precisely what values are shared is still a matter of some controversy, both within the lesbian feminist community and between lesbian and non-lesbian feminists. One controversial issue is the affirmation of differences between women and men, regardless of whether such differences are seen as socially constructed or as essential to the "nature" of women and men. As Taylor and Rupp note, "Explanations aside, belief in fundamental differences between male and female values permeates lesbian feminist communities. Indeed, this emphasis on difference serves to justify the existence of a 'woman's community' (1993, 41). Drawing boundaries between male and female promotes a certain kind of oppositional consciousness, one that they, like many lesbian feminists, feel is "necessary for organizing one's life around feminism" (43).

Within the lesbian feminist community, this emphasis on difference leads to conflicts between separatists (those who have the goal of building an all-woman world) and those lesbians who favor alliances with men committed to social justice. Some separatists will exclude all males (even boys over the age of three) from their activities; they argue that maleness itself represents the source of violence against women (Anderson 1994). Lesbian mothers of sons have usually disputed this claiming that it is both possible and necessary to raise sons who do not themselves exploit women and who actively work to prevent the oppression of women. The debate between lesbian feminists and nonlesbians has more often focused on the extent to which cultural affirmations of a "woman's community" tend to marginalize heterosexual women, including women who share with men their political commitments to confronting racism or class oppression, as many women of color and working-class women do. Indeed, as the gay rights movement has developed and come under attack from the New Right, and as AIDS has increasingly devastated the gay male population, ever more lesbian feminists are committed to finding a collective identity that supports their shared political work with gay men.

Thus, the gay/straight division of the 1960s has been replaced by a more complex and shifting set of conflicts in the 1990s. Although some, particularly heterosexual, women who have not participated in the growth and development of the "women's community" in the 1970s and 1980s tend to see it as "cultural" and apolitical, lesbian feminists point out the significance of such networks for sustaining identity and activism over the long-term, even though they may discount alternative ways by which feminists not in this community also find support for their long-term commitments. The conflict over values, how much to stress women's difference and separateness from men, has become a broad issue in feminism, as we will see in later chapters. Because of the gay rights movement, lesbian activists are more likely to be "out" (open about their sexual orientation) than in the past, so their straight colleagues and co-workers are more likely to be aware of their contributions and more able to recognize the differences among them. Lesbian activists themselves are more likely to recognize their own diversity and the problems of divisiveness that emerge when organizing emphasizes a politics of identity or implicit sameness.

Perhaps most important, however, the violently antigay position of the New Right has taught all feminists a great deal about the need to confront homophobia directly. Because the linking of feminism with lesbianism, in a climate of intolerance, has been used to discourage young women from speaking out, the future of feminism depends on the effectiveness with which the movement takes the sting out of the label lesbian (Schneider 1991). While the political positions that some lesbian feminists endorse are quite properly debated within movement circles, the presence and value of lesbians in the New Feminist Movement is beyond debate.

Pornography.   One of the least debatable goals of contemporary feminism is an end to violence against women, and as there is evidence linking pornography to such violence (e.g., Donnerstein 1980), it may seem strange that pornography has become a point of conflict among activist women. For some feminists the key issue shaping their attitude is the sexual content; for others, it is the antifemale violence found in most pornography. The former are reluctant to condemn pornography; the latter have no hesitation in doing so.

The law reflects the sexual view; pornography is legally defined as depiction of explicit sexuality that is offensive to community standards. As sexual taboos have weakened, "normal" nonviolent sexuality has become progressively less offensive, so what receives the label pornographic today is increasingly violent and women-hating. Yet, outside feminist circles, objections to pornography still largely focus on its explicit sexuality. Feminists who share this focus on sexuality rather than violence are likely to see pornography as a positive force in liberating women's repressed sexuality.

Movement women who wish to protest the dehumanization and violence against women in contemporary pornography often hesitate to make common cause with antisexuality campaigners who have in the past used antipornography statutes to suppress birth control information and otherwise to keep women ignorant of their bodies (Diamond 1980; Bessmer 1982). Nonetheless, radical feminists and right-wing moralists find themselves on the same side of the pornography issue, although their reasons differ: traditionalists are worried about pornography's threat to the sexual control and moral purity of the male consumer; while feminists fear that this material legitimates and encourages violence against women in general. At times, feminist antipornography activists such as Catherine MacKinnon and Andrea Dworkin have joined with right-wing moralists in campaigning for local ordinances restricting the distribution of pornographic materials.

The pornography debate within feminism has taken on a troubling dimension as feminists on all sides of the issue have accused the others of betraying the movement by adopting the sexual ethics of patriarchy. This debate reflects a basic tension within contemporary feminism between its moral reform and liberal traditions. Moral reformers affirm a personal, caring, nonexploitive vision of sexuality and therefore campaign against dehumanizing pornography, while also emphasizing the value of sexuality to the development of the whole person. Sexual liberationists reflect a hands-off stance, bolstered by the liberal ideology of individual choice and appeals to freedom of expression.

Feminist support *for* laws to control pornography is based on defining the harm done to women as a form of sex discrimination. This harm can come either directly through coercion or abuse in the production of pornographic material or indirectly in the effect on consumers who are encouraged to force women to reenact degrading scenarios. The feminist case *against* such laws is based on First Amendment grounds, namely that freedom of speech and of the press protects even the most hateful material, whether the women-hating of pornographers or the racism of the Ku Klux Klan. The fear here is that once one type of expression is declared unprotected, other forms can be as well, including women's assertive definitions of their own sexuality. Depictions of lesbian sex, for example, might be censored. For some lesbian feminists, "bad girl" sex magazines such as *On Our Backs* are an important aspect of sexual expression that they find threatened by what they call "anti-sex" organizing against pornography.

The feminist debate over pornography has spilled over into other areas where the link between words and actions is problematic, as in, for example, attempts to regulate "hate speech" on campus, or in attempts to deal with sexual harassment that is verbal rather than physical. In other words, much of the feminist debate over pornography has been carried on in terms of the "pro-sex" or "anti-sex" labels that more properly characterize the way the law understands pornography (as explicit and offensive sexuality) rather than in terms that reflect the core feminist concern with violence. The real feminist dilemma in the 1990s is emerging as a problem of how to relate speech that encourages and condones violence to the actual acts of violence themselves. Sometimes acts that are speech (such as verbal sexual harassment) are defined as discriminatory in themselves; sometimes even the most historically dangerous types of "hate speech" (such as Klan rallies) are protected. Pornography (understood as depicting violence against women approvingly) may well contribute to anti-woman acts of violence, but recognizing it as an expression of woman-hating is also grounds for seeing it as politically protected speech. The paradox is that the more "deviant" pornography is perceived to be, the more easily the law can be used to regulate it, but the presentations of violence against women that are seen as normal and rewarding are the ones that are most likely to be dangerous.

Racism and Anti-Semitism.   Another divisive issue that has periodically recurred within the women's movement is tension produced by racism and anti-Semitism. Fear and hatred of Jews and the oppression of persons of color are not new in the world; but black anti-Semitism and Jewish racism are especially dangerous for the women's movement as they pit two strongly feminist constituencies against one another. Far beyond their proportion of the population, Jewish women have been prominent in the New Feminist Movement, as they were in both the Civil Rights movement and the New Left. For many, their religious identity and their feminism are of a piece with their commitment to movements of liberation everywhere, including the Near East. African-American women have also been disproportionately feminist in their attitudes and have been crucial to the success of the women's movement, especially in broadening the feminist perspective to take account of racial and ethnic oppression (hooks 1990; Collins 1990). Thus, it has been doubly painful to observe strains between the two valued partners.

Although many African-Americans identify the Israeli–Palestinian conflict as an issue of minority rights against a dominant, if numerically smaller, Israeli population, the basic tension between Jews and people of color in the United States is rooted in their different history and experiences of social mobility. Both are well aware of the effects of discrimination, prejudice, poverty, and marginality. Jewish women, however, have attained a level of economic security and educational privilege from which most women of color remain excluded. For African-American women, minority status refers to legal and social barriers and to limited economic prospects. For Jewish women today, being a "minority" means being an outsider in a Gentile culture. Much of the most vocal opposition to affirmative action, however, has come from the men who dominate Jewish organizational life, and the result has been to reinforce the impression that Jewish concern for civil rights extends only to the limits of their self-interest.

Jewish women have also come under attack by the extreme left wing of the women's movement, whose primarily white members identify with the Palestinian cause, as well as by other feminists who feel that the strong Jewish presence in the movement has reduced its chances of success (a charge that has also been leveled against lesbians). Vocal anti-Semitism on the part of some prominent African-American men, such as Louis Farrakhan or Leonard Jeffries, has also made Jewish women concerned about the extent to which such attitudes are shared in the black community.

Within the New Feminist Movement, African-American women have faced racism in a variety of forms: indifference to their concerns, disregard of their contributions, patronizing efforts to "recruit" and "educate" them to support goals and priorities established by white women. The feeling on the part of women of color that movement leaders were unwilling to support them in decision-making roles received confirmation in a number of incidents, ranging from the failure of NOW to endorse the presidential candidacy of Congresswoman Shirley Chisholm in the 1970s to the firing of an African-American staffer in the central office of the National Women's Studies Association (NWSA) in 1990s (Leidner 1993). Both of these events caused open conflict among movement activists. In the latter case, NWSA was brought almost to the point of collapse as it struggled with issues of accountability and democratic process. Some women of color accused the organization of being actively racist and formed a splinter group, while other women of color (including the current president,

Vivian Ng) defended the NWSA, while also acknowledging that it did not always live up to its own high standards of inclusiveness.

Clearly, it is potentially destructive of the movement, literally and symbolically, if the price for maintaining minority group and radical representation is the exclusion of any other group of women. A diverse feminist movement must welcome and accommodate women of all backgrounds and encourage each member to listen sensitively to the concerns of others. This is precisely why racism, agism, homophobia, anti-Semitism, and discrimination against the disabled are fundamentally incompatible with the feminist commitment to respect for all women. Although there is no feminist debate over the crucial importance of inclusiveness, it is structurally very difficult to achieve.

Moreover, the priority that individual women give to overcoming historical patterns of racism and anti-Semitism often reflects the extent to which their own friendship networks are segregated (Russo et al. 1991). Because most white feminists still do not live racially integrated lives on a day-to-day basis, it is easy for a gap to develop between their abstract moral commitment to inclusiveness and their concrete actions to challenge racism and to create a climate of practical equality, even within the movement. Taking such segregation for granted allows the costs of a lack of diversity to go unremarked. It is also easy for white women not to notice the benefits they derive from racism, just as men take the privileges arising from sexism as their due. In this, as in so many feminist issues, the personal and the political are intertwined. Although the New Feminist Movement has gradually built up a premise of a shared moral commitment to eradicating racism, anti-Semitism and other forms of discriminatory privilege as part of the feminist agenda (for without it, only some women are freed), the continuing gap between this abstract principle and the practices of individual feminists and feminist organizations makes charges of hypocrisy seem well taken. Rather than true hypocrisy (false professions of concern), we think the problem the movement often faces today is the absence of institutionalized antiracist practices that would serve to address these concerns effectively.

Summary and Conclusions

The spread of feminist ideas and groups at the beginning of the 1970s made the ensuing decade one of tremendous organizational growth and diversity. Organizations that had been dormant since the suffrage struggle were reactivated on behalf of an expanded agenda for women's rights, while new organizational forms appeared. Direct action/self-help groups appealed primarily to socialist and radical feminists; the more structured political and educational associations drew mostly from the ranks of liberal and socialist feminists; while cultural/entrepreneurial efforts attracted radical and career feminists. But all three strategic forms brought together women of varying persuasions.

The most marked change of this decade was a muting of the distinctions between the collectivist and bureaucratic strands as they became increasingly interwoven into the different strategic forms of association. Self-help groups were often transformed into service providers, operating with a flattened hierarchy and minimal bureaucratic trappings, but also developing the procedures of accountability and record keeping expected by clients and funding agencies. Educational/political associations carried out their networking functions with a mix of consciousness-raising and formal programs. The cultural/entrepreneurial groups remained collectivist in style, but as they grew in size and profitability adopted those bureaucratic procedures necessary for managing their complexity and diversity. In contrast to the 1960s, the meaningful distinction in this decade was in strategic orientation rather than organizational style.

As the bureaucratic and collectivist strands became intertwined, many activists with a collectivist history became concerned about co-optation, while those from the bureaucratic tradition worried about the impracticality of trying to change outcomes for women without recognizing how the larger societal systems worked. Both fears were well founded, as we see in the next chapter. Nonetheless, the period 1973–82 was a decade in which women from both sides of the issue learned from one another as they constructed organizational forms that drew selectively from both traditions. As Remington (1991) has pointed out, these hybrid organizations continue to experience structural strains: they are not yet ready to envision women as powerful rather than merely seeking empowerment; they have not developed mechanisms to foster and reward long-term organizational commitment or leadership; and they too readily allow conflicts to be personalized. The problem of power in feminist organizations remains a sensitive and understudied issue, but one that must eventually be confronted.

So, too, is the issue of diversity and dissent. Conflicts within the movement have repeatedly generated new groups and renewed efforts at consciousness-raising. In many respects, this has been a productive process for the movement as a whole, producing a diversity of groups and strategies into which individual feminists could devote their efforts. Moreover, internal conflict has sometimes moved the feminist agenda in the direction of more inclusiveness. Without these struggles, it is unlikely that the movement would have adopted the previously "extreme" position that homophobia is a form of sexism or recognized the invisible assumption that the experience and goals of white women were the "norm." In strengthening its commitment to social diversity and economic justice, the women's movement has deliberately begun to address the biases in participation and leadership that were built into its initial mobilization, and to confront the legacy of racism and anti-Semitism in the this country and worldwide. These shifts toward relatively radical substantive positions went hand in hand with changes in the direction of increasingly institutionalized structures that may appear to be co-opted and more conservative in style. This paradox will also be explored further in the next chapter.

The sheer number and diversity of feminist organizations has brought a degree of institutionalization to the movement, without, however, significantly blunting feminism's radical edge. The mainstream political and educational organizations that were reactivated into feminist activity, such as the Young Women's Christian Association, the National Council of Jewish Women, and even the Girl Scouts of America, pursued nonmainstream or "outsider" issues with "insider tactics" (Spalter-Roth and Schreiber 1994). Many of the goals of direct action groups have been adopted by civic and professional associations, although the explicitly feminist organizations continue to provide a more radical political critique and more forceful advocacy than do other service providers. Cultural and entrepreneurial groups sustain a feminist community that is sometimes faulted for being too marginal to be effective; some of these settings offer emotional sustenance to long-term activists, and others encourage the development of new forms of consciousness-raising.

As more and more women become committed to "careers in feminism," they come to appreciate the variety of movement organizations and the complementary strengths those organizations encourage. As a result, the once-fierce conflict between self-defined radicals and other feminists has been muted, even if it has not disappeared entirely (Daniels 1991; Ryan 1992). At the ideological level, there has been a coming together on certain goals, despite the diversity of organizational structures and practices. In the next chapter, we examine in depth two of the major issues that have shaped the movement, the Equal Rights Amendment and reproductive rights, as these struggles played out in the tumultuous decade of the 1970s.

Although it is commonly assumed that feminism is a young women's issue, this delegate to the International Women's Year conference in Houston illustrates the universality of concern for equality. *Photograph © Bettye-Lane.*

Chapter 6

Interest Group Politics: Triumphs and Tensions, 1973–82

The growth and transformation of feminist groups in the 1970s had special significance for those organizations whose major goal was changing the American political system to make it work for women. By mid-decade, many of the political and educational associations joined forces in Washington and the various states to lobby for legislation and enforcement of existing laws that extended and protected women's rights, and to seek greater representation of women among policymakers at all levels of government. Although women's interests were represented in part by the leadership elite of the women's policy network that emerged at this time, this mobilization of the feminist movement into a broad-based interest group was also visible at the grass roots, as millions of individual feminists became active in support of the Equal Rights Amendment and reproductive rights.

Choosing to work within the system, however, raises issues of co-optation. As long as feminists remained invisible or were seen as merely ridiculous, the possibility and contingent problems of seeking allies, funding, and political influence did not arise. This situation changed dramatically as the women's movement became a recognized political force. The growth of support for feminist positions and acceptance of the label "feminist" (discussed in chapter 4) provided the context in which women's organizations could coalesce and claim credibility as representatives of the interests of all American women.

In this chapter we trace the transformation of some of the educational and political organizations of the movement as they grew from small, marginalized groups at the periphery of American politics to players in the political mainstream. In so doing, we also follow the changing American political agenda, as issues such as the Equal Rights Amendment (ERA) and reproductive rights took on a central position in partisan political struggles. We date this period from the beginning of the struggle for the ERA and close with its defeat.

Just as the ERA became the rallying point for feminists, it also served to awaken and unite a backlash movement, which has concentrated its energies on opposing legal abortion and gay rights, and defending what it calls "family values." Organized antifeminism has become closely identified with the right wing of the American political spectrum and with conservative religious forces. The struggle between these two sides has increasingly defined party politics in the United States and has become a forum for symbolic claims about the position of women, families, and the role of the state in everyday life choices. In effect, the once-radical claim that "the personal is political" carried the day during this decade, as issues of family structure and personal freedom rose to the top of the agenda of both political parties. The chapter closes with a detailed discussion of the emergence of the backlash movement.

Entering the Political Arena

In a democratic society, the ultimate success of a social movement depends on the ability of its organizations to use and manipulate the political system. Otherwise, members continue to be without a voice in policymaking, and movement issues continue to be perceived as irrelevant or illegitimate. To the extent that it succeeds, however, the movement is transformed into an "interest group" participating in institutionalized political processes. To become players in this system, feminist organizations needed a mobilized constituency and access to decision-makers—both of which appeared distant goals, given the low levels of gender consciousness and political organization among women at the beginning of the decade. Between 1973 and 1982, however, significant gains were made in each of these dimensions.

Women's Gender Consciousness.   Generating a sense of solidarity and shared fate among American women has been a long and slow process. Simply dividing the population by the variable "sex" does not capture the politicized consciousness of identification of women as a group with common interests and a collective identity as women. In one sense, of course, women are not *a* group but a portion of *every* group, whether group boundaries are drawn on lines of race and ethnicity, or age, or political party. In another sense, however, women are a group insofar as they define their fortunes as interdependent; the sense of solidarity, positive affect, and shared agenda that this represents can be called a *politicized gender consciousness,* and this consciousness increased throughout the 1970s, especially among white women (Gurin 1982; Rinehart 1992). As the public opinion data cited in chapter 4 indicate, there was a sharp shift in the early 1970s toward egalitarian attitudes. This made legislators more receptive to feminist goals at a time when several relevant issues, from equal pay to the ERA, were before Congress. But not all women who considered themselves part of the population called "women" embraced such egalitarian norms. As we will see, antifeminists also attempted to mobilize women to press for what *they* defined as women's rights—support for women as full-time homemakers, for example. Nonetheless, egalitarian gender consciousness rose from 22 percent among white women and 26 percent among women of color in 1972 to 44 and 39 percent, respectively, by 1982 (Rinehart 1992). Here was a large and growing constituency of women with a shared interest in achieving higher status and equal rights that movement organizations could now claim to represent.

As Mueller (1988) points out, even a high level of gender consciousness in the 1920s would have gone unnoticed because public opinion polling did not exist to identify differences between women's and men's voting patterns. When first-wave feminists did not rush to support women candidates following suffrage, politicians discounted the women's vote and feminists as an effective interest group. With the revitalization of the movement in the 1970s, women could become a significant political force, but realizing this potential required further organizing effort.

The Women's Policy Network.   The core set of organizations that took the representation of women's political aspirations and strivings for equality as their mandate included both those formed in the 1960s, such as NOW and WEAL, and reactivated organizations originally founded early in the century, such as the National Women's Party (NWP), the National Federation of Business and Professional

Women's Clubs (BPW), and the League of Women Voters (LWV). By 1973, NOW, WEAL, and the National Women's Political Caucus (NWPC) had all established Washington offices to be close to the action.

From this beginning, a "woman's lobby" soon developed, as the core organizations and other national voluntary organizations such as the National Council of Jewish Women, United Methodist Women, and the American Association of University Women joined in an effort to build grassroots support on a variety of issues and to influence legislators. In the course of the ERA struggle, described later in this chapter, other associations representing women and girls—e.g., Soroptimists, Girl Scouts of America, and the Young Women's Christian Association—added their support to feminist efforts, creating a broad and strong coalition.

In general, the contemporary feminist network "inside the Beltway" (the superhighway that circles Washington, D.C.) consists of three elements: the mass-membership organizations mentioned above; increasing numbers of lobbyists for direct action groups throughout the country (e.g., the National Coalition against Domestic Violence); and newly founded research institutes such as the Center for Women's Policy Studies and the Institute for Women's Policy Research (Spalter-Roth and Schreiber 1994). Leaders of these varied organizations have coordinated their activities through a "Council of Presidents" in order to enhance their influence on legislation, policy initiatives, and federal appointments (Gelb and Palley 1987).

The similarity in social background characteristics among both feminist and traditional organization members made possible a shared realm of discourse (Costain 1981). There was also a co-optable network of friendships and common organizational memberships between women in the established and the new women's groups (Gelb and Palley 1982; Rossi 1982).

The established women's organizations had mastered the art of lobbying. They put their knowledge and expertise, and the political legitimacy of their large memberships, to the service of feminist goals. They also provided a large pool of community activists, women well versed in local politics and organizing. This coalition achieved a number of significant victories in the mid-1970s: minimum wage for domestic workers, educational equity, access to credit, admission to military academies, job protection for pregnant workers, and funds for the observance of International Women's Year. Major defeats included failure to override President Nixon's veto of comprehensive childcare legislation and to preserve federal funding for abortions for poor women. The importance of the coalition between feminist groups and traditional women's organizations is underscored by the fact that at this time the movement received little support from such powerful sectors as the business community, unions, or the national administration.

The Political Environment. In addition to the benefits of increasingly favorable public attitudes and a coordinating council of women's organizations, Congress itself became more supportive of women's movement issues in the 1970s. A dozen activist congresswomen and several male colleagues introduced and guided bills through the complex legislative process, taking on a role that has since been formalized in the Congressional Caucus on Women's Issues. Experts from the new research centers provided statistical ammunition and monitored the enforcement and effectiveness of statutes already on the books (Davis 1991; Gelb and Palley 1987).

With only a low-level lobbying effort by NOW, WEAL, and NWPC, Congress had already passed legislation designed to improve the status of women. The Equal Rights Amendment passed by a vote of 354 to 23 in the House of Representatives in October 1971, and by 84 to 8 in the Senate in March 1972. The ERA was viewed as so noncontroversial that no public opinion polls were conducted until 1974. Its easy passage through Congress convinced many feminist skeptics that lobbying could be effective and that traditional tactics could foster support by the general public.

However, the ERA would not long remain so free of controversy, and as the struggle for ratification at the state level intensified, feminists were increasingly drawn into the conventional political arena where the amendment's fate would be decided. Washington-based feminist organizations experienced a dramatic expansion in membership, funding, and staff throughout this period. But Washington was only one site of feminist politics, and many of the same issues before Congress were introduced into state legislatures, forcing feminists to become active at this level also. These transformations in political involvement and in the locus of activity were particularly evident in the changing structure and fortunes of NOW.

Changes in NOW. In its original structure, NOW consisted of two almost disconnected parts: an elite lobbying group in Washington, D.C., and a network of autonomous local units whose members engaged in a variety of task forces and direct actions. By the mid-1970s, however, decision-making was increasingly concentrated in the national office. NOW became a mass-membership organization, with most joiners only active enough to write a check. The vast expansion of this relatively passive membership provided the credibility and funds for the organization to hire staff and to augment its lobbying effort, especially on behalf of the ERA campaigns that were mobilizing feminists throughout the country. These bureaucratic tendencies created tension within the organization because the few thousand members who attend NOW's annual meetings remained committed to egalitarian, participatory processes, while the great mass of members had only a weak connection to the decision-making apparatus of an organization they joined in order to produce concrete political results.

NOW not only grew dramatically in size and resources (see Table 6.1) but also found itself increasingly involved in electoral politics at both the national and the state level. It appealed for funds through political action committees (PACs) and distributed money and endorsements to selected candidates. The membership was divided over this growing emphasis on mainstream politics, and the future direction of the organization became the focus of a series of divisive national conventions. In 1982, delegates seeking a return to the radical goals and unconventional tactics of NOW's earlier years rallied behind the candidacy of Sonia Johnson, a Mormon excommunicated by her church for supporting the ERA. They were defeated by the forces favoring a more pragmatic political strategy, lead by political scientist Eleanor Smeal. In 1984, Johnson ran for President of the United States as a consciousness-raising gesture. Thus, even as they rejected "politics as usual," the more radical faction was drawn into the electoral arena, for that was the forum where feminist issues were debated and often decided (Ryan 1992).

TABLE 6.1.

Growth of NOW: 1972–92

	1972	*1977*	*1982*	*1992*
NOW Membership	15,000	40,000	220,000	200,000
Annual Budget	$160,000	$500,000	$13,000,000	$8,000,000
Public Support for ERA	(not available)	56%	63%	(not available)

Source: National NOW Times *October 1982 and 1992; Carden 1974, 196.*

Playing Party Politics. In the early 1970s, as the component elements of the women's policy network were poised to enter the electoral arena, neither major political party was particularly identified with feminism. Throughout the 1940s and 1950s, the Republican party had been the prime supporter of an Equal Rights Amendment; while Democrats, at the urging of labor leaders, opposed the ERA in favor of legislation giving special treatment to women workers. When the Supreme Court struck down such protective measures in the 1960s, unionists and Democratic candidates were free to embrace the amendment as well as other "women's" issues. At the same time, during the presidency of Richard Nixon (1969–74), the Republican party adopted a "southern strategy" of appealing to white conservative voters angered over changes in race relations, school desegregation, affirmative action, and welfare dependency.

Nonetheless, the presidential election of 1976, between Republican Gerald Ford and Democrat Jimmy Carter, was not marked by a strong polarization of feminists along party lines. The candidates' wives, Betty Ford and Rosalynn Carter, openly supported the ERA, which was also endorsed by the platform of each party. Feminists lobbied both candidates, winning concessions from Carter that he honored after his victory—namely, the appointment of women to the cabinet and an advisory committee on women's affairs. But Carter's relationship with feminists deteriorated throughout his term; the more outspoken members of the advisory commission resigned in anger, and many faulted him for the stalemate over ratification of the ERA. As a result, feminist support for his second-term candidacy was lukewarm, even though the climate for feminists in the Republican party had turned positively chilly. For the first time, the Republican platform failed to endorse the ERA; on the contrary, it called for a constitutional amendment banning all abortions and for the selection of judges opposed to reproductive rights (Costain 1991).

In 1980, Ronald Reagan was elected on this platform despite the appearance of a significant "gender gap" in voting patterns, with women more likely than men to vote Democratic. This gap has persisted and even widened in both state and national elections, reflecting not only women's reaction against the Republican party's anti-ERA and antiabortion stands, but also their positive support for Democratic policies on such "traditional" women's issues as education, social welfare, environmental protection, and peace (Mueller 1988).

Yet for some feminist activists, the Democratic party has proven to be a weak and inconsistent ally, more concerned with winning back the increasingly conservative lower-middle-class whites who voted for Reagan than with maintaining the allegiance of its "core constituencies" (feminists, urban voters, minorities, labor union members). Feeling excluded from either major party, some feminist activists have been attracted to insurgent political movements such as the Rainbow Coalition in 1988 and former NOW President Eleanor Smeal's effort to form a new National Women's Party in 1989. Many feminists may yet lend their support to a new third party should the Clinton administration be too inconsistent an ally.

Other Alliances.   Throughout the 1970s, feminist ties to Civil Rights organizations, organized labor, and the liberal wing of the Democratic party were strengthened, though still somewhat fragile. One study (Rossi 1982) of delegates to the National Women's Conference in Houston in 1977 identified two distinct subgroups of feminists with weak links to one another: one had strong economic and social welfare priorities; the other largely focused on issues of sexuality and violence against women. This distinction reflected the different routes through which the women had come into the movement. Feminists with experience in the Civil Rights movement, unions, or the New Left tended toward a socialist perspective in which race and class were crucial variables; they were also more likely than other feminists to be women of color, from working-class backgrounds, and to value ties with Civil Rights organizations and unions as a matter of principle rather than as a strategic choice.

Radical feminists, particularly those from the moral reform tradition, are most deeply concerned with women's special qualities and experiences, particularly those of exploitation and violence. Many are also members of world peace and disarmament groups, and active in the ecology and antinuclear movements. It is in these directions that they then look for allies; in turn, long-established women's peace groups (e.g., Women Strike for Peace) have drawn new support from the revitalization of feminism.

Liberal feminists are most likely to favor alliances with established civil rights organizations, particularly the American Civil Liberties Union (which has funded a women's rights project), and with the family planning movement, as exemplified by Planned Parenthood. On other issues, liberals have made joint cause with minority lobbies— blacks, the aged, the handicapped, and children's rights advocates.

As a consequence of all these different interests among feminists, the New Feminist Movement has established a broad range of links to other political interest groups, but these alliances typically do not encompass the entire movement. While there is a vulnerability to such "weak ties," there are also strengths (Granovetter 1973): greater flexibility for broad-based feminist organizations such as NOW to maneuver among potential allies and to balance goals and priorities of the many constituencies within the movement. An important aspect of NOW's activities in recent years has been to educate its members to expand their vision to encompass a variety of feminist perspectives, and to support one another's issues.

The Struggle for the Equal Rights Amendment

The single issue that most fully defined the movement in this period, 1972–83, was the battle for ratification of an equal rights amendment to the United States Constitution. Although its eventual failure has obscured many impressive legislative victories achieved throughout the decade, the struggle for the ERA symbolized and embodied all the currents discussed in this chapter, and the crucial role that it played then will continue to shape the future of the New Feminist Movement.

History of the ERA.   The ERA was first introduced in Congress in 1923, at the urging of the National Women's Party (NWP) and its indefatigable leader, Alice Paul. Despite continual pressure from the NWP, the legislation remain locked in the Judiciary Committee for the next three decades, in part because many women's groups believed it would invalidate laws protecting women industrial workers, and in part because male union members feared added job competition from women (Harrison 1988; Mathews and DeHart 1990). Indeed, the bitter division among feminists over the relative merits of the ERA and existing legislation that singled out women alone for protection in the workplace paralyzed feminists' efforts to exert political influence from the 1920s to the early 1960s.

When this issue was finally laid to rest with the Civil Rights Act of 1963 and various court decisions that overturned discriminatory legislation, however well intended, the NWP began to convince second-wave feminists that the amendment was a worthy cause. Its text was simple and to the point, and seemingly unambiguous:

The Equal Rights Amendment

Sec. 1. Equality of rights under the law shall not be denied or abridged by the United States or by any State on account of sex.

Sec. 2. The Congress shall have the power to enforce by appropriate legislation the provisions of this article.

Sec. 3. This Amendment shall take effect two years after the date of ratification.

In 1972, the ERA was finally called out of committee, passed by the House of Representatives with barely an hour's debate, and quickly ratified by the Senate. Speedy endorsements followed in thirty-four of the thirty-eight states required for the amendment to be adopted. But hopes of a quick and easy victory dimmed as the amendment became stalled in fourteen state legislatures, mostly in the South. The unexpected strength of resistance to the ERA marked a major turning point in the history of the New Feminist Movement.

Feminist forces needed to shift their attention to state-level politics in order to secure the necessary ratifications, and this change of focus had an enduring impact on the movement. Heretofore, the movement had been embodied in a multiplicity of grassroots, local direct action, educational, and cultural groups, in addition to the elite Washington-based network, with minimal state-level organizing. Now, however, resources began to flow from both the local-and national-level, converging in efforts to build state-level organizations. This happened most intensively in the contested states in which ratification seemed possible (e.g., Illinois, North Carolina), but state-level organizing also blossomed in other states, to fight against attempts to rescind earlier ratification votes or to pass equal rights amendments to state constitutions (Boles 1979; Mathews and DeHart 1990).

Secondly, internal struggles became muted as even those feminists who originally had been less than enthusiastic about the ERA (radical and socialist feminists particularly) saw this modest liberal goal in danger of going down to defeat. Pragmatically, feminists in state coalitions learned both to work with each other and to play legislative politics with a diverse set of allies. They developed strategies and tactics that were independent of the national-level organizations, such as NOW, and more responsive to the political climate of their individual states

(Mathews and DeHart 1990). Alliances forged in the battle for the ERA could henceforth be mobilized in the struggle over other women's issues, whether reforms in rape law or mandated parental leave. The working definition of a feminist became "someone you can count on to support your issues."

At the national level, feminist groups reached out to other organizations to form an ERA Ratification Council that eventually included over a hundred national organizations, from the Amalgamated Clothing Workers of America to Zonta International. Participants in the ratification drive, from flight attendants to Catholic nuns, acquired more familiarity with feminist activists, and feminist organizers learned some important lessons about women's diversity.

At the same time, a newly energized opposition also sought to broaden and solidify its support among religious and political conservatives. The efforts of these forces, which we will examine in more detail later in this chapter, were so successful that by 1978 it was clear that the original seven-year period for ratification would expire without the needed approval (Boles 1979). An intensive lobbying effort by the pro-ERA coalition, highlighted by a massive demonstration in Washington, prodded Congress to extend the deadline for three more years, but to no avail. In 1982, following narrow defeats in Florida and Illinois, all hope for ratification faded. Underscoring the strength of the opposition, several similar amendments were defeated at the state level.

Why Did the ERA Lose?   Since all that the amendment guaranteed was "equality of rights under the law," what grounds could there be for opposing such a minimalist reform? Several scholars have tried to explain the variety of factors that doomed this effort. One common thread in these analyses is a recognition of the strong symbolic meanings that became attached to the amendment. For example, the so-called "potty-issue," that is, the superficially silly claim that the ERA would mandate gender-integrated restrooms, can be best understood in the context of southern white resentment of racial integration of restrooms, lunchrooms, and schools (Mathews and DeHart 1990). "Forced busing" and other desegregation orders that overrode state and local decision-making were analogies that the anti-ERA forces could exploit to increase state legislators' anxieties about where this amendment might lead.

Second, it is generally easier to awaken fears about the loss of the familiar than to convince people of the benefits of change (Conover and Gray 1983). Anti-ERA forces successfully fed people's fears that women would lose the protection of their husbands, that men would lose control over wives and daughters, and that once the firm boundaries assigning women and men to their "proper" places were challenged, gender itself would become unstable and women "unsexed." Where advocates saw equality and freedom, opponents foresaw sexual license, competition between women and men, and personal irresponsibility (Mathews and DeHart 1990; Marshall 1994). Such highly polarized symbolic contests are rarely won by advocates of change, even when they outnumber adherents to the status quo (Berry 1986).

A third symbol-laden issue was the claim that the ERA would require not only conscripting women into the armed forces but sending them into combat (Mansbridge 1986). Although, in practice, "combat" has been defined to exclude military women from sitting in a missile silo in Kansas but not from nursing roles in war zones, the image of women as warriors has always been highly unsettling, stirring up anxieties about female aggression. Members of Congress sought to allay some of these fears by suggesting a long list of exemptions and exceptions. Even if these limitations could have made the ERA more acceptable, the very idea of treating men and women differently would have negated the symbolic meaning of the amendment. But by insisting that "equal treatment" meant just that, and that the ERA would allow women to be drafted and sent into combat on the same basis as men, its proponents handed legislators a credible reason to vote against the amendment.

By the time of its defeat, it is not clear what practical effect the ERA might have had. The Supreme Court was applying the equal protection clause of the Fourteenth Amendment to strike down such obviously discriminatory practices as refusing social security benefits to male dependents of female wage earners. Other rights could be protected by specific federal law—for example, the Pregnancy Discrimination Act of 1978 demanding that employers treat pregnancy the same way as any other "temporary disability." At the state level, many statutes guaranteed women the same rights that they would have gained with the passage of the federal ERA, although the variation in women's status from one state to another is now greater than ever before. Even the symbolic values of an equal rights amendment were realized without its enactment, including a growing realization that women can perform well in combat and deserve no different consideration than men in military service.

Thus, while the ERA continued to be introduced in Congress during the Reagan and Bush administrations, there was little serious effort to pass legislation that would surely have faced a presidential veto that Congress could not override. The threat of presidential veto so stalemated Congress on all types of gender and civil rights issues in the 1980s that feminist energy for legislative change was largely redirected to the states. In some states, the feminist coalitions forged in the ERA struggle continue to post impressive victories; in others, the battles are more defensive and the progress more discouraging. But after the defeat of the ERA, the primary arena for gender politics clearly shifted to state legislatures, where the growing representation of women as members is encouraging, although wide disparities between the numbers of men and women remain.

Dangers of Co-optation

Playing politics increases the possibility of "co-optation," that is, being absorbed into the policy structures that one has been fighting against. When the feminist movement or its leaders are used only to promote the goals of other groups and political leaders rather than those of women, co-optation has taken place. Making compromises and trading support, however, should not be seen as only a danger. Coalitions and compromises are also the route that movements take to co-opt other interest groups, government agencies, and political candidates. There are three areas where control and co-optation are at issue in conducting interest group politics: setting agendas, acquiring and making endorsements, and receiving funding.

Agenda-Setting. The increased visibility of a New Feminist Movement placed women's concerns on the political agenda in a way they had not been since suffrage was won. This was evident not only in specific legislative victories, but in the increasing attention paid to women's issues at all political levels, from the global to the local community.

The resurgence of feminism around the world began to be felt in international politics as the United Nations declared 1975 "International Women's Year" and 1975–85 the "Decade for Women," ushering the new decade in with a conference in Mexico City. At this conference men in national governments set the agenda for the two thousand delegates they appointed, and more time was spent debating colonialism and disarmament than discussing gender equity or women's needs. Nonetheless, it was a tremendous consciousness-raising experience, alerting women in affluent countries to the limitations of their perspectives and encouraging women in developing countries to speak out more forcefully on gender inequity in their own context. Delegates developed a plan of action and set future U.N. conferences for Copenhagen (1980) and Nairobi (1985).

Although as Bunch (1980, 83) put it, "Copenhagen is a government conference about women—not a women's conference," the U.N. plan that emerged from that event did put national governments on record as needing to improve the status of their female citizens. Combined with the consciousness-raising effects of so many different women coming together and sharing their experiences, these national studies and commissions energized feminists around the globe to put their own issues on the agenda in their home countries. By the time of the Nairobi conference, both government delegates and nongovernmental organizations (NGOs) that met in parallel to the official conference were discussing feminist concerns about political representation, gender equity, and affirmative action (Nelson and Chowdraty 1993) and reporting on a wide variety of grassroots feminists organizations around the world (Cagatay, Grown, and Santiago 1986).

In the United States, in anticipation of the International Women's Year conference of 1975 President Ford appointed a national commission to study and report on the status of women. Under the leadership of Jill Ruckelshouse, perhaps the most openly feminist Republican woman, the commission held public hearings and miniconferences all over the country that drew new recruits to the movement. The commission's final report, "To Form a More Perfect Union . . . Justice for American Women" (1976), amply documented the continuing barriers to equal opportunity for American women.

The commission also organized a National Women's Conference in Houston, Texas, in 1977. Despite the presence of organized antifeminists dominating a few state delegations, most of the delegates were feminists, and women of color were represented in greater measure than either their proportions in the general population or their presence in feminist organizations up to this point. Diversity in attitudes and social background was the hallmark of the conference (Rossi 1982), but the overall plan that the convention strongly endorsed was clearly an expression of feminist goals. Both Republican (Ford) and Democratic (Carter) administrations tried to control the mood and direction of the conference by their selection of commissioners, while state-level political struggles (especially over the ERA) determined the composition of state delegations. Nonetheless, the overall tone of the convention was feminist. As feminists collaborated with mainstream women politicians on the successful ratification of the plan, antifeminists organized a "counterconvention" a few blocks away that drew considerable media attention in the name of "equal time."

Because the more radical positions were endorsed when controversy arose, there is little evidence here that feminists had been co-opted into the nonfeminist mainstream. Indeed, in order to preserve a united front, many delegates overcame personal reservations to support majority positions on sexual orientation and reproductive rights. In addition, the Houston conference facilitated the creation of state-level coalitions among feminists concerned with different issues (e.g., sexual violence or economic justice for poor women), thus broadening state political agendas beyond the ERA. As we will see in chapter 7, these coalitions grew in significance in the following decade of reaction and retrenchment.

Although the Houston conference helped place gender on the national agenda, it failed to move national politics in a more feminist direction. President Carter appointed a National Advisory Committee on Women, chaired by Bella Abzug and Carmen Delgado Votow, but when the committee publicly criticized increased defense spending in the 1980 budget, Abzug was fired and the other members resigned immediately. NOW and other feminist organizations withdrew their support from Carter. The Reagan administration was even more committed to increased military outlays at the expense of funding for social services, of which women and children are the prime beneficiaries. In contrast to the token endorsement of feminist goals by both Democratic and Republican administrations up to 1980, the Reagan presidency was committed to seeking support from antifeminist organizations. As fighting feminism became a key element in the Reagan administration's domestic political agenda, the feminist cause became part of an overall opposition to "Reaganomics" (Amott 1993). This was not co-optation, but *realignment,* as both sides changed to put feminist issues squarely in the center of the political agenda for the coming decade.

Endorsements.   To the extent that any social movement pursues goals that must be accomplished through legislation, it is advantageous to have allies in both major political parties and to avoid making enemies among sitting legislators. Thus whether or not to endorse any specific candidate becomes an important strategy question.

In the early 1970s, the endorsement issue led to a major policy dispute between the National Women's Political Caucus and NOW, with only the NWPC endorsing and doing fund-raising for individual candidates. Members of the NWPC, often drawn from the ranks of women party activists, were frequently accused of "careerism," that is, using the movement for personal advancement (the same type of charge leveled at the "media stars" and talented writers in collectivist groups) or of "selling out" for the sake of electability. By the mid-1970s, however, NOW reversed its policy as it became ever more involved in mainstream politics. But deciding that endorsements can be important tools is simpler than making decisions about whom to endorse.

Three different sets of priorities were advocated by feminists: (1) to support more women for political office, regardless of their specific stands on crucial issues; (2) to support "your friends," that is, candidates, especially incumbents, who have taken strong pro-feminist stands on these issues, even if they are men being challenged by women; and (3) to support a progressive platform, that is, a broad agenda of political stands that provide a basis for coalition among race, class, and gender interest groups. That these priorities could conflict in specific cases became evident in a number of state races. In North Carolina, a strong male supporter of the ERA who had taken abuse for this position was challenged by a progressive woman (Mathews and DeHart 1990); in New Jersey, Millicent Fenwick, a female role model of national reputation and a Republican supporter of feminist causes, was challenged by a Democrat who would help maintain Democratic control of the Senate; in Connecticut, Lowell Weicker, a Republican supporter of abortion rights and gay rights faced a challenge from Toby Moffett, a candidate who represented a broad coalition of progressive economic reformers. In each of these cases and many others, feminist organizations split their endorsements, with the national organizations preferring one candidate and the state-level groups lining up behind the other—a sure recipe for ineffectiveness and frustration. When national NOW withdrew its endorsement of Jimmy Carter in 1980 because of its frustration with his fitful support, they found themselves powerless to confront the Republican party's shift to the extreme right, represented by the nomination and election of Ronald Reagan. Although the National Women's Political Caucus remained committed to supporting women candidates in both major parties, it became increasingly difficult to find Republican women willing to make even a token endorsement of feminist positions.

Funding.   The risk of co-optation also arose in the course of seeking funding for feminist self-help and direct action projects. Throughout this period, several issues new to the political arena became defined as social problems. For example, concern over wife abuse and the need to provide an alternative for women wanting to leave a violent partner led to the creation of battered women's shelters. But it takes money to establish and operate such a facility. Appeals were made for public and private contributions to defray the costs of building, staffing, publicizing, counseling, and providing childcare. More important, direct action groups were committed to going beyond assisting individual women to challenging the systems that permit such abuse in the first place. This meant that in addition to seeking support for shelter services, feminists sought to change the institutions that legitimated male violence (e.g., laws that defined marital rape as impossible) or that blamed women for their own victimization, as when police departments defined "domestic disturbances" as a private matter and probably justified. Wishing to influence legislators as well as to provide services, feminist activists sought access to the judicial and political systems in general. National coalitions representing local groups active in providing services to battered women, rape victims, and displaced homemakers joined the Washington-based women's policy network in lobbying for both legislative change and stable funding.

The use of government money for feminist programs poses a number of problems: to whom should the project be accountable—the funders or the women being served? How much bureaucracy is compatible with the goal of empowering women? Whose criteria for eligibility should be used? And what sort of records should be kept? (Matthews 1994; Reinelt 1994). What, indeed, should the problem behavior be called? For example, at the beginning of the decade, assaultive husbands were labeled "wife-batterers," but legislators and funders preferred the less overtly feminist terms "domestic violence" and "spousal assault," which obscure the issue of women's subordination.

As feminists made inroads into the higher ranks of state agencies, these new feminist bureaucrats were able to adopt rules sensitive to the concerns of grassroots activists, but there is a conflict of loyalties for those who would wage a feminist struggle from "the terrain of the state" while the state as a whole remains dominated by male interests (Eisenstein 1990; Reinelt 1994). Another dilemma arises when requests for funding transform the movement into another "special interest group" for whom a legislator does a "favor" in return for feminist support on other issues.

At the local level, feminist groups have tended to focus on matters relating to sexuality, including sexual violence, rather than political and economic issues. Local feminist groups are more likely to engage in direct action than in lobbying. Yet direct action groups, including rape hot lines, shelters for battered women, and health-care clinics, share problems and needs that render them vulnerable to co-optation and distortion of priorities ("goal displacement").

One factor is the sheer cost of direct action. Whether resources are given as in-kind services (volunteer labor, rent-free space) or in cash (from foundations or government agencies), group members must direct their energies to keeping these resources flowing. The time spent on fund-raising and public relations comes at the expense of the group's original goals.

Often the problem is more subtle, involving the crucial distinction between self-help and community services (Withorn 1980). Feminist principles of community organizing emphasized the need to develop structures in which women could help themselves resist their subordination. Hot lines, shelters, and clinics relied on the voluntary labor of women rather than on the services of certified "experts." In addition, programs were to be run collectively by staff and clients alike. Volunteers were to engage in consciousness-raising, helping victims to place their personal experience in a larger political context, and encouraging them to build self-esteem through helping themselves and others.

These egalitarian self-help principles were rarely shared by the funding sources to which the feminist groups appealed. Foundations, charitable organizations, and government agencies demanded clear lines of accountability, evidence of expertise (degrees, diplomas, certificates), and rigorous bookkeeping, all of which gradually introduced bureaucratic norms into a collectivist structure. Moreover, the longer feminists worked in these settings, the more they came to distinguish service providers from clients, and to approve increases in staff power. Once such compromises are made, few obstacles remain to the transformation of the original radical organization into a conventional community service, complete with an executive director, a board of trustees, and a fund-raising/public relations specialist. Such changes often provoked angry confrontations among staff members, some of whom would move on to other, purer feminist community projects (Ahrens 1980).

Foundation funding poses another set of problems. As a rule, foundations prefer to grant "seed money" to experimental projects rather than to support established and successful programs. As a consequence, many feminist community organizations lost their funding when they were no longer new; unable to replace these funds, the services were discontinued. Other organizations struggled to find new projects to interest foundation sponsors, or tailored their programs to the current fad among funders; either way, priorities were distorted. Very few local action groups have been able to survive and maintain their original goals for as long as five years, but new groups continue to form around a growing range of issues. Feminist-founded rape crisis centers and battered women's shelters remained more political in their analysis and more dedicated to community education than did their nonfeminist counterparts, as both types expanded through the period 1972–83 (Martin 1993; Matthews 1994).

Conclusions.   Insofar as feminists wanted to shape policy on issues of concern to them, they needed to become "players" in the political system as a whole. In the early 1970s, some feminist groups were already at the margins of the political playing field, for example, the various state Commissions on the Status of Women, which dated back to the 1960s and had often been able to fund special projects or studies. In addition to feminists who brought their growing expertise on specific issues into state agency jobs, women in many agencies and political positions became converts to feminism; in Australia the word "femocrat" was coined to describe the phenomenon of women working in government for women's rights (Eisenstein 1990). This trend meant that the movement had more "insiders" as well as more outside organizations pressing for new projects, studies, and legislative changes. Insiders and outsiders do not necessarily share the same priorities, and the movement as a whole becomes increasingly vulnerable to having its agenda co-opted by those who have control over the purse strings.

These examples suggest the dangers of trying to work within the system at any level: co-optation, trivialization, banishment, and goal displacement. But remaining on the outside has its hazards: ridicule, indifference, marginalization, and powerlessness. The leaders of organized feminism have moved in the direction of creating a political force out of the diverse elements that compose the contemporary movement. Yet as feminist mobilization brought women's issues into mainstream politics, a countermobilization of groups opposed to this agenda was activated (Mueller and Dimieri 1982). Such polarization has worked to the disadvantage of feminists, whose goals appeared more controversial and less consensual than originally perceived (Boles 1979; Gelb and Palley 1982).

Backlash Movements

Social movements invariably produce countermovements based on resistance to change, producing a "loosely coupled tango of mobilization and demobilization" in which movement and countermovement mutually affect one another (Zald and Useem 1987). Countermovements are typically reactive both in structure and ideology, focusing on narrow goals, namely preservation of the status quo, rather than embracing a broad plan of social transformation (Ferree and Miller 1984). The antifeminist backlash, however, became more than a defensive reaction to the ERA and legalized abortion, as its leaders and ideals have been absorbed into the larger countermovement called the New Right (Himmelstein 1990).

Organized Antifeminism.　　The New Right, as defined by one of its founders (Viguerie 1980), consists of all those opposed to high taxes, government regulation, sex in the media, abortion, and weakness in foreign policy. Central to its philosophy are traditional conceptions of masculinity, including displays of male strength, control over others, hierarchical power relations (from God to husbands and fathers to women and children), and competitive success—all of which are rejected by the new feminism. The New Right program calls for a return to an idealized past when government was small and military service honored, when children obeyed their parents and wives depended on their husbands, and when Protestant prayers were in the schools and sex education was out. In essence, members of the New Right seek a massive repeal of real and imagined social trends of the past four decades.

Many of the fears raised by the New Right are shared by many Americans who are dismayed over what they perceive as the breakdown of all social institutions, but most particularly the family. In the face of what is seen as a collapse of traditional authority, some social scientists even blame feminists for undermining the power of men as husbands and fathers (Moynihan 1965; Lasch 1977; Bellah et al. 1985). The common message of the New Right is that many of our current social and economic problems could be solved if only American women would return to the kitchen and bedroom, for their own good as well as that of the nation, if not Western civilization itself.

Opposition to feminism also arises from a romanticization of the family. When the family is perceived as the only legitimate source of sexual and emotional fulfillment, anything that threatens its stability is a personal loss and a public danger. Since women are charged with the maintenance of family life, they bear responsibility for its apparent breakdown. Blame is then placed on the promises of feminism: that women can have an identity apart from family roles, that they can find fulfillment in the world of work, that marriages should be egalitarian rather than patriarchal, that relationships with other women could be as satisfying as those with men, and that one's body need not be placed at the service of God or country. These promises are seen as tempting but ultimately dangerous. No wonder, then, that the New Feminist Movement has aroused such a passionate backlash!

Opposition to the ERA began with the John Birch Society, an ultra-right-wing organization devoted to saving America from communism. Since the John Birch Society has limited influence even within the New Right, the anti-ERA cause needed a more mainstream image and charismatic leadership, both of which were provided by Phyllis Schlafly, an energetic and articulate Republican party activist from Illinois. When her efforts to influence defense spending, foreign policy, and other "men's" issues were rebuffed by Republican party leaders in the early 1970s, she picked up the Birch Society suggestion that women themselves could provide the troops needed to defeat ERA. Schlafly formed an organization called the Eagle Forum, with branches across the country, and assumed a leadership role in the STOP-ERA coalition. When the defeat of the ERA was celebrated, she was the undisputed star.

How did Schlafly do it? In the first place, she had resources: money from various New Right funding sources (such as the owners of Amway Enterprises and Coors Beer, and members of the National Chamber of Commerce); assistance from "old Right" organizations, such as the Birch Society, the American Legion, the Daughters of the American Revolution; the active support of fundamentalist Protestant ministers, including the growing numbers of "televangelists," leaders of Orthodox Jewry, the Mormon Church, and large segments of the Roman Catholic hierarchy and their associated organizations such as the Knights of Columbus. Second, she had high visibility in the press.

The media's need for "balance"—which means finding only two sides to any issue and treating both as equally important and legitimate— gave Phyllis Schlafly reams of valuable publicity, and since antifeminists were not concerned about the hierarchical implications of her media stardom, she dominated the "debate" throughout the late 1970s as feminist leaders came and went (Marshall 1994). Third, and no less important, like the feminists she opposed, she had the impassioned support of women organized at the grassroots level in "Right-to-Life" (antiabortion) as well as anti-ERA groups. They appeared at every public meeting, pressured candidates, handed out literature, wrote letters to the editor, and showed up in the voting booth on election day.

Who are these women who actively oppose feminism? Several studies of active antifeminists agree in describing them as disproportionately likely to be married, to be involved in church activities, and to be conservative in both religious ideas and politics in general (Mueller and Dimieri 1982; Mathews and Dehart 1990; Marshall 1991). The consistency with which they support the fundamentalist view of biblical truth, for example, is greater than the consistency of their opinions on women's issues, some being willing to support equal pay or anti-rape programs while being firmly opposed to reproductive rights or equality in hiring. Antifeminist attitudes are related not only to religion and marital status, but also to more general beliefs, such as denying the social causes of poverty and opposing black civil rights (Smith and Kluegel 1984), and anxiety over trends that legitimate open expressions of sexuality (Mathews and Dehart 1990). Some fear that advances for women will come at the cost of men's status (Spitze and Huber 1982); while others are afraid that feminism will result in women being exposed to the same exploitation as men on the job or in the armed forces. Indeed, the "women in combat" issue has been a powerful organizing weapon for antifeminists (Mansbridge, 1986). In general, those who have actually mobilized to act on these beliefs are, like active feminists, a selective subsample—in this instance, drawn from the co-optable social networks of fundamentalist Protestant and conservative Catholic churches, and from the extreme right of the political spectrum (Mueller and Dimieri 1982).

To a surprising extent, antifeminists recognize many problems that feminists also address, but frame their proposed solutions quite differently. The antifeminist view of men, for example, is in many ways more mistrustful than that held by feminists. STOP-ERA leader Phyllis Schlafly plays eloquently upon women's economic dependence and consequent fear of divorce by demanding a return to punitive alimony for "guilty husbands" and urging women to be "better," that is, more submissive, wives, while feminists look for economic independence and marriage based on affection rather than fear of punishment as the solution for the same insecurities.

Class tensions are also exploited by antifeminist organizers, who play upon the perception of feminists as upper-middle-class Yuppies with career options, contrasting this stereotype with that of the "unselfish" wife and mother for whom children are never "unwanted," only "unexpected" (Luker 1984; Marshall 1994). It can be seen as a mark of feminist accomplishment that even Phyllis Schlafly has modified her vision of "traditional" womanhood to affirm women's paid employment, although she continues to insist that it can only be legitimate when it does not involve a "career" or suggest that taking care of her family is not her core priority (Marshall 1991). Since most women do not have realistic options for advancement in the work force and since most working-class men and women place their family before their job in personal importance, Schlafly can use social class language to suggest that job discrimination and childcare are Yuppie issues rather than mainstream concerns (Marshall 1994). As feminists increasingly recognize, the language of "choice" resonates more with concerns of relatively affluent and educated women who can take advantage of opportunities that the movement has opened up for them (Stacey 1983). Insofar as abortion rights and the ERA can be cast as a referendum on the meaning and importance of families, the advocates of "family values" have framed the issue in a way that puts the feminist position on the defensive (Ginsburg 1989).

The strength of the backlash can thus be interpreted as evidence of the salience of the issues raised by the feminist movement: not simply jobs, or pay, or childcare, but the authentic liberation of women from dependence on men, from involuntary childbearing, from confinement to the home, and from conformity to a punishing image of beauty (Wolf 1991). The New Right correctly realizes that, when carried to its logical conclusion, the feminist agenda challenges every established, male-dominated authority structure: religious hierarchies, governing bodies, corporations, financial institutions, and school systems from kindergarten to universities. It should be no wonder, then, that resistance has been so intense and so successful in delaying the implementation of laws already enacted and in resisting further changes, despite overwhelming public support for specific feminist goals. Nowhere has the power of resistance been more forcefully displayed than in the area of reproductive rights.

Abortion and Reproductive Rights.   The other major focus of resistance to feminism emerged in the mid-1970s, following the Supreme Court's decisions in *Roe* v. *Wade* and *Doe* v. *Bolton* that declared unconstitutional existing abortion laws in Texas and Georgia. These and similar state statutes had denied abortions under *any* conditions, leaving the pregnant woman and her physician open to criminal prosecution if an abortion was performed. Indeed, up to the early 1960s, not only was abortion outlawed in most states, but so was access to contraceptive information, much less the actual devices, even for married couples. Only in 1965, in *Griswold* v. *Connecticut,* did the Supreme Court recognize the existence of a right to marital privacy that superseded the interests of the state in regulating morality. And it was not until 1972 that state laws banning the sale of contraceptives to unmarried adults were struck down, on grounds of the Fourteenth Amendment's equal protection clause.

During this period, as noted in chapter 4, public opinion on state laws prohibiting abortion under all circumstances had undergone a major shift: from overwhelming opposition to change to a slim plurality in favor of leaving the decision to a woman and her physician. In part, this shift was the result of highly publicized cases of women forced either to seek out an illegal abortionist or to bear a deformed child as a result of an epidemic of German measles in the 1960s or as a result of having taken the drug thalidomide (Condit 1990). Public opinion was also influenced by the emergence of the New Feminist Movement and the demands of a new generation of politically engaged, primarily college-educated young women. By 1972, the movement to reform state laws on abortion had made slow but steady progress, with one-third of the states adopting less restrictive statutes, based on medical considerations rather than a woman's right to choose.

Then, on 22 January 1973, quite unexpectedly, and by a vote of 7 to 2, the Supreme Court ruled that outlawing abortions under all circumstances violated a woman's right to privacy. But because this right to privacy was inferred rather than clearly stated in the Constitution, *Roe* v. *Wade* has generated much controversy ever since. The justices themselves stopped short of a full guarantee of the right to privacy by also recognizing the states' interests in protecting the health of the mother and the life of a potentially viable fetus. Thus the Court ruled that during the first three months of pregnancy, the state could not intervene in a woman's decision; but during the second trimester, states could enact regulations only for the purpose of protecting maternal health; and in the final twelve weeks of pregnancy, the state's interest in protecting life could permit banning abortions except to preserve the life or health of the pregnant woman.

Roe v. *Wade* had the immediate effect of striking down the most repressive state laws, even though it fell short of defining an absolute right to reproductive choice. The decision also activated a powerful and sustained antiabortion movement that united conservative political and religious forces at both the grassroots level and the level of national organizations. Over the next decade, the National Right to Life Committee and its various offshoots and allies, most notably the Roman Catholic hierarchy and the newly prominent fundamentalist Protestant preachers of the "electronic ministry," were able to erode the reach of *Roe* v. *Wade* through pushing for highly restrictive state legislation that met with protection from federal courts that were increasingly filled with Reagan appointees (Staggenborg 1991).

At the national level, Congress passed the Hyde Amendment denying Medicaid funding and restricting military and federal employee health insurance coverage for abortions. When these laws were upheld by an increasingly conservative Supreme Court, the reproductive rights forces turned again to the states for relief. Several states voted to pay for Medicaid abortions with their own funds, but others enacted even more severely restrictive regulations on when, where, and under what circumstances abortions could be performed.

Yet pro-choice forces still felt relatively confident, as it was clear that public opinion remained on their side, and in 1983, the Supreme Court reaffirmed the basic principle of *Roe* v. *Wade* by finding most of the newly enacted state restrictions unconstitutional. But the Court also left the door open for the states to figure out how to restrict access while not totally denying the Constitutional right to an abortion. By now, Ronald Reagan was under strong pressure from the antiabortion forces that had supported his election not only to make this issue the litmus test for all nominees to the federal courts, but also to push for a constitutional amendment declaring that life begins at conception. Yet despite Reagan's many supportive gestures, antiabortion leaders came to feel that he had not placed his full political weight behind the Human Life Amendment. They were angry and highly mobilized at a time when the pro-choice organizations were relatively demobilized and reactive, blocking state-level restrictions when they could, but generally relying on the Supreme Court to protect a woman's right to privacy (Staggenborg 1991).

Having expected more from a friendly White House, and increasingly frustrated with the slow pace of legislative and judicial change, antiabortion activists gradually turned to more direct, and often violent, means of restricting access to abortion services. Between 1977 and 1983, there were thirteen instances of arson, eight bombings, and over one hundred instances of vandalism and physical invasion at women's health facilities. A medical director and his wife were kidnaped, and clinic personnel were routinely threatened and assaulted—and such actions escalated over the following decade, as we will discuss in the next chapter (National Abortion Federation 1992).

Although the antiabortion movement is most closely linked to the radical right wing of American politics, criticism of the abortion rights movement has also come from the political left. For many liberals, this position stems from a basic commitment to nonviolence and pacifism, and from a concern for the conditions of poor women, rather than from anxiety over teenage sexuality (Hall and Ferree 1986; Ginsburg 1989). Left-wing activists accept the necessity for legal abortion as a means of keeping the procedure medically safe, but at the same time they deplore the social injustices that make it the only alternative for some women. Both the socialist and moral reform traditions in feminism also encourage a distinction between the legal right to a safe abortion and the desirability of abortion per se (Petchesky 1980). The need for abortion, they point out, is socially determined by poverty, by the stigma attached to unmarried motherhood, by the anonymity of current adoption practices, and by repressive sexual attitudes that limit the use of reliable contraception. From these perspectives, the way to reduce the incidence of abortion is not through restrictions that drive needy women to risky alternatives, but through change in the social/economic factors that have produced the need for an abortion in the first place. Although feminists had long organized and fought for this wider vision of reproductive rights—for example, in CARASA, the Coalition for Abortion Rights and Against Sterilization Abuse—the growing strength of the antiabortion mobilization pushed most feminists into a reactive, defensive position. With their limited gains under siege, few movement activists could pursue the broader proactive goal of enabling all women, including the poor and the nonmarried, to have only the children they want and to be able to raise them in health and dignity. In 1994, in recognition of this broader goal, the National Abortion Rights Action League (NARAL) changed its name to National Abortion and Reproductive Rights Action League.

The Men's Movement.   A third element in the backlash has been the emergence of a "men's movement" to resist the cultural as well as political gains made by feminists over the past few decades. The first men's groups organized in the 1960s and early 1970s to explore the need for change in men's roles in work and family through personal self-examination and consciousness-raising, and many of these early groups were sympathetic to the transformations that feminists desired (e.g., Kimmel 1987). The feminist men's movement spawned a journal, *Changing Men,* annual conferences, and a variety of grassroots action groups (e.g., groups dedicated to changing rapists and batterers) that are still in existence. However, to an increasing extent in the 1970s and 1980s, men began to organize to resist the social changes implied by feminism.

One aspect of this countermovement is the "divorced men's movement," which is struggling for enhanced rights for fathers in custody and visitation and fewer financial obligations to divorced spouses and dependent children (Coltrane and Hickman 1992). The media began to celebrate the "new father" in movies such as *Kramer* v. *Kramer* and *Three Men and a Baby,* which showed many of the themes that the divorced men's movement would stress: mothers either abandon their children emotionally for a career or are financially incapable of providing for them and thus do not deserve custody, while caretaking unlocks a new dimension of personal growth in men (Chesler 1986).

Another aspect of the counterfeminist men's movement is the celebration of a mythic, primeval masculine self that can be released only by bonding with other men (Bly 1990). These groups define men as oppressed by women and feminized by deskbound American culture, and they celebrate physical strength and tests of courage as being uniquely masculine during all-male weekend retreats. They, too, celebrate change in men but in a direction opposite to that of the custody movement: this mythopoeic (myth-making) men's movement encourages men to "get in touch" with an aggressive, physical, nonfamily-oriented self through rituals of "male bonding."

Both the divorced men's movement and the mythopoeic men's movement were but small and relatively uninfluential forces in the

early 1970s. By the end of the decade, however, many of their premises had drawn considerable media support. As Faludi (1991) shows,
the ideas of the backlash that were rooted in these male anxieties had
become staples of talk-show culture. As men's movements made
expressing antifeminist attitudes more legitimate, what it means to be
labeled a feminist became more controversial.

Conclusions

The decade between 1973 and 1983 was one in which feminist questions and issues rose to the top of the national agenda, only to be met
by a surprisingly strong backlash from a variety of forces and interests. Although feminist organizations grew, gained legislative victories, entered the political arena, and co-opted others' political agendas
at least as often as they were co-opted themselves, the decade as a
whole cannot be seen as one of unmitigated victory. Two major negative developments—the defeat of the ERA and the ascendency of the
New Right in the Republican party and in the Reagan presidency—
were marks of a shift in national priorities that posed new challenges
to feminists. The growing backlash, evident in the Stop-ERA campaign, the support for "right-to-life" groups, and the politicization of
"family values," provided testimony to the strength of feminists in placing their issues on the nation's agenda but also highlighted a fundamental fault-line in feminist thought that would come to characterize
the women's movement itself.

The shorthand phrase "equality vs. difference" captures the nature
of the debate within the movement on the importance of women's
"special" characteristics—their needs as bearers of children, their
capacities for empathy and intimacy—in relation to political claims for
equal rights and equal treatment (Vogel 1993; Kaminer 1991).
Heralded at the beginning of the 1980s by Betty Friedan's *The Second
Stage* (1981), Jean Elshtain's claim that the movement should politically recapture "a woman's world of concern and care" (1982), and Carol
Gilligan's contrast between women's "ethic of care" and men's ethic of
impersonal rights (1982), feminists' demands for greater respect for
women's traditional obligations for family care, as well as practical
measures to support women and men doing this work heightened
debate. On the one hand, this was a response to the backlash that
defined feminists as cold, selfish careerists and attempted to show
instead what the positive vision of feminist families could offer all

women. On the other hand, it reopened questions about the balance between protection and opportunity that the equal treatment claims of the ERA ignored.

In general, reactive movements stress protection against danger and threat; while proactive movements stress opportunity and change. As the backlash grew and the dangers to women in the still male-dominated system loomed larger in all women's consciousness, women's need for protection in their current circumstances began to seem more significant to feminists. The stress on new opportunities typical of the first decade of feminism was less evident at the end of its second decade; while concern with the continuing dangers of sexual violence, impoverishment, and economic exploitation grew. As the balance of political power shifted to the right, the protection of women's existing status became ever more urgent. As we will see in chapter 7, these realities shaped the politics of the reproductive rights struggle in the 1980s and brought out more defensive elements in the feminist perspective as a whole.

The debate over equality vs. difference, however, also reflected the long-standing ambivalence in feminism over the demand for rights within the existing system versus a desire for an entirely different system of values and rewards (Gordon 1991; Lunneborg 1990). One such debate centered on the role of women entering the "man's world" of politics: How critical can women be of the rules of the game if they are playing it to win? Does women's exclusion make it easier for them to take moral postures condemning war, cutthroat competition, and sexual dehumanization? If so, should women try to change the system from the outside or try to get in? Although the dangers of co-optation are real, so too are the possibilities for influence and change, as this decade demonstrated. As noted in the previous chapter, feminists continued in the 1970s and early 1980s to offer alternative visions of politics in their direct action/self-help, educational/political, and cultural/entrepreneurial organizations at the grassroots level (Christiansen-Ruffman 1994). But the view of women as a political constituency with interests to be represented within the system also became better established. The resistance that women's mobilization provoked in these years was one measure of its effect. In the next chapter, we look at the struggle that feminists waged in the next decade to protect their gains and accomplishments from the attacks of the backlash movement.

The issue of abortion rights has been a major focus of the movement, from (clockwise) the first rally for a liberal abortion reform law in New York in 1972, through rallies to defend *Roe* v. *Wade* in 1977, demonstrations against the Human Life Amendment in 1982, and protests against the *Webster* decision in 1989. *Photograph © Bettye-Lane*

Chapter 7

Two Steps Forward, One Step Back: Defending Gains, 1983–92

With the election of Ronald Reagan in 1980, the national political agenda shifted markedly toward the Right. In the following decade, under both Presidents Reagan and Bush, many fronts on which feminist gains had been realized in the 1970s came under direct attack. Outspoken antifeminists were appointed to the judiciary and placed in charge of civil rights enforcement; social programs benefiting poor women were cut or abandoned; and reproductive choice was openly opposed. For the New Feminist Movement, the major challenges of the 1980s included maintaining public approval for positions that a popular president and the federal government no longer supported; resisting efforts to reframe feminist concerns in hostile language; and defending feminist organizations and their members from direct, sometimes violent, attack.

In this chapter, we argue that the hostile climate in which the New Feminist Movement existed in this period led to major changes in organization, strategy, and emphasis. We call this decade one of "defensive consolidation" because much of the movement's efforts were directed at defending feminist perspectives and programs, and because such efforts required more extensive consolidation among feminist organizations regardless of their specific form of feminist perspective (radical, socialist, liberal, or career) or organizational strategy (educational/political, direct action/self-help, or cultural/entrepreneurial). Much of this consolidation occurred along substantive lines.

That is, whereas in previous decades one could more easily speak of "the" women's movement, there now appeared to be many specific movements—the battered women's movement, the reproductive rights movement, the antirape movement, the pay equity movement, to name just a few—and these specialized movements drew on the organizational strengths and individual skills of feminists in a variety of social locations to effect progress on specific issues.

For example, the battered women's movement came to include the following: openly feminist public officials and legislators working on this issue; managers, employees, board members, and volunteers at community-based shelters; people who turned out for demonstrations or wrote checks or letters of support for programs; community activists and educators; supportive law enforcement personnel and lawyers. The variety of their efforts meant that laws were passed, implemented, and monitored for effectiveness; programs were funded and staffed; public consciousness was raised. Thus, the movement that consolidated around a specific issue—ending woman battering— engaged an enormous variety of feminist activists at all levels from grassroots to federal with strategies that ranged from institutional to confrontational.

Because this was already the third decade of the active mobilization of the New Feminist Movement, it is appropriate to speak of it as a *mature* movement. Maturity does not imply that the movement has ceased to grow or develop, but rather that many of the early organizations were now institutionalized, that is, they had developed regular patterns of interaction with individuals and groups in their environment. In contrast to previous decades, the movement's energies were at this time less directed to founding new groups (organizational proliferation) than to accomplishing unfinished goals. Many activists had a base of experience in a variety of feminist organizations on which they could draw for both good ideas and bad examples. Some of the organizational problems facing the movement in this decade included recruiting new generations of activists into existing organizations and passing on the lessons learned in the 1960s and 1970s.

In the first section of this chapter, we examine three specific struggles waged by feminist organizations in this period of defensive consolidation: reproductive rights, sexual violence, and economic justice. These issues dominated the political agenda of the 1980s, and each issue posed both serious threats and new opportunities for mobilization. The second section looks at how changes in the political environment affected recruitment among young women, and how the defensive demands of the period shaped the organizations and strategies of the movement.

Old Problems, New Issues

Gains made in previous decades combined with the resistance to change by the New Right and the federal government placed feminists in the position of having to defend what they thought they had already won. In many cases, this led to a broadening and deepening of alliances, but it also made feminism more of a reactive movement—that is, one that responded to threats rather than setting its own agenda for the future (proactive). These threats came in a variety of forms. Each of the three issues considered in this section posed different types of dangers in equally varied arenas. The battle over reproductive rights has been waged largely in the courts and on the streets; the struggle over sexual violence has been carried out largely in the media; and the conflict over economic priorities has been played out primarily in state and federal legislatures.

Reproductive Rights. *In the courts.* As we saw in chapter 6, by the early 1980s, the abortion issue had been radically transformed by the mobilization of anti-choice constituencies at both the grassroots and the national level, supported by the White House and many friendly state governments of both parties. The initiative now passed to those seeking to limit severely or totally ban abortion, placing reproductive rights activists on the defensive. Feminists could no longer rely on a protective Supreme Court, as justices supporting *Roe* v. *Wade* were replaced by justices selected precisely for their antiabortion views. By the late 1980s, a majority of the Court was ready to undermine the premises of *Roe,* if not overturn it completely. Three major decisions between 1989 and 1991 eroded women's right to reproductive choice and spurred reactive mobilization among feminists.

In *Webster* v. *Reproductive Health Services* (1989), the Court left standing a Missouri statute that barred public hospitals and employees from performing abortions, required physicians to test for fetal viability, and stated that human life "begins at conception." In effect, the

Court invited other states to enact ever more restrictive legislation. Many states, mostly in the South, but also Pennsylvania, Utah, and the Territory of Guam, responded immediately with laws that raised obstacles for women and health-care providers, including the mandate of a twenty-four- or forty-eight-hour waiting period after the woman was informed about fetal development and the requirements that a minor secure permission from one—or even both—parents and that a married woman inform her husband.

The first of these increasingly restrictive state statutes reached the Supreme Court in the case of *Planned Parenthood of Southeastern Pennsylvania* v. *Casey,* decided in July 1992. A bare majority of justices upheld the basic right of a woman to control her reproductive life but nonetheless left standing virtually all of the Pennsylvania law. The Court also enunciated a new standard by which to judge the constitutionality of similar statutes: whether the restrictions constitute an "undue burden" on the woman. The practical outcome will be a wide disparity among the states in the availability of legal abortion, depending in part on how effectively feminists mobilize in each state to resist these laws in the future.

The Reagan and Bush administrations also issued regulations that subverted the intent of laws they were charged with carrying out. One such rule barred workers in family planning clinics receiving federal funds from even mentioning abortion as a possible option for their clients. In *Rust* v. *Sullivan* (1991), the Supreme Court upheld this regulation, declaring that the government had no obligation to "support" speech of which it disapproved. Despite the decision's implications for free speech in all areas of public life, its practical effect was limited, since this regulation was rescinded in early 1993 by newly elected President Clinton. Clinton also reversed policies that banned abortion in military hospitals, denied Medicaid funding for abortions for poor women, and barred approval of the abortifacient drug RU486, although Congress has the power to restore such barriers.

Clinton's first appointment to the Supreme Court, Ruth Bader Ginsberg, reflected a commitment to reproductive rights that may guide lower-level judicial appointments as well. But because it will take many appointments to reverse the conservative tilt of the federal judiciary, pro-choice advocates have shifted their attention back to Congress in order to seek protection of reproductive rights. In 1991, a Freedom of Choice Act was introduced by 32 Senators and 132 Representatives but had made only halting progress toward enactment by early 1994. NOW and some feminist legislators withdrew their support from the bill when limitations on abortion funding were added, since this would mean fewer reproductive rights for poor women than for the middle class.

On the streets. Antiabortion forces have not depended solely on the courts or the federal administration to achieve their goals. Demonstrations and protests at hospitals, clinics, and physicians' offices escalated throughout the 1980s, so effectively harassing providers that most hospitals and doctors no longer perform the procedure. By the end of the 1980s, only 10 percent of all abortions were performed in hospitals, compared to almost half in 1974. This was originally considered a positive trend by feminists who favored the more client-centered and less expensive treatment offered in freestanding clinics. However, as the practice of abortion became isolated from the medical mainstream and localized in the hands of a few providers in separated facilities, antiabortionists were able to concentrate their attacks on these small and relatively unprotected sites (Beam and Paul 1992). At the same time, medical schools and residency programs stopped training students in the techniques of safe abortion. As a consequence, in the United States today, abortion services are not available in 80 percent of counties, especially in the Rocky Mountain states and in the South (Henshaw 1991; Lewin 1992).

The aggressive confrontational mode of the antiabortion movement began in 1984 with the first "Action for Life" training conferences, which evolved in 1987 into an organization called Operation Rescue (OR), under the leadership of Randall Terry and Joseph Scheidler. Operation Rescue employs coercion and intimidation to close clinics, harass health-care personnel, and deter women from seeking abortions, as vividly illustrated by its 1988 "siege" of family planning facilities in Atlanta, Georgia, during the Democratic National Convention.

A typical OR performance includes obstructing clinic entrances with a human chain of protesters (often locked to doors and to each other), laying down (or telling their children to lay down) in front of cars, aggressively confronting clinic clients and personnel with threats and moral condemnation, and resisting arrest by going limp and refusing to give their names. Despite obvious differences between some of these tactics and the nonviolent protests of the Civil Rights movement, antiabortion protesters have successfully framed their actions as borrowed from this tradition. Other protesters may follow clients or providers to their homes, threaten their families, make harassing phone calls at all hours, and throw bricks through their windows.

In the five years between 1987 and 1992, there were over five hundred blockades at hundreds of clinics around the country. Other, more violent actions over the decade included 390 cases of criminal vandalism, dozens of burglaries, physical assaults on providers and patients, and hundreds of fires, bombs, and noxious gas attacks (National Abortion Federation 1992). Physicians who provide abortion in their private practice have also been harassed at their homes as well as at their offices. Even before the 1993 murder of Dr. David Gunn, one of the few physicians serving family planning clinics in Florida, fewer and fewer doctors were willing to perform the procedure. As anti-choice violence escalated, so did the cost of insurance and security, forcing some clinics out of business and other providers to decide that this was too risky and unpleasant a way to practice medicine (Hyde 1994; Simonds 1994). The result is that the availability of legal, safe abortion has been substantially curtailed. By 1991, only 7 percent of rural counties had even one abortion provider (Beam and Paul 1992).

The successes of the anti-choice mobilization activated all sectors of the women's movement to defend clinics and their clients. An alliance was also forged between feminists and the family planning network, despite the latter's initial concerns about their public image and tax status (Staggenborg 1991). The National Abortion and Reproductive Rights Action League (NARAL) and Planned Parenthood are now strongly allied with NOW and the women's policy network, and feminist organizations at all levels have placed the defense of reproductive rights at the top of their agenda, diverting valuable resources from proactive fights on other issues.

At the local level, feminists have responded creatively and energetically to Operation Rescue by training crisis intervention teams to defend clinics and to provide protective escorts for clients. These countertactics have proven successful in turning back OR assaults in many cities, but once the immediate crisis is over and the national media have left the scene, lower-level harassment continues day after day, week after week (Simonds 1994). Involvement in ongoing clinic defense have thus become an important form of feminist activism. New defensive organizations have sprung to life, such as Students Organizing Students, founded after the *Webster* decision and already counting 150 campus chapters in 1991 (Kamen 1991).

Conclusion. In the twenty years since *Roe,* regardless of national administration, public opinion has steadily favored the pro-choice position (see chapter 4). Such support is not without its nuances and ambiguities. While endorsing a general right to choose, many Americans make distinctions among the reasons women have for terminating a pregnancy. Although 80 to 95 percent favor the right to a legal abortion in cases of rape, incest, fetal deformity, or threat to the mother's life or health, only about half support legal abortions for reasons such as being poor, unmarried, or not wishing to have another child. However, 43 percent feel that a woman should have the right to choose under any circumstance, compared to under 20 percent who would deny abortion in all cases. Polls also indicate that most Americans do not support the obstruction of family planning clinics, nor do they wish to see *Roe* v. *Wade* overturned (Schmittroth 1991). In fact, pro-choice organizations received a record number of contributions in the months immediately following the *Webster* decision, and membership in NARAL doubled (to 400,000).

At the same time that most Americans support woman's right to legal abortion, many also express strong personal reservations. In her reanalysis of national survey data, Scott (1989) found women are more likely than men to express moral reservations but equally likely to endorse the legal right. While individuals may be ambivalent, the public debate has become polarized. Feminist scholars' efforts to hear women's voices and represent their complex decision-making processes (e.g., Ginsburg 1989; Gilligan 1982) are drowned out by the anger and violence of the confrontation. Thus the simple need to defend choice rather than a proactive and inclusive vision of reproductive rights (e.g., Petchesky 1984; Rothman 1989) has dominated women's movement politics in this decade.

Sexual Violence. While the struggle over reproductive rights has often been physical, the battle between feminists and the New Right over sexual violence has been a war of words. Both sides are actively engaged in contesting the media's framing of the issue. One significant achievement of feminist organizations in the 1970s was the building of a substantial consensus in the United States that women ought to be able to walk the streets in safety and to feel secure in their homes and workplaces. Over the past decade, feminists have offered new labels, arguments, and strategies addressing various behaviors on the continuum of sexual violence: workplace harassment, physical abuse in the home, rape, and incest. At the same time, the antifeminist backlash has attempted to trivialize these issues with claims that date rape is a myth and that women are "whining" about outcomes that they have either invited or imagined (e.g., Roiphe 1993). Debates over whether women or men are to blame for the undeniable prevalence of sexual violence have intensified, and the feminist attempt to build a consensus that would hold men accountable for their actions now seems in danger of slipping away.

Sexual Harassment. This term covers a wide range of behaviors that were viewed as the inevitable result of "natural sexual attraction" until the late 1970s. Even though "sex discrimination" as a broad category was outlawed by the Civil Rights Act of 1963, it took almost two decades for sexual harassment to be reframed as an actionable form of unlawful discrimination.

The first cases claiming that workplace demands for sexual favors constituted sex discrimination were filed by African-American women in the late 1970s (MacKinnon 1987, 60–65). In 1980, the EEOC ruled that harassment on the basis of sex was a violation of the Civil Rights Act. Among the actions so defined were unwelcome sexual advances and requests for sexual favors; other verbal and physical conduct when submission is either explicitly or implicitly made a condition of employment or the basis of employment decisions; conduct that interferes with an individual's work performance and creates an intimidating, hostile, or offensive working environment (Seals, Jenkins and Manale 1992). In 1986, the Supreme Court affirmed the illegality of sexual harassment in *Meritor Savings Bank* v. *Vinson.*

Although the language of the statute is gender neutral, the great majority of the victims are women for several reasons: women are still perceived as legitimate targets for male attention and aggression; harassment is part of the "normal" working conditions of many sex-typed jobs such as waitressing and nursing; male co-workers can use sexual harassment to defend their turf from women trying to enter male sex-typed jobs; men are more likely than women to be in supervisory positions with the power to harass subordinates (Martin 1989).

Most feminist attention has been directed toward raising awareness of the issue in the courts and among victims. The well-publicized confirmation hearings of Clarence Thomas as Justice of the Supreme Court in 1991 greatly raised consciousness on the issue, but the hearings also revealed the obstacles to bringing a successful sexual harassment suit. Anita Hill, a law professor who had worked for

Thomas both at the Education Department and when he directed the EEOC, charged that he had created a hostile environment and engaged in unwelcome sexual conversations. Her claims were ridiculed and her character and sanity attacked. According to public opinion polls, the hearings initially left women as well as men more convinced by Thomas's denial than by Hill's testimony. However, as the television images faded, opinion dramatically reversed, with a majority in 1992 believing Hill (Gallup October 1991 and December 1992). In effect, the hearings were a national consciousness-raising session on sexual harassment, demonstrating how sexist assumptions affect a woman's credibility and how she is treated by authorities, as well as the personal costs and political significance of speaking out (Morrison 1992).

Anita Hill was blamed for not reporting the behavior of her boss at the time it happened (when it was not clear the courts would treat it as illegal), but her response was more typical than not. A survey of federal government employees found that 42 percent of the women (but only 14 percent of the men) said they had been sexually harassed, yet only 5 percent took any kind of formal action (Tangri, Burt, and Johnson 1982). Similarly, a national poll in 1991 found that four out of ten women had experienced unwanted sexual advances at their workplace, but only 4 percent reported the incident (Kolbert 1991). Use of legal remedies is inhibited by cumbersome reporting procedures as well as a lack of clear-cut penalties (Seal Jenkins, and Manale 1992), a situation that feminists are attempting to remedy through their unions and state legislatures. At the urging of the women's policy network in Washington, the Civil Rights Restoration Act of 1991 included explicit penalties for sexual harassment, but they were relatively mild compared to penalties for other infractions.

Feminist organizing on college campuses in the 1980s has focused on sexual harassment, with the goals of raising consciousness among actual and potential victims and changing administrative codes and penalties. One study of college women found that 30 percent had experienced sexual harassment from at least one male instructor during their undergraduate years (Dziech and Weiner 1984). Peer harassment in college is also common, ranging from acts such as loudly "rating" the attractiveness of women passers-by to physical attacks (Paludi and Barickman 1991). Because the courts have held that the absence of a specific antiharassment policy implicitly condones such behavior, institutions of higher learning are attempting to define standards of inappropriate conduct. For example, in 1993, after much controversy, the University of Virginia instituted a policy forbidding instructors to have any sexual contact with students under their supervision.

The general public and school authorities often view sexual harassment and assault as somehow caused by the woman or girl. "Boys will be boys" and "she must have asked for it" are still common responses (American Association of University Women 1992), as was evident in reactions to well-publicized sexual attacks on schoolmates by young men in New York, New Jersey, and California in the early 1990s. Given the pressures not to report such incidents, most feminists believe that these practices are far more widespread than the few highly visible cases suggest—that is, that these are not the extreme or unusual events that the public and press have assumed, but everyday reality for young women.

In another well-publicized case, the 1991 convention of an organization of U.S. Navy fliers known as the Tailhook Association, several hundred officers assaulted more than eighty women. Although previous conventions were characterized by similar levels of sexual violence, this one came to public notice when one of the women, a naval officer herself, reported the incident to her superiors who in turn began an investigation. By this time, thanks to years of feminist organizing in the military, investigative procedures and penalties were in place that made it possible for the officer to seek redress; still, top Navy personnel attempted to hush up the scandal and excuse the perpetrators.

While there can be little doubt that the well-publicized Hill–Thomas hearings and the Tailhook Association orgy raised public awareness of the pervasiveness of the problem, they also stimulated backlash. Antifeminists claim that statutes and policies against sexual harassment violate freedom of speech; that what women perceive as sexual advances or a hostile environment are merely men doing "what comes naturally," and if women are offended by it, they should stay out of the places where it occurs; and that men are now so afraid of being falsely accused that their rights are being violated. Yet the feminist definition of sexual harassment seems to be holding up against this attempt to reframe the issue.

In the Democratic primary elections of 1992, unexpected victories were won by half a dozen candidates whose campaign was largely based on reaction to the Hill–Thomas hearings, and several of these candidates went on to win national office. Sixty-two percent of the public agrees that if more women had been in the Senate, the

Hill–Thomas hearings would have been conducted very differently. As MacKinnon concludes, "if the question is whether a law designed from women's standpoint and administered through this legal system can do anything for women—which always seems to me a good question—this experience (with sexual harassment cases) so far gives a qualified and limited yes" (1993, 146).

Domestic Violence. The women's movement of the 1970s defined violence against children and wives (and partners in unmarried unions) as battering, a form of illegitimate and illegal abuse, and provided alternatives such as shelters for women attempting to flee such attacks. Prior to that point, domestic violence had been largely veiled by the curtain of privacy drawn around the nuclear family. Breaking through this shield of secrecy was a difficult task, and it is still far from complete. Many Americans continue to support a man's right to coerce obedience or sexual compliance from his wife, and because women are expected to keep the peace within the home, wives are often blamed (and blame themselves) when men erupt in anger. Although gender-neutral language has become customary in speaking about the problem, much of the violence is clearly predicated on gender-specific expectations of authority and submission.

This has not prevented an ongoing debate over the prevalence and gender distribution of violent acts in the home. The most commonly used estimates of the frequency of assault come from the National Family Violence Surveys of 1975 and 1985 and suggest that 16 percent of all couples (married or not) experience at least one episode of violence a year. These data are widely criticized, however, because they indicate that men are as likely as women to be assaulted, information that antifeminists have seized upon to minimize the extent of wife-beating as a social problem. Feminists point out that even if both strike out, it is the wife who is more likely to be seriously injured, and she is typically responding defensively to a history of spousal violence (Brush 1990; Kurz 1989; Yllo and Bograd 1988). Department of Justice data show that women are three times as likely as men to be violently assaulted by someone with whom they are intimate (Harlow 1991), and that between 22 and 35 percent of women treated in hospital emergency rooms are victims of ongoing abuse (National Coalition against Domestic Violence 1991).

In the 1980s, feminist organizations began to devote more attention to the problems of women who actively defend themselves against further assaults. Not fitting the stereotype of the passive and innocent victim, such women often end up in prison for their attempt-ed self-defense. One television docudrama, "The Burning Bed," did much to raise consciousness of this issue. Focusing on the actual case of a long-term battering victim who finally killed her husband while he slept, the dramatization may have helped the general public to grasp a point that was being raised by feminist legal scholars: under a "reasonable woman" standard of self-defense, women in con-stant fear of their lives are not acting with excessive force when they strike back, even against a disarmed or sleeping man (Smith 1993). Not all juries have accepted this defense, but the feminist reframing of the issue has persuaded several governors to commute the sen-tences of women who killed their batterers. Although there is evi-dence that the presence of resources for battered women—shelters, hotlines, legal aid—reduces the likelihood of killing an abusive part-ner (Browne and Williams 1993), such resources are neither univer-sally available nor sufficient to stop the abuse. The numerous cases in which ex-husbands or ex-boyfriends have killed former wives or girl-friends after years of stalking and harassing them, often when protec-tion orders issued by the courts barred them from contacting the victim, indicate the depth of the problem.

In sum, despite adopting the less political language of "domestic violence" in the 1980s, feminists have continued to frame issues of bat-tering in ways that make men's responsibility for these assaults under-stood. Although women are still far from secure from assault by family members, feminist organizations have developed consciousness of the problem and of a woman's right to self-defense when society fails to protect her.

Rape and Sexual Abuse.   Against the force of custom and renewed efforts by antifeminists to define sexual assault as a harmless game, feminists have continued to frame sexual assault, even between inti-mates and family members, as a crime. Victim blaming assumed new dimensions in the 1980s, as attention has shifted from assaults by strangers in dark alleys (the stereotypical but much less common case) to attacks by acquaintances, friends, and even fathers. The issues of incest and date rape that have become prominent in the 1980s evoked a conservative response aimed at discrediting the vic-tims by suggesting that adult survivors of incest are victims of "false memory syndrome," and that women who are raped in dating situa-tions are "asking for it" (Estrich 1993).

In all rape trials, including those with celebrity defendants such as

William Kennedy Smith or Mike Tyson, the jury's verdict still largely depends on whether the victim is successfully presented as a naive innocent or as a sexually experienced woman, as well as how threatening the alleged perpetrator looks to the jurors. Press coverage plays on these themes, and there are additional biases based on the race of both victim and defendant. The media sensationalize the rare instances when a white woman is raped by a nonwhite man, giving support to the popular myth of the minority rapist and obscuring the reality that most women are raped by men of their own race and class. Conversely, the media's tendency to ignore rapes, even serial rape-murders, of women of color creates the illusion that these women are not victims (Benedict 1992; Hall 1983).

The press often stereotypes rapists in terms of class, race, and ethnicity instead of focusing on the gender violence of the crime. In the 1980s, several well-publicized rape cases made this particularly evident. Coverage of a 1983 gang rape in New Bedford, Massachusetts, (dramatized in the movie, *The Accused*), denigrating the Portuguese-American rapists on the basis on their ethnicity, succeeded in mobilizing their ethnic community to defend the men (and blame the Portuguese-American victim). Similarly, the institutionalized racism of the mainstream press in the Central Park Jogger case led to their portraying the African-American teenagers as wild animals and blaming the perpetrators' brutality on their family structure, social class, and the ghetto culture, while ignoring the similarities to cases of gang rape by white men and boys. The African-American press responded by redefining the boys as innocents being lynched (Chancer 1987; Benedict 1992). In both cases, race and ethnicity diverted the media from covering the basic issue of sexual violence.

Press treatment of victims continues to discourage women from reporting rapes. In the 1980s, the policy of not printing the name of rape victims (unless another paper has done so first) came into question, with some feminists arguing that anonymity perpetuated the idea that rape was shameful and others claiming that it merely acknowledged the fact that the coverage was often demeaning and shaming. Silence about rape continues to create uncertainty about its prevalence. In 1991, the Department of Health and Human Services funded a broad-based survey of American women in which respondents were asked about both attempted and completed rapes in the past year and at any time in their lives. Extrapolating to all American women, their estimate is that 680,000 women were victims of forcible rape each year, over 12 percent had been sexually assaulted at some time, and that 60 percent of sexual assaults occur in childhood (National Victim Center 1992).

Other data confirm the frequency of sexual assault in American families. For example, a survey of sixth- through twelfth-graders in a middle-class Los Angeles school district found that nearly 20 percent of the girls had experienced an unwanted sexual encounter, almost all involving an older relative or family friend (Erikson and Rapkin 1991). Antifeminists cast doubt on the credibility of children's accounts but also refuse to believe adult survivors, returning to Freud's claim that such numbers must represent fantasy and false memory rather than real experiences.

The most extensive debate has been generated by feminist attention to acquaintance rape in general and date rape on campus in particular. As more young women define sexual encounters that included force or threats as being rape, antifeminists blame the women's movement for having changed the rules of the game—for having imposed a "politically correct" sexuality that takes the "natural" excitement and risk out of dating (Paglia 1990; Gibbs 1991; Roiphe 1993). Camille Paglia, an academic favored by conservative intellectuals, has used the media effectively to propound her view that men do indeed suffer blue balls and only a naive or stupid woman would allow herself to be raped. Women college students are apparently not persuaded; many have organized in their collective defense (from using bathroom graffiti to identify potential rapists to holding demonstrations demanding harsher penalties than the college administration had imposed). Along with improved lighting and locks, educational programs for male students about what "no" means are being provided on many campuses, usually through the college's women's center or committee on the status of women. The infrastructure of feminist organization created on many campuses in the 1970s is responding vigorously to the challenge of date rape in the 1980s.

Conclusion. Patricia Smith (1993), a noted legal scholar, concludes that in all three crimes of sexual violence—harassment, battering, and rape—great social change and legal progress for women has been seen, but that the pervasiveness of these abusive practices attests to the continuing sexism of society. Police and prosecutors, judges and juries, reflect the attitudes of the general public and continue to minimize the harms done to women. Changes in the law achieved in this decade are only a small part of a broader social challenge to norms legitimating male violence and male domination that will surely take many decades to accomplish.

Economic Justice.   The Republican administrations of the 1980s cut back social services and reduced the real income of welfare recipients and low-wage workers while providing massive tax cuts and transfer payments for businesses and wealthy Americans on the theory that the benefits of elite investment would "trickle down" to create prosperity for all. Vast military expenditures created both a short-term economic boom and a quadrupling of the federal debt but failed to trickle down to women, then as now on the bottom of the economic ladder. Instead, the gap between rich and poor widened, and many women's basic economic survival was placed at risk (Amott 1993). Conflict between feminists and the New Right on this issue played out primarily in the legislative arena, where social policy is set, and where the recession brought on by the national economic policy in the 1980s greatly reduced revenues available for social programs.

Affirmative Action.   Despite the gains made by women professionals and college graduates in the 1970s in entering high-prestige male-dominated occupations (see chapter 1), almost half of the female labor force, especially women of color, remains concentrated in the low-paying service sector. Comparing the median incomes of year-round full-time workers in 1991, women earned 74¢ for every dollar earned by a man (up from 60¢ in 1979), but a good proportion of the decline in the size of the wage gap was due to a fall in men's wages rather than a rise in women's incomes. Studies continue to indicate that sex and race discrimination play a major role in income inequality (Baron and Newman 1990; England 1992).

Such discrimination had been the target of civil rights legislation and executive action in the 1960s, which sought to redress the effects of decades of preferential hiring of white males. Executive Order 11375, issued in 1967 under President Lyndon Johnson, required that companies receiving federal contracts take positive steps ("affirmative action") to recruit and train women and minority men, to set goals and timetables for compliance, and to demonstrate that they were making good-faith efforts to meet these objectives. Affirmative action policy does *not* require setting quotas for hiring, nor does it mandate preferential treatment of unqualified or less qualified candidates. That most

Americans are misinformed about these points is due in part to media carelessness and in part to an intentional effort by conservative politicians to win votes from working-class white men by playing on their anxieties about unemployment and job competition.

The media failed to distinguish "affirmative action" from "affirmative relief," which is a court judgment that finds that a particular employer has actively discriminated and orders a remedy in the form of accelerated hiring or promotion of the affected category of workers. In carrying out affirmative relief, a judge may set a quota and timetable to remedy a past pattern of illegal actions, just as back-pay awards are made to offset the effects of salary discrimination. Between media misrepresentation and conscious efforts by conservative groups and politicians to depict all affirmative action as "reverse discrimination," the continuation of patterns of discrimination against women and minority men has not been seriously challenged for over a decade.

Throughout the 1980s, not only did the Justice Department withdraw from even minimal enforcement of equal opportunity statutes, but it argued successfully before the Supreme Court that more of the burden of proof should fall on the *victims* of discrimination. Evidence of a pattern of disadvantage was no longer enough to shift to employers the burden to provide proof of a nondiscriminatory cause for the pattern; plaintiffs had to show evidence of "malicious intent." Such evidence of a frame of mind is extremely difficult to find, especially since most employers today know better than to put their discriminatory thoughts into writing.

In addition, in the *Grove City* case, the Court ruled that higher education institutions receiving federal funding could discriminate in programs other than the specific one being funded; for example, the chemistry department was free to indulge in discrimination if only the financial aid office got federal money. Presidents Reagan and Bush personally campaigned against affirmative action, referring to employment targets as "quotas" and remedies for past discrimination as "reverse discrimination" against whites, and suggesting it was difficult to find more than a few "qualified" white women or persons of color.

In response to these attacks, the women's policy network joined with other civil rights groups to press for an act of Congress reaffirming the original intent and interpretation of the 1963 Civil Rights Act. After civil rights and feminist organizations spent several years energetically lobbying for it, the Civil Rights Restoration Act passed Congress, only to be vetoed by President Bush. Although Bush eventually signed a much diluted version of the law in 1991, the final version was so weak on remedies for gender discrimination that many women's organizations withdrew their support for it.

At this writing the stance of the Clinton administration is still unclear, but twelve years of failure to enforce equal opportunity policies already jeopardizes the labor force gains women made in previous decades. Discrimination cases are harder to win, and more costly to bring. Regulatory mechanisms have been dismantled, and incentives for true affirmative action are virtually nonexistent. Although the backlash movement would like to blame feminists for women's economic struggles, feminists are committed to convincing the general public that the remedy for their problems in the workplace is more equality, not less.

Pay Equity/Comparable Worth. Because of sex segregation, women and men rarely hold the same jobs, and the work historically done by women is paid much less on average than that performed by men. The concept of pay equity, or comparable worth, is based on the principle that people who do jobs that (1) require a similar level of skill and effort, (2) take place under similar working conditions, and (3) involve a similar level of responsibility should receive similar paychecks. The 1980s saw major battles, primarily in the public (government) sector, to reevaluate all jobs and set wage scales based not on the historic gender of the occupation but on its comparable worth to the employer (Steinberg 1987; Acker 1989). By the end of the decade, many state governments had made adjustments in their wage-setting policies, and a number of local governments were engaged in conducting comparable worth studies or had already implemented some pay equity proposals. The outcome was typically a compromise among unions, employing agencies, feminist lobbies, and state legislatures that stopped well short of full equity but nonetheless established the principle of cross-gender comparison and improved wages for employees in female-dominated jobs (Acker 1989; Evans and Nelson 1989). By mobilizing union women in particular, the pay equity movement highlighted the relation between gender and class and raised feminist consciousness among working-class women (Blum 1991). Although elite women have been important sponsors of comparable-worth legislation, their interests lead them to try to limit the cost of settlements, to advocate technocratic rather than democratic decision processes, and to defend managerial control over wage-setting (Acker 1989; Blum 1991).

Not only has the pay equity issue enhanced the potential for working-class feminism that the career feminism of earlier decades slighted, but it has encouraged cross-class alliances among feminists and others concerned with economic justice. For example, the National Committee on Pay Equity (NCPE), a lobbying and information clearinghouse, is a coalition of religious, labor, civil rights, legal, professional, and women's organizations in the United States and Canada. Other new groups include the Women's Economic Agenda Project in California, the Women's Agenda in Pennsylvania, and the Women's Lobbyist Fund in Montana. These organizations held their first national conference in 1987. With Clinton's election in 1992, one Washington lobbyist noted that "the faxes are flying" among women's groups that are trying to formulate a national agenda on economic justice for women, with pay equity as a crucial element.

The backlash movement has attacked comparable worth in the same ringing tones it applied to the ERA and reproductive rights; Clarence Thomas, while still head of the EEOC, called it "the looniest idea since loony tunes." But these denunciations do not appear to have found much resonance among the general public, where strong majorities favor some sort of pay equity measures (National Committee on Pay Equity 1992).

Family Policies and Poverty. Beginning in the late 1970s, feminists concerned with economic justice directed attention to the fact that the majority of Americans living in poverty were women and children, and this phenomenon came to be termed "the feminization of poverty" (Pearce 1978). They highlighted several causes of women's impoverishment, such as divorce, low wages, and declining opportunities for blue-collar jobs.

Studies in this decade showed how often divorce drove even middle-class women to welfare for a few years, and how the lack of alimony and minimal levels of child support left single mothers penniless (Weitzman 1985; Sugarman and Hill 1990). Judges had been quick to turn the feminist claim that women should be economically independent into a myth that women actually were financially self-sufficient and so required only the most modest levels of transitional support.

Feminist responses included organizing displaced homemakers—midlife women divorced after a long period of full-time homemaking and child rearing. The National Displaced Homemaker Network coordinated efforts by similar networks on the state level to direct funds for job training to centers for displaced homemakers (e.g., twelve such centers were operating in 1992 in Connecticut alone). To date, very lit-tle federal support has been forthcoming, although some states have imposed a fee on marriage licenses to pay the costs of programs for battered women and displaced homemakers, a formal recognition of the risks women face in conventional marriage.

Another response to the poverty of women and children was to seek more energetic enforcement of court-ordered child-support pay-ments from absent fathers. However, the means that state legislatures have used to implement such programs have often led to invasion of the privacy of divorced or unmarried women and to defining women in terms of economic dependence on some man. These policies also do very little to raise the standard of living of most single mothers. In some states welfare benefits are cut by the amount collected from absent fathers. Feminist opinion is increasingly divided on the merits of even lobbying state legislatures to experiment with such programs.

But many women are poor even if they are not divorced or out of the labor force, and this is particularly true for women of color. Many women have critiqued the "feminization of poverty" concept, arguing that women of color had always been poor, and that neither marriage nor a job was a reliable route out of poverty. Men of color also have low wages and high unemployment, and the jobs available to women of color themselves often pay such low wages that even year-round full-time work (itself hard to find) is inadequate to bring a family out of poverty. In 1992, a full-time job at just above the minimum wage pro-vided an annual pretax income of less than $10,000. Feminists have thus joined a wider coalition arguing for a higher minimum wage, an earned income tax credit, universal health insurance, and an expanded Headstart program for preschoolers as practical steps to bring many women out of poverty and to reduce its effects on their children (Bergman 1986).

Conclusions.   The framing of economic justice as a feminist issue grew throughout the 1980s. The need to defend reproductive rights is, however, a competing concern, and the drive for gender equality in the workplace is also increasingly presented as a "family issue" rather than one of feminism (Spalter-Roth and Schreiber 1994). Most femi-nist organizations see poverty as a women's issue, and many activists have targeted women's poverty as their primary focus in legislative lobbying (Boles 1991). Although those career feminists who had a nar-row vision of economic opportunity were able uncritically to applaud gains made by a small number of professional and managerial women, most feminists found much to criticize in the limited opportunities and growing poverty of a large segment of the female population. The national administration in the 1980s was so apparently indifferent to the needs of real families and real children, while trumpeting support for "family values" and "unborn children," that many feminists made defeating these politicians a major goal. The change of administration in 1993 was thus most welcome, but the achievement of actual changes in policy remains a challenge for the coming decade.

Political Strategies and Dilemmas

Although feminist organizations were put on the defensive by the backlash movement, issues such as reproductive rights, equal opportunity, violence against women, and the welfare of the family increasingly came to be the main lines of political and cultural conflict (Freeman 1993). Both the high salience of feminist issues and the reactive position of feminist organizations played a major role in shaping the nature of the women's movement in this decade.

In this section, we look at how the "culture war" over feminism has shaped public perceptions of the movement and particularly the orientations and activism of young women. We see it especially manifest in what we call "the myth of the postfeminist generation." We then turn to an analysis of the defensive transformations of organizations and the continuation of proactive strategies throughout this decade.

The Myth of the Postfeminist Generation.   As we saw in chapter 4, about 30–40 percent of all Americans now define themselves as "feminist," a historically impressive percentage. Nonetheless, critics have rushed to proclaim (yet again) the "death" of feminism and the advent of a "postfeminist generation" (e.g., Bolotin 1982). This new generation is described as (1) disillusioned with what they perceive to be the feminist promise of "having it all"—a fulfilling career, a happy marriage, and accomplished children—and (2) worried that to be labeled "feminist" is also to be seen as "unfeminine." In the late 1980s, news magazines and advertisers hailed the dawn of a postfeminist era characterized by a return to conventional patterns of marriage and domesticity. This conclusion was based largely on anecdotal evidence and wishful thinking; the public opinion data reviewed in chapter 4 show instead a continuing trend toward more feminist opinions and higher levels of self-identification with feminism. Susan Faludi argues that this presentation of feminism as passé or dangerous was a part of a media backlash (1991), but there are a number of additional reasons why the image of feminism was changing in this decade.

One change is the baseline for comparison: in the late 1960s and early 1970s, journalists assumed feminists were wild-eyed fanatics with whom few if any women would identify; whereas in the late 1980s and early 1990s, many media pundits seemed puzzled that not all women were feminists. The label "feminist" was still felt to be somewhat risky, implying a person who was angry and "shrill," but the disavowal of feminism also seemed dangerously behind the times, suggesting a lack of awareness of discrimination and/or a repudiation of equality as a goal (Kamen 1991). Somehow, the ideal seemed to shift to being "feminist" (in the sense of being enlightened about and emancipated from past forms of subordination) but not "a feminist" (in the sense of being angry about continuing inequality). As Stacey (1989) documents, many of the assumptions of feminism have passed into the common wisdom; the life that even conventional young women expect to live today is not that of their mothers or foremothers.

A second change is in the visibility of criticism of the movement by academic women, both feminist and not. The media were quick to publicize economist Sylvia Hewlett's (1986) charges that the New Feminist Movement was to blame for the failure of American institutions to correct the conditions that disadvantage and impoverish single mothers. More recently, the media has celebrated the deeply misogynist views of art historian Camille Paglia (1990). Paglia, who has been warmly welcomed into the conservative establishment and funded by its foundations, claims that male domination, including sexual assault, is natural, necessary, and secretly desired by women. Also, blaming women and the feminist movement for women's failure to achieve full equality has become commonplace among journalists.

As Faludi (1991) also documents, motion pictures and television programs began to portray unmarried women with professional careers as homicidally dangerous while celebrating what the media claimed was a "trend" toward well-paid professional women throwing over their careers for full-time motherhood. Although individuals can always be found to exemplify a purported "phenomenon," there is no statistical evidence for such a general tendency. Biased and uncritical reporting of the supposedly low probability of marriage for unmarried women in their thirties or the high level of infertility of women who defer childbearing, and of a myriad of other dangers of careerism undoubtedly affected how younger women thought about their future.

Such a negative view of feminism in the media was, of course, nothing new: solemn proclamations of the editors' wishful thinking that the movement was dead date back to 1971 (*Ms.* "No Comment" 1982). But if young women were actually rejecting feminism, where did all the enrollments in women's studies courses come from? One conservative response was to label the trend toward more inclusive curricula on college campuses as a conspiracy of "political correctness," in which faculty pressured or mandated enrollment in "intellectually shallow" courses (Bloom 1987; D'Souza 1991). It was evident to these critics that there could be no intellectual merit in courses focusing on women, ethnic minorities, or others whose works had been traditionally excluded from the conventional curriculum.

Ironically, it was the newcomers, such as women's studies programs, who were declared to be intolerant, ideological storm troopers, imposing their perspective on the university's "impartial" and "apolitical" decisions about who and what should be studied. The backlash refrain was to label women's studies and ethnic studies programs "victim studies," mocking the oppression and exclusion these groups had endured. These intellectual attacks spilled over into an increasingly intolerant and nasty mood on campuses toward people of color, feminists, lesbians, and gays. Physical attacks and campus hate crimes increased.

In this climate, it hardly seems surprising that many college women are hesitant to express their feminist views in class or in peer groups (Schneider 1988; Kamen 1991). However, attitude change among college women and men has also gone less deep than many feminists expected. College women continue to expect their husbands to earn more than they do (even while saying they believe in equal pay for women and men); they still expect to compromise only their own careers in order to raise children (even while they endorse shared child rearing in principle); and they expect to be supported by a man's income for some portion of their life (even though they assert the value of economic independence for women) (Machung 1989).

Some observers see parallels between the resistance to feminism in the early part of this century and the claim that young women are less feminist today, and argue that the women's movement is once again "in abeyance" (Taylor and Whittier 1993). Although feminism was expressed in a strong and well-organized social movement in the 1920s, its organizational strength withered in the following decades. Few young women born in the 1920s or 1930s were exposed to feminism as a coherent or comprehensive perspective. Observers soon noted that the average age of women identified as feminists was relatively high and rising. Feminism was perceived as something "old-fashioned" and feminists as out of touch with modern "emancipated" women and the new realities of expanding opportunities and more egalitarian marriages.

This pattern led Alice Rossi (1982) to suggest that feminist accomplishments are achieved in a repeating, two-phase multigeneration process. The first generation, chafing at the limitations clearly imposed on them as women, struggles for structural change. The modest changes they achieve are part of the social environment of women of the second generation, who are able to explore opportunities and experience freedoms that are still new and perceived as remarkable progress. The third generation then takes such accomplishments for granted but again experiences the limits and restrictions that remain and, chafing against these boundaries, becomes another first generation mobilizing for change.

Rossi argues that changes on the structural level are not sufficient for lasting progress; only when changes are assimilated into women's everyday life can the need for further changes be known. Her argument is based both on the historical record and on the theoretical premise that feminist demands arise from women's daily experiences and that without such resonance, feminist claims will fail to awake a supportive response. When change is rapid, however, "generations" could be very short.

From a different perspective, Gloria Steinem (1983) argues that the apparent conservatism of some young women ten years ago was a reflection of their stage in the life course. Unlike men, for whom youth can be the period of radical experimentation ultimately tempered by the responsibilities of work and family, women are more likely to be radicalized by age. It is misleading to extrapolate a universal pattern from the male model, because it is women's direct experience of marriage, motherhood, employment, divorce, and aging itself that underscore the difficulties of being female and transform conventional women into feminists. The status of women—and their rewards for accepting the male-defined criteria of value—may be highest when they are young. As Carolyn Heilbrun (1988) has also argued, women may only realize their radical disagreement with the status quo as they discover themselves living a life for which they never had models and no longer seek others' approval. The women who seemed conservative a decade ago may have already been radicalized by the events of their lives.

Does this add up to an authentic "postfeminism" in the current generation? Although antifeminist opinions are more evident in the media, the attitudes of young women remain just as feminist as their mothers' views (see chapter 4). Moreover, the increasing numbers of young women in established feminist organizations, as well as a proliferation of new organizations focused on mobilizing the younger generation of feminists, suggest that the complacency of the late 1970s has already been replaced by an urgency and anxiety to defend gains already won. Many established feminist groups have "young feminist" networks (e.g., NOW's Young Feminist Conference and the Center for Women's Policy Studies' Feminist Futures Project). Some of the organizations founded by and for this younger generation have contributed to the revival of grassroots, confrontational feminist politics in the later part of this decade (Kamen 1991). Other young feminists are seeking academic degrees that will enable them to pursue a career in feminist law or community work or education, as seen in the continuing expansion of women's studies–inspired graduate programs in fields as diverse as public policy and theology. Young feminist professionals in Washington have organized their own Women's Information Network (WIN) for both career networking and political support (Kamen 1991). Women's studies is also a means by which activists can pass on the organizational lessons they have learned from their past decades of experience to the women—regardless of their ages—who have not shared that history.

A major challenge facing the feminist movement in the 1990s is moving from the reactive stance of the 1980s to a more proactive vision of the future. If that vision is to find resonance, it will need to incorporate the concerns of women born after the New Feminist Movement had already mobilized and made its mark. Rather than "postfeminists," this cohort could be appropriately called "second-generation feminists." Some call themselves the "Third Wave" (Manegold 1992). Their lives are not as restricted as their mothers', but they face an abundance of challenges and obstacles to achieving political and social equality and self-determination. The perspectives and issues of the second-generation feminists who become activists will play a major role in shaping the agenda and priorities of feminism in the coming years; the hard-won lessons of inclusiveness and diversity are part of the legacy on which they will have to build (Pfister 1993).

Defensive Adaptations and Organizational Maturity.   The reactive, defensive stance feminists adopted in the 1980s also had organizational consequences for the movement. First, the hostile political climate encouraged the development of broad coalitions, since allies were necessary to prevent erosion of significant employment and reproductive rights. Second, when all were under attack, differences among varieties of feminism became far less significant and similarities more important, so that ideological conflicts declined sharply. Because the New Right was trying to make feminism an unspeakable "*F*-word," variations in feminist identity became less defining of individuals or organizations than ever before (Heilbrun 1988). Indeed, varieties of visions for the future are primarily important for proactive movements; when feminist priorities are centered on defending gains already won, such visions are increasingly irrelevant. As Hyde (1994) points out, ideology does play a part in defensive movements by suggesting a preferred strategy and providing a network of past allies to mobilize against attacks; in the struggle to survive, some feminist organizations she studied became more conservative and professional, and others became more embedded in broad political resistance movements.

But to a greater extent than ever before, in the early 1990s there was a single feminist community, characterized by strategic cooperation of direct action/self-help, political/educational, and cultural/entrepreneural groups in activist networks organized to target specific issues such as women's health, battering, or reproductive rights (Boles 1991). The proliferation of feminist organizations in the 1970s reached a stage in the 1980s in which institutionalization and long-term survival rather than growth dominated the agenda, a stage of movement maturity. Part of the price of this necessary institutionalization was specialization—that is, the increasing autonomy of "submovements" with specialized concerns such as the battered women's movement, the antirape movement, the pro-choice movement, or the women's health movement (Tierney 1982; Matthews 1994; Morgen 1994; Staggenborg 1991).

In fact, these different "submovements" had by the 1980s established unique sets of relationships—whether hostile, supportive, or mixed—with the funding agencies, foundations, and local communities with which they routinely dealt. They also competed for the scarce resources available from the government, and for the time, energy and commitment of individual feminists. Over the 1980s, involvement with specialized submovements became increasingly important in defining the identity of feminist organizations and activists. Gelb (1989) shows how the American form of politics (weak parties and a strong lobbying system) encouraged this development; whereas Boles (1991) argues that the emergence of broad coalitions at local, state, and federal levels also reflects the principle of federalism embodied in the American system. Much policymaking important to women is not centralized but requires coordinated efforts at all levels to be effective.

We further argue that the hostility toward feminism expressed by the national administration in the 1980s encouraged an organizational shift toward state-level, coalition politics. As we saw in the previous chapter, the original focus of feminist organizations was on grass-roots direct action and women's community building at the local level, or on bureaucratic organizations lobbying for political gains on the national level. In the 1970s, the long, bruising struggle over the ERA gave birth to a third level of organization—namely, in the individual states, since the amendment needed ratification by state legislatures (Mathews and DeHart 1990; Berry 1986). As the federal climate became increasingly chilly in the 1980s, feminists turned more of their attention to the state legislatures to defend gains and pursue goals other than the ERA.

By 1989, feminists in forty states had created ongoing and diversified coalitions to address women's issues; one of the first such networks, the Wisconsin Women's Network (founded in 1979) is supported by sixty-seven dues-paying member organizations and over a thousand individual members and has two paid staffers and over a dozen policy task forces (Boles 1991, 46). In several states, such coalitions produced policies and laws that expanded women's rights well beyond the national baseline, although in others, feminists simply struggled to resist increasingly punitive and restrictive laws. The variation between states in feminist strategies and successes is a topic that requires further research.

Within each submovement, state-level coalitions connected direct action service providers with each other and with politicians, administrators, and educators concerned with each specific issue (Boles 1991). Because states are relatively small, their emergent women's policy networks depended heavily on the local direct action groups and feminist cultural community, as well as on formally organized political groups (Taylor and Whittier 1993). By 1990, there were over two hundred local-level commissions on the status of women, which Boles describes as "quite similar to the small groups of the radical branch of the women's movement, but with a difference: much of their activity now is undertaken in cooperation with governmental bureaucracies" (1991, 47). Thus, boundaries also blurred between self-help groups, political organizations, and individual entrepreneurs and professionals.

At the same time, it became increasingly clear that feminist commitment was not for a brief battle, but for a lifetime of struggle. Change would not come easily or soon. Mature feminist organizations were faced with the challenge of making sustaining a career in feminism possible, both emotionally and financially (Daniels 1991; Whittier 1994; Remington 1990). In the face of an increasingly angry and violent countermovement, abetted by the inaction of federal and many local authorities, problems of emotional burnout were heightened (Simonds 1994). Great financial strains were created by the federal government's efforts to take funding away from women's health centers (Hyde 1994). Individual activists needed not only adequate income but also interpersonal support and opportunities for personal growth in their work—requirements that not all feminist organizations could meet (Morgen 1994; Remington 1990). Nonetheless, the women's community forged by cultural/entrepreneurial groups in the previous decades had become strong enough to sustain the commitment of those engaged in direct action/self-help and political/educational activities in the 1980s (Taylor and Rupp 1993). Lesbian feminists have always played a major role in maintaining this community, and their efforts were increasingly central to many feminist organizations (Whittier 1994).

Proactive Feminist Mobilizations.   The wide reach and increasingly integrated structure of mature feminist submovements defensively addressing issues high on the public agenda should not conceal feminist mobilization in other areas. Although when under attack from the Right, organizations' success could often be measured by sheer survival, the New Feminist Movement also developed strategies for change. Some of the feminist initiatives that bore fruit in the 1980s and early 1990s were the result of decades of earlier mobilization; others represented a return to styles of feminist activism that were more characteristic of earlier decades. We look here at three types of proactive feminist politics: unobtrusive mobilization within institutions, electoral politics, and the new grassroots direct action groups that formed in this decade.

Unobtrusive Mobilization. As examples of what she calls unobtrusive mobilization within institutions, Mary Katzenstein (1990) examines the development of feminist consciousness, organization, and strategy in two improbable contexts: the U.S. military and the Roman Catholic Church. Although both institutions are large, bureaucratic, strongly hierarchical and male-dominated, they nonetheless experienced substantial internal feminist activism that indelibly changed their structure and practices. Such unobtrusive mobilizations occurred in other institutions as well; we also look briefly at the judiciary and academia.

In the case of the military, the introduction of the All Volunteer Force (AVF) in 1973, with its competitive wages and career opportunities, brought an influx of female recruits. In the first few years, the expansion in women's numbers and rights was dramatic: the percentage of women serving in the armed forces tripled between 1972 and 1976; ROTC and the service academies were opened to women; mandatory dismissal for pregnancy was ended; and dependents' benefits were extended to their families. By 1980 the backlash began to be felt, as military leaders announced a need to "pause" in recruitment efforts and reassess the role of women (Stiehm 1989). Although women increased from 2 percent of the military in 1972 to 11 percent in 1992, this increase represented less than the increase projected in the 1970s. The coordinating body for women's affairs, the Defense Advisory Commission on Women in the Service (DACOWITS), began to exert pressure on the separate services to remove obstacles to women's rising through the ranks, most particularly the rules barring them from direct combat. The gains made, as evidenced by the greater visibility of women in the Panama and Desert Storm campaigns, further convinced the public that women can and do serve with distinction in all roles opened to them. Lobbying by women overturned the congressional prohibition on women in combat, and in 1993 the Clinton administration shifted the burden of proof to the military to demonstrate why a particular job should be closed to women and dropped most restrictions on women in aerial and naval combat roles.

DACOWITS has also focused on developing enforceable procedures for responding to cases of sexual harassment; when the Navy's own procedures were not followed, the assaults at the Tailhook convention became a public scandal. The integration of women in military roles also opened up a broader discussion of military values, sexuality, and gender stereotyping. "Witchhunts" directed against women—accusing them of being lesbians and threatening them with dishonorable discharges—had often been used to punish women for counterstereotypical behavior or for refusing men's sexual advances. Such accusations increasingly invoked an active defense from women's organizations such as WEAL and raised consciousness about the damaging effects of antihomosexuality policies on both men and women in the military, fostering a wider debate on sexuality and the double standard (Stiehm 1989).

In the Roman Catholic Church, women's extremely limited access to formal positions of leadership encouraged Catholic feminists to concentrate on changing the way women think about hierarchy and status (Katzenstein 1994). For some, the answer lies in "woman-church," small nonhierarchical groups of women reclaiming the church as a house-based community of believers (Ruether 1986; Farrell 1991). The long-term decline in the number of men in holy orders opened up some ceremonial and administrative church roles to women at the parish level, but the more profound change has come as both nuns and laywomen have rethought conventional answers to why the church is so male-dominated. Debates over inclusive language have led feminists to discuss more inclusive practices and to speak out strongly on issues of social justice. In some cases, this outspokenness has led to a visible split with the male hierarchy, which often places a higher priority on antiabortion activities than on ministering to the poor (Katzenstein 1994).

In the judiciary, change is evident as over half the states have at least one female justice on their highest court, and in Minnesota women constitute a majority on the state supreme court. Both as individuals and as members of the caucus of women on state court benches, these judges have spurred nearly every state to conduct a serious review of practices in the courtroom and in the law that constitute gender bias. Training programs have been set up in many states to help male judges become more aware of ways in which they may be discriminating against lawyers who appear before them, plaintiffs and defendants in the cases they hear, jurors they empanel, and staff they employ (Gender Bias Task Force Reports from Connecticut, New Jersey, Maryland, and New York are good examples). Moreover, law schools have gone beyond merely admitting more women to recognizing the importance of feminist issues in the law. Between 1986 and 1992, the number of law school courses focusing on women has grown from 30 to 145, and nine law schools (including Harvard, Yale, and Chicago) publish journals devoted to feminist jurisprudence (*About Women on Campus* 1993, 9).

In academia, there is probably no discipline, from accounting to zoology, that has not been affected by unobtrusive mobilization over the past two decades. It is projected that by 1995, 40 percent of all doctorates will be awarded to women, compared to 14 percent in 1970 (U.S. Bureau of the Census 1993, 172). With the increased representation of women in all fields of study, feminist caucuses and task forces in many disciplines have actively directed attention to gaps in knowledge, the gendered nature of course content, and the chilly classroom climate for future generations of scholars.

Feminist caucuses and task forces are also concerned with the status of women within the profession as a whole. Although in 1992 women constituted 27 percent of America's higher education faculty, they remain clustered disproportionately in lower ranks, less prestigious institutions, and in stereotypically feminine fields. Furthermore, the research topics pursued by feminist scholars are not typically those that receive the highest rewards in their discipline, where the "canon" of worth is still monopolized by a predominantly upper-middle-class, heterosexual white male elite. This can be seen in publishing patterns in sociology, for example, where female scholars and gender issues remain marginalized, though less so than in the past (Grant and Ward 1991; Ferree and Hall 1990).

The feminist struggle within academia, therefore, is not just over jobs and promotions, though these basic needs have been difficult enough to attain. The financial costs and personal difficulties of bringing a sex discrimination suit, the veil of secrecy around much academic decision-making, the falsification of records, and the lack of administrative accountability have often made pursuit of job equity an exercise in futility (Theodore 1986; Pleck 1990). But the challenges to women in academia also include gaining greater control over standards of evaluation of scholarship, input into decisions about curricula and requirements, and better conditions for professional development for both faculty and students.

In conclusion, we can see that there has been a mobilization of feminist pressure groups and caucuses within a variety of institutions. The focus of such groups has not been restricted to achieving the personal advancement of their members alone, as some observers of career feminist initiatives in the early 1970s would have predicted. In many diverse institutional contexts, feminist mobilization has also challenged the standards and practices of parent organizations in fundamental ways.

Electoral Politics. The 1980s backlash mobilized a feminist response at both national and state levels, which included an increase in the number of women running for political office. The heightening of gender consciousness in the general public and the salience of specific issues such as sexual harassment and reproductive choice also increased the chances of electoral success among women candidates in the early 1990s. Funding, traditionally a problem for women candidates, grew substantially when the Hill–Thomas hearings starkly illustrated the overwhelming control of men in congressional committees. Organizations raising money for pro-choice women candidates in 1992 reported record donations. EMILY's List, founded in 1985 to support pro-choice Democratic women, was a major contributor to some campaigns. By 1993, women constituted 20 percent of all state legislators, 11 percent of the members of the U.S. House of Representatives, and 7 percent of the Senate—still not impressive numbers, but a substantial increase from 1971, when women constituted a mere 5 percent of state legislators and fewer than 3 percent of members of Congress.

The 1980s saw the emergence and spread of a gender gap in voting behavior; women were significantly more supportive of Democratic candidates than were men. Beginning in the presidential election of 1980, in which women were 6–9 percent less likely to vote for Ronald Reagan, the gap grew throughout the decade, reflecting women's negative experiences with Reagan-era policies. Thus in 1988, most men saw their fortunes as improving (52 percent), while most women did not (56 percent reported that their lives were getting worse or staying the same). Reagan's appointments were also more male-dominated than the previous administration's: whereas 15 percent of President Carter's appointments to the federal bench were women, the proportion of women among Reagan's appointments fell by half, to 8 percent. Top policymaking appointments show a similar pattern: 18 percent were women under Carter, 12 percent under Reagan, and a slightly lower percentage under Bush (Tillet and Krafchek 1991). The early appointments by President Clinton show a sharp reversal: There are highly visible women in top posts in the Departments of Justice, Commerce, and Environmental Protection, as well as Health and Human Services.

The increasing importance of women in politics reflects in part their growing strength as voters. Before the reemergence of feminism, women had voted at a significantly lower rate than men, but by 1980 women matched and then exceeded the turnout of their male peers. Because adult women outnumber men, women voters hold the key to electoral success: In the 1992 election, women accounted for 54 percent of all voters. Women's priorities on average differ from those of men; women are more interested in heath, education, welfare, and the link between work and family, and they are less concerned than men about national defense, taxes, and foreign affairs. The voting strength of women as a constituency surely played a role in the passage of the Family and Medical Leave Act of 1993, for example, which Clinton signed after two years of Bush vetoes. The lobbying for this law was led by the Council of Presidents, a coordinating body for the heads of forty-nine different Washington-based women's organizations, first founded in 1985. Passing this law is thus a significant long-term proactive victory for the movement.

The 1992 election also tripled the number of women in the Senate. Women's share of the House rose to forty-seven seats, a tiny percentage, but nearly twice the share held in 1990. At state and local levels women also ran well, capturing twenty-one major state offices and increasing their representation in state legislatures from 18 to 23 percent in just one year. Many of these candidates had shaped their campaigns to highlight issues raised by the New Feminist Movement; several anti-choice referenda were also defeated at the state level.

Not only has a crucial corner been turned, so that the presence of a woman candidate is no longer a novelty in itself, but the increasing visibility of women as a voting constituency has brought salience to some previously ignored issues. Although not all women elected to office are feminists, and not all politicians will support a more woman-centered agenda, there are now certain key prerequisites in place for feminist political influence to grow over the next decade. The parental leave bill enacted in 1993 was only the first item on the Council of Presidents' Women's Agenda, which includes issues such as childcare, health care, pay equity and reproductive rights.

Grassroots Direct-Action. In addition to electoral victories and mobilization within institutions, the New Feminist Movement also made gains in the 1980s at the local level, producing new forms of direct action at the grass roots that often engaged young activists. To an extent that surprised the media pundits who are so eager to declare the death of feminism, radical direct action groups actually increased in this decade. The Women's Action Coalition (WAC), formed in January 1992 in New York City, was soon followed by similar groups in Minneapolis, Houston, Toronto, Los Angeles, and other cities. As one member put it, "Anita Hill was our founding member. . . . [T]he catalyst in large part was seeing an all-white-male Senate Judiciary Committee grilling a black man and a black woman. There was this feeling of 'I'm going to take it to the streets. I'm angry'" (Saltpeter, cited in Hoban 1992). A "Guide to Direct Action Groups," published in *Harper's Bazaar,* brought an avalanche of letters from women throughout the country who were looking for a way to express their outrage over the Hill–Thomas hearings and anxious to found local chapters (Sheppard 1992).

Composed primarily of women in their twenties and early thirties, WAC has turned media attention to issues as diverse as nonpayment of child support in the United States and the widespread rape of Muslim women in Bosnia. WAC tactics include street theater, demonstrations, and other public protests reminiscent of the zap actions of the 1960s. New York's WAC has its own Drum Corps for marches, and a snappy logo—an eye, with the slogan "WAC is watching. We will take action." In the words of one activist, "We are oppressed but we are not going to be victimized" (Murray, in Hoban 1992). WAC has targeted family law courts for protests on Mother's Day, challenged Operation Rescue in front of abortion clinics, marched in front of courthouses where rape cases are being tried, demonstrated in front of museums that do not show women artists, and held regular vigils in front of the United Nations to protest the systematic use of rape as a terrorist tactic in the former Yugoslavia (Hoban 1992; Manegold 1992).

Although WAC is the most visible sign of the "new" grassroots energy of feminism, it is not the only one. WHAM, the Women's Health Action Mobilization was formed in 1989, taking its inspiration for street protests from the demonstrations staged by the radical AIDS protest group ACT-UP. Within a year, WHAM had a mailing list of three thousand names and held dozens of local meetings on issues from herbal medicine to abortion rights. Most of the members are under age thirty, and many are willing to risk arrest for their cause (Manegold 1992). Guerrilla Girls, founded in New York in 1985, calls itself "the conscience of the art world" and uses anonymous hit-and-run tactics to highlight sexist practices in museums, advertising, and media in general. Their posters, stickers, and street theater (in which they don gorilla masks and leather jackets) are aimed at art shows that virtually exclude women artists (Withers 1988). Direct actions, such as Take Back the Night marches, which were first held in San Francisco in 1978, spread to working-class communities such as Waukegan, Illinois, where four hundred people turned out for the 1990 march organized by their local coordinating council against sexual assault (Kamen 1991, 299). Such marches are virtually institutionalized on many campuses.

Other local direct actions may not be coordinated by an ongoing group but spring from the desire to protest specific actions dramatically. For example, Taylor and Whittier (1992b) report on a group of feminists in Ohio who sent pig testicles through the mail to a judge who had said that a four-year-old rape victim was "a promiscuous young lady." Other dramatic forms of public protest are also invented. For example, in Arizona, after charges of acquaintance rape against a basketball player were dropped, women protesters were arrested for outlining their bodies on the sidewalk in chalk with the slogan "rape is not a sport" (*About Women on Campus* 1993).

Third Wave is a new organization of "twenty-something" African-American and white feminists that has attempted to bridge the gap between spontaneous local protest actions, ongoing direct action groups, and more conventional forms of political action. Drawing on the language of the Civil Rights movement, Third Wave sponsored "Freedom Summer '92," a voter registration drive for pro-choice young people (Manegold 1992). Similar goals characterize the Fund for a Feminist Majority (FFM), founded by former NOW President Eleanor Smeal, and attracting a less age-specific membership. FFM provided an alternative to NOW when NOW's own leadership seemed to be abandoning the electoral arena in the mid-1980s. Both Third Wave and FFM—and increasingly, NOW—are committed to combining the "insider" strategies of lobbying and voting with the "outsider" tactics of taking to the streets.

Conclusions

In this chapter we have examined the issues and organizational changes that characterized feminist activism in the period of defensive consolidation. During the openly hostile administrations of Presidents Reagan and Bush, the feminist agenda was dominated by struggles to preserve reproductive choice, to combat sexual violence, and to protect poor women from some of the worst economic consequences of "trickle-down" economics. Despite a sense of shared adversity and some limited successes in broad coalition building, the major thrust of this period was specialization, that is, organizing around specific issues. Feminists of very different perspectives and organizational affiliations were able to unite around particular policy concerns, raising funds and activating networks toward this goal, creating a vast web of submovements. In some ways, opposition strengthened the movement, creating a need for state organization and shattering some young women's complacency about gains already won. But constant defense took a toll as well, both in individual burnout and organizational collapse.

Unobtrusive mobilizations within many institutions changed organizational practices and challenged conventional thinking on many issues. Increased victories in electoral politics in the 1990s and a rebirth of direct action tactics at the grass roots provided the foundation for further mobilization in the coming decade. The new burst of energy and activism from second-generation feminists suggests that they are already defining their own agenda for the future of feminism. In the final chapter, we survey the accomplishments and unfinished agenda of the past three decades.

The testimony and treatment of Prof. Anita Hill during confirmation hearings for Supreme Court Justice Clarence Thomas occasioned widespread outrage among women throughout the country and led to a resurgence of feminist activity in conventional politics and on the streets. *Photograph © Bettye-Lane*

Chapter 8

Looking toward the New Millennium

After three decades of contemporary feminist activism, it is paradoxical to call these efforts the "New" Feminist Movement, especially as the struggle continues into the next millennium. The term does help us to remember the earlier phases of intense feminist mobilization (before the Civil War and before the passage of women's suffrage) that American history books still forget to mention (see Flexner 1959; Buechler 1991). But the phrase also obscures the duration, extent, and institutional maturity already achieved by the current wave of feminist organizing efforts. In this chapter, we review the changes in the status of women and the practices of the contemporary feminist mobilization while it could still be described as "New" and then venture a look into the future of feminism, as a changing but continuing struggle to achieve the full equality and self-determination of all women.

Thirty Years of Struggle

Eleanor Flexner titled her classic study of the battle that led to the passage of the women's suffrage amendment *Century of Struggle* (1959). The contemporary feminist mobilization is not yet that old, but it already has brought about changes that reach across generations. In the period between 1945 and 1963, higher levels of education and increase in labor force participation of women combined with continuing discrimination and changing family relationships set the stage for the rebirth of widespread feminist activism in the United States. Women's own political experiences, the example of African-American Civil Rights activists, unprecedented prosperity, and liberating cultural currents provided material resources and cultural frames that encouraged feminist mobilization. By the mid-1960s, all the essential elements were in place: widespread grievances, the rudiments of an organizational structure, and ideological frames with strong historical roots and increasing contemporary resonance. Three major traditions of thought and action—moral reform, liberalism, and socialism—fed into the emerging feminist critique.

But troubles and ideas alone do not create social movements. The emergence of the New Feminist Movement hinged upon specific events of the 1960s. President Kennedy's Commission on the Status of Women produced a network of activist women that in turn gave birth to NOW and other bureaucratic organizations. The Civil Rights movement began a cycle of protest that involved younger women and helped them develop their own consciousness of oppression, and these women ultimately formed consciousness-raising groups and collectivist organizations. Feminism became strikingly visible on the streets, while behind the scenes, lobbying and litigation brought important changes as well.

The rapid growth of support for the movement in the early 1970s strained its fragile organizational structure. Both the movement's own information outlets and the mass media spread the message of feminism, but what the two understood by feminism was not always the same. Depending on their preferred means and vision of the ultimate goals of social change, feminists tended to define themselves and be defined in "hyphenated" ways: as socialist-feminist, liberal-feminist, radical-feminist, or even career-feminist. Conflicts within and among feminist groups made the term "sisterhood" seem almost ironic.

Growth in the number and size of movement organizations was only one way in which feminism expanded rapidly in the late 1960s and early 1970s. Public awareness and public opinion about feminist issues changed especially dramatically in these early years and have continued to move in a more feminist direction. However, as feminist consciousness spread to working-class communities and women of color developed critical perspectives on their multifaceted oppression, both growth and fragmentation occurred. Building truly inclusive women's organizations proved an elusive goal. Although no one organization adequately achieved the desired inclusiveness of the new feminism, the full set of groups and organizations described in this chapter reflected the array of interests and diverse constituencies activated by the movement. From the early 1970s, together and separately, working-class white women and women of color were organizing effectively on their own behalf—efforts that strengthened the movement as a whole, even though membership was fragmented in a spectrum of organizations.

By the mid-to-late 1970s, it had become difficult to speak of bureaucratic and collectivist strands of feminism as separate tendencies because they had been woven together in a complex tapestry of feminist organizational life. Organizations, such as NOW, that had originated as bureauratic groups were pulled toward less hierarchical and more participatory styles by incoming streams of grassroots members. Conversely, the more collectivist groups, such as local feminist newspapers, developed more formal structures in order to survive. New hybrid associations, such as women's studies programs, began to emerge. Links were forged between grassroots groups and national organizations, giving the movement a unique vitality and scope. The often bruising controversies over homophobia, racism, and anti-Semitism were also important means for heterosexual, Christian, white feminists to question their unconscious privileges. The debate over pornography produced conflicting tenets of feminist orthodoxy and highlighted the problems of exclusionary thinking, while the conflicts over diversity led most activists to realize that homophobia and racism are incompatible with their understanding of feminism.

By the late 1970s the important distinctions among feminist groups were no longer to be found in organizational type (collectivist or bureaucratic) but in organizational strategy (political/educational, direct action/self-help, cultural/entrepreneurial). Local groups providing health care, legal services, sexual assault counseling, shelter for battered women, and other services expanded. As they grew in size as well as number, these groups evolved into increasingly formalized organizations, receiving regular funding, employing paid staff, and planning their operations over a longer time horizon. The "women's community" offered both cultural events (such as music festivals) and services (e.g., feminist carpenters and therapists) that provided a supportive environment and vision of the future to "women-identified" women. Thus in most cities, and even in many smaller towns, it was possible to imagine a life and career anchored in feminism.

The political/educational arm of the movement developed in two directions. The political groups coalesced into a strong and visible policy network in Washington; the occupational and educational groups developed into widespread organizations in a variety of specific professions, from flight attendants to engineers, and in institutions ranging from labor unions to universities. At the national level, the women's policy network became a significant political interest group united in the struggle for the ERA. At this time a countermovement from the Right emerged, creating a growing political polarization over such issues as the nature of the family, reproductive rights, and childcare. Women's concerns that in the 1960s had only been defined as political by small groups of feminists rose ever higher in salience for all politicians and parties. Internationally, also, the feminist mobilization was spreading. Women's movements appeared in virtually every nation, international networks proliferated, and a genuinely global conception of feminism began to emerge.

In the United States, by the early 1980s, with the defeat of the ERA and the growing threat to reproductive rights, the strength of the backlash movement also became unmistakable. Twelve years of conservative Republican administrations created a hostile environment for feminism that changed the movement in many ways. Differences among feminist visions (radical, liberal, socialist, and career) became virtually irrelevant as the movement as a whole consolidated to defend gains already won. State-level organization grew as support from Washington vanished and as the Supreme Court shifted the power to preserve or restrict reproductive rights by returning jurisdiction for these matters to the states. Coalitions and networks reached across differences in organizational strategies and coordinated efforts to defend women's interests in a variety of specific areas. It was the backlash movement that determined the arenas of conflict: in the courts and on the streets over reproductive rights; in the media over sexual violence; and in the legislatures over economic justice.

The antifeminist positions of Republicans in the 1980s led many activists to hope that a corner had been turned with the inauguration of a Democratic president in 1993, despite skepticism over the depth of support for feminism in the new administration. Significant increases in women's representation in electoral offices at all levels and continuing feminist mobilization within institutions provided a basis for limited optimism. New mobilizations of young feminists taking to the streets as well as working through existing institutional channels offered further evidence that this was no "postfeminist" generation. Despite extensive media coverage, the backlash failed to make significant inroads into public opinion on many significant issues, ranging from reproductive rights to the willingness to call oneself a feminist.

With 30–40 percent of American women saying they are feminist, over 4.5 million individuals claiming to have at some time given money to the women's movement, and approximately one in every three hundred women saying that they had participated in some type of feminist activity, the level of feminist mobilization in this country remains impressive (Boles 1991). Unlike the mass media, social movement scholars (e.g., Knoke 1990; Zald 1988) regularly conclude that the New Feminist Movement remains exceptionally broad-based and active. Comparing feminism with other social movements, for example, Zald concludes that it has "the best chance for continued high levels of mobilization and activity" (1988, 29).

Although the contemporary feminist movement has already come a long way, it still has a great distance to go if it is to accomplish its goal of making this a "woman-friendly" society. Women are still far from equality and self-determination, and the backlash of the previous decade led many activists to adopt a reactive, defensive stance. Yet without a proactive vision of the future, the movement will never move beyond its present position. With the next millennium just around the corner, there is a great need for feminists to think in terms of what the next few decades can and should bring for women. In thinking about where we want to go as we enter in the next century, it is useful to pause and take stock of where we are at the end of this one.

Feminist Success in the Twentieth Century

Staggenborg (1994) suggests that social movements produce three types of outcomes that should be counted as successes. First, movements change the policy and practices of formal organizations, especially governments. Many times these outcomes are the most observable forms of success or failure: a law is passed, or a constitutional amendment fails; women are admitted, appointed, nominated, or promoted to take on new responsibilities; penalties for discrimination, abuse, assault, or harassment are imposed. Gamson (1975) calls these outcomes gaining "advantages," in contrast to what he labels gaining "acceptance," which means being able to influence future outcomes.

Staggenborg (1994) divides the ability to win future advantages into what she calls her second and third type of success: organizational survival and cultural change.

Staggenborg calls organizational survival a form of success because the movement has thereby created new resources for the continuing representation and mobilization of its constituency. Given that most people, most of the time, are coping with their daily lives rather than struggling to change the basic conditions under which they live, it is essential to have mechanisms in place that make it possible to mobilize quickly for occasional, intensive political activity. Such preparedness may even minimize the necessity for emergency campaigns. Other social movement scholars have noted that although such continuing organizational resources often go unnoticed when they are not activated, creating structures that survive over the long term provides succor in bad times and opportunities for further change when the situation improves (Morris 1984; Taylor 1989b).

Staggenborg's third form of success appears when a social movement changes the underlying culture of a society. "Culture" in this sense is more than the sum of individual attitudes, as expressed, for example, in public opinion polls. Although polling can be an important means of tapping cultural shifts, especially when they are emerging and still contested, many cultural beliefs are so taken for granted that no polling organization would ever ask about them, nor would variation in answers be found if they did.

Cultural change is the least observable but perhaps the most enduring form of transformation, because culture provides the basic "tools" for organizing experience and giving meaning to the actions we take (Swidler 1986). For example, whether sending someone a preprinted birthday card should be understood as a positive gesture (thinking of you) or a negative one (too unconcerned or lazy to write a few lines of your own) depends on the culture of the society and not on the individual attitudes of the sender or recipient (unless they are known by both to differ from the culture at large). And a preprinted birthday card won't be available in stores unless it is a culturally acceptable form of greeting. Although an individual may resist pressures to conform to culture (be "deviant"), true cultural change represents the invention and spread of new ways of interpreting actions. Such a collective challenge produces new possibilities for behavior and new meanings for old behaviors.

The first three decades of the New Feminist Movement have produced substantial successes of all three types. Although we have already described many of the individual victories and losses, we now review the key dimensions of change in the latter half of the twentieth century.

Changes in Policy.   The legacy of nineteenth-century feminism provided a bedrock on which twentieth-century gains could be built: access to higher education and, in more limited numbers, to the professions, as well as the right of women to keep their own earnings, get a legal divorce, and keep their children. Feminists in the early part of this century built upon this foundation, especially when they attained the right to vote and hold political office. In the latter half of this century, other advantages have been won that will continue to be significant in women's lives in decades to come.

The most recent educational and occupational advances were secured in part by the passage of Title VII of the Civil Rights Act in 1963 and in part by continuing litigation and lobbying. Literally tens of millions of dollars in back-pay awards have been won in court cases and out-of-court settlements (Gelb and Palley 1987). Educational gains, particularly fostered by Title IX of the Education Amendments of 1972, which barred sex discrimination in schools receiving federal funds, provide an important base for future feminist activism. For example, women constituted 45 percent of law and 35 percent of business school students in 1993 (U.S. Dept. of Education 1993), which means that many will have the skills and motivation to work for further legislative and occupational gains. White women in particular have made gains in the professions, especially those that were expanding (such as accounting, law, and pharmacy), and therefore, could offer women opportunities that did not come at the expense of men (Sokoloff 1992). Where women were entering, there was also a strong probability that the occupation was losing status and income (Reskin and Roos 1990). Women of color closed the gap between themselves and white women in occupational access and rewards, but all women remained well behind white men in job status and income.

As Table 8.1 shows, some headway has been made in opening up a wide variety of male-dominated occupations to women, even though the great majority of women continue to work in lower-paying, female-dominated jobs. Even among professionals, there are still approximately twenty times as many women working as nurses than as physicians and ten times as many women teaching elementary and

TABLE 8.1

Women Employed in Selected Occupations, 1970, 1981, and 1991
(Numbers in Thousands)

Occupation	Number		Women as Percent of All Workers in Occupation		
	1970	1981	1970	1981	1991
Professional-technical	4,576	7,173	40.0	44.7	50.0
Accountants	180	422	25.3	38.5	51.5
Computer specialists	52	170	19.6	27.1	34.0
Engineers	20	65	1.6	4.3	8.2
Lawyers-judges	13	80	4.7	14.0	18.9
Physicians (osteopaths)	25	60	8.9	13.8	20.1
Registered nurses	814	1,271	97.4	96.8	94.8
Teachers, except college and university	1,937	2,219	70.4	70.6	74.3
Teachers, college and university	139	202	28.3	35.3	40.8
Managerial-administrative, except farm	1,061	3,098	16.6	27.4	40.0
Bank officials-financial managers	55	254	17.6	37.4	44.7
Buyers-purchasing agents	75	164	20.8	35.0	33.9
Sales managers–department heads; retail trade	51	136	24.1	40.4	42.1

TABLE 8.1
(continued)

Occupation	Number			Women as Percent of All Workers in Occupation		
	1970	1981	1970	1970	1981	1991
Sales workers	2,143	2,856		39.4	45.4	48.8
Sales clerks, retail	1,465	1,696		64.8	71.3	66.7
Clerical	10,150	14,645		73.6	80.5	80.0
Bank tellers	216	523		86.1	93.7	90.3
Bookkeepers	1,274	1,752		82.1	91.2	91.5
Cashiers	692	1,400		84.0	86.4	80.9
Office machine operators	414	696		73.5	73.7	73.2
Secretaries-typists	3,686	4,788		96.6	98.6	98.5
Shipping-receiving clerks	59	116		14.3	22.5	29.6
Craft	518	786		4.9	6.3	8.6
Carpenters	11	20		1.3	1.9	1.3
Mechanics, including automotive	49	62		2.0	1.9	3.4
Operatives, except transport	4,036	4,101		38.4	39.8	40.1
Assemblers	459	599		48.7	52.3	n/a

TABLE 8.1
(continued)

Occupation	Number			Women as Percent of All Workers in Occupation		
	1970	1981	1991	1970	1981	1991
Laundry and dry cleaning operatives	105	125		62.9	66.1	64.5
Sewers and stitchers	816	749		93.8	96.0	89.2
Transport equipment operatives	134	304		4.5	8.0	9.0
Bus drivers	68	168		28.5	47.3	n/a
Truck drivers	22	51		1.5	2.7	4.2
Service workers	5,944	8,184		60.5	62.2	59.8
Private household	1,132	988		96.9	96.5	96.0
Food service	1,913	3,044		68.8	66.5	59.3
Cooks	546	723		62.5	51.9	46.9
Health service	1,047	1,752		88.0	89.3	88.6
Personal service	778	1,314		66.5	76.1	81.6
Protective service	59	145		6.2	10.1	15.2

Source: U.S. Department of Labor 1982 U.S. Bureau of the Census, 1992b.

high school students as standing before college and university classes. Nonetheless, on average, women's wages for year-round full-time work rose from under 60 percent of men's, where they had been stuck from 1950 to 1970, to over 70 percent by 1990 (England 1992, 24). Better job prospects and higher incomes make women's commitment to the labor force more secure; the probability now is that a woman will stay in the labor force all or most of her adult life, whether or not she has children (U.S. Bureau of the Census 1990).

The difficulty of rolling back such gains is illustrated by the resistance of employers to the Reagan administration's efforts to relieve them of their affirmative action obligations. Just as it has taken decades to change patterns of discrimination that were imbedded in the bureaucratic practices of personnel management in government and corporations (Bielby and Baron 1987), once less discriminatory policies were in place, bureaucratic inertia resisted their removal. Women were extremely well qualified for their new positions and, even in a period of backlash, employers were not anxious to lose them. Under conditions of recession, when competition for scarce jobs intensifies, the tendency to prefer male applicants could undercut women's recent gains in nontraditional occupations. But women today are in a stronger legal and occupational position to challenge discriminatory hiring and promotion decisions.

The real progress in the integration of women in a profession or position comes with the move beyond mere tokenism. Just as in the nineteenth century a few exceptional women became the first women doctors and first women lawyers, the past three decades have witnessed a large number of highly visible "breakthroughs": the first woman jockey, the first woman firefighter, the first woman astronaut, the first woman Supreme Court Justice, the first woman vice-presidential nominee of a major party, and so on. Women in such positions soon realize that their successes and failures will be taken as an indication of the capabilities of all women, as conveyed by the concept of "tokenism"—something that represents the whole. The token also represents an employer's minimal compliance with nondiscriminatory hiring practices. Equally significant, though less publicized, is the appointment or promotion of a second, third, or seventeenth woman to a male-dominated occupation. As with other minorities in the workplace, a critical mass must be achieved before working conditions are normalized for women (Kanter 1977).

The policy gains most difficult to achieve have been those that address the problem of combining paid work and motherhood. The structure of the "normal" workplace assumes a "normal" worker: a male with a wife at home to raise his children, provide his meals, and organize his private life so that he can devote the majority of his waking hours to meeting the employer's demands without interference (Acker 1990). Many European countries have policies that offer special protections or benefits to women (such as extended paid maternity leave) to acknowledge the special burden of women's "dual role," but policymakers have never challenged the assumption that only *women* have the responsibility of managing a family and a job. Even extending benefits legally to men, as several countries have recently done, has not challenged the social expectation that these policies have little to do with most men's lives. Thus only a very small percentage of men have taken them up—about 10 percent of Swedish men, for example (Gelb 1989).

American social policy has only recently addressed this issue, but it is doing so in a distinctive way. Court decisions and legislation combine the insistence on gender neutrality characteristic of U.S. feminism with at least some benefits geared to gender-specific needs, such as maternity. This approach affirms a commitment to shared child rearing and gender equality in the workplace (Vogel 1993). Struggles to define and defend appropriate policy for women workers have highlighted the continuing tension between feminists who stress women's fundamental equality with men and feminists who emphasize women's differences, particularly in the area of reproduction. The varying emphases of "equality feminists" and "difference feminists" that produced acrimonious debates over social policy in the 1930s and 1940s have reemerged as a point of contention in the 1980s and 1990s (Vogel 1993). The common goal is to achieve equality through different treatment only insofar as necessary to acknowledge that women are not in reality "similarly situated" to men. While woman-specific "protective legislation" in employment has always led to discrimination on the job, reforms such as the Family and Medical Leave Act are designed to offer at least minimal protection to workers with family needs, whether men or women.

Without an expansion of such policies to provide income replacement for workers who cannot afford to consider an unpaid leave, many women will continue to depend on men's wages to support them through periods of intensive unpaid family labor. Others enjoy no such support; many of them depend on welfare benefits that are increasingly inadequate for raising children. The economic risks of divorce continue to be disproportionately borne by women. As a result of the poverty of women, nearly a quarter of all children (22 percent) and almost half of African-American children (46 percent) were being raised in poverty, and cutbacks in public services (e.g., libraries, parks, and recreation) make it even harder for poor children to get what is not available at home (U.S. Bureau of the Census 1992a). Thus, the growing social inequality of the past fifteen years has made women's child-rearing labor harder to carry out and has increased the risk that they and their children will fall through an ever-weaker "safety net."

Overall, the social policy changes produced by the New Feminist Movement, like those spurred by the Civil Rights movement, have worked to the advantage of those who had more resources to begin with—that is, education, job skills, self-esteem. But those with fewer resources to begin with have fallen further behind, and the gap between the "haves" and the "have-nots" has increased, both among white women and among persons of color; while some women and minority men have fallen through the cracks, others have acquired vested interests in the status quo. This is not the fault of feminists, as some have claimed (e.g., Hewlett 1986) but reflects more fundamental barriers to equality in the American system. Feminist activism, effective as it has been in some policy areas, has still been unable to remove these constraints.

American social policy has embraced an "independent" model of the individual—imagining a person who does not provide care for others nor require care (even temporarily as a child, sick or elderly person, or permanently because of physical or mental disabilities) to be the only truly worthy worker. Persons with caregiving responsibilities are at a disadvantage in such a system, whether they are men or women. In this system, more affluent women can take the social role of "husband" and hire a poorer woman to be the "wife" who takes care of children and the home (leaving her own children and home behind). But the system ignores the needs of the "wife." Women who do caregiving, either as unpaid labor or as paid domestic work, are shortchanged in pay, pensions, insurance, and other benefits (Romero 1992). Feminist social policy also needs to address the social need for and value of caregiving work and reward and support caregivers. Among the countries with active feminist movements, Norway has perhaps made the most dramatic steps in this direction. Not coincidentally, Norwegian women also led the world in political representation; in 1993, the prime minister was a woman, and a third of the parliament members were women. Both gains resulted from women's own efforts to organize and use their voting strength (Chapman 1993).

Organizational Changes.   As we have seen in previous chapters, the proliferation and consolidation of feminist organizations over the past thirty years has been a striking feature of the movement's development. The varied and diverse feminist organizations existing today on every level from neighborhood to global are crucial resources for securing future change. The contributions of such groups to the achievement of a variety of specific policy and cultural gains should not obscure the fact that the organizations themselves are a successful outcome of feminist labor.

More important than any specific policy outcome is the fact that these organizations have come to represent women collectively, having a legitimate role in shaping public policy and in meeting women's needs directly. When movements produce "institutionalized participation" (i.e., access and organizations), this gain is both more durable and more productive of further reforms than is merely winning specific rights (Tarrow 1983). Many formal policy gains would be hollow without continued monitoring and pressure for enforcement from women as an organized interest group. But not only large, national, policy-focused groups are important organizational achievements; even those organizations that proved ephemeral often provided significant learning experiences that members carried into other settings, built upon, and transformed into more permanent contributions to the organizational landscape (Strobel 1994).

Other particularly valuable assets are the coalitions and networks formed over these decades. The early years of feminist organizing produced diversity and decentralization, which is advantageous for social movements because a variety of strategies can be pursued simultaneously, so that if one strategy reaches a dead end, another can still be pursued (Gerlach and Hine 1970). But such proliferation also runs the risk of repeatedly reinventing the wheel. The most effective structures for a social movement are not merely decentralized but *reticulate*— that is, they have a strong network structure, with many linking lines of communication and coordination. It is just such a reticulate form that gradually emerged in the New Feminist Movement. Rather than single, centralized organizations that completely dominate the definition of issues or articulation of strategies, feminist organizations have built up interlocking networks of coalitions. Such linking bodies range from the Council of Presidents of forty-nine national, mass-membership women's organizations, in Washington, D.C., to local coalitions on specific issues, such as the Alliance to End Violence Against Women, in St. Louis, Missouri, which brings together a dozen local activist groups. The networks are then tied together across levels: the National Coalition against Domestic Violence (NCADV, founded in 1978) connects fifty-two state-level coordinating committees (some states have more than one) and also hundreds of local groups and citywide networks (Arnold 1994). The NCADV is itself linked into Washington policymaking networks that cut across issues, and many state-level groups are part of broader feminist coalitions (e.g., the Wisconsin Women's Issues Network). There is thus a very dense fabric of interwoven lines of communication and assistance so that feminist organizations can readily share information and innovative ideas without a centralized decision-making structure.

Such organizational density is also an asset when it is necessary to turn out supporters at a mass rally or demonstration. Activism is always strengthened when personal ties as well as abstract issues encourage participation (Klandermans and Oegema 1987). The massive size of reproductive rights demonstrations, for example, is facilitated when women do not merely read about them in the newspaper but are personally invited to attend by others in their network. The extensive contemporary feminist network thus provides enhanced opportunities for noninstitutional forms of protest as well as more effective delivery of services and more forceful lobbying.

Networks are also critical in constructing a feminist movement that is truly diverse and inclusive. As we have seen, women of color, working-class women, young women, older women, Jewish women, Catholic women, professional women, and women in unions have found it useful to form organizations that address their specific interests. While none of these individual organizations reflect the true diversity of women's experiences and perceptions, networking among them makes it possible for the movement as a whole to do so. City groups such as Hartford's Coalition of 100 Black Women or the Seattle Women's Funding Alliance provide connections among the various special purpose projects that they sponsor (e.g., shelters run by and for African-American women or lesbian women's spirituality groups) and are themselves linked into larger coalitions. Diverse organizations

This February 1992 rally, which brought together activists from ACT UP (AIDS Coalition to Unleash Power) and WHAM! (Women's Health Action and Mobilization) just before the New Hampshire primary to protest President Bush's inaction on AIDS and women's health issues, is an example of an issue-oriented coalition of organizations. *Photograph by Marilyn Humphries.*

with very specific goals are not an alternative to feminism; they are the characteristic expression of American feminism at the local level. It is when all these different expressions of feminism come together that the collective strength of the movement is manifest.

Coalition structures, strong and flexible as they are, are not without their drawbacks. Because coalitions provide little incentive for groups to work through rather than around the differences in perspective and commitment of their members, it is often difficult for coalition members to develop a shared collective identity as feminists. Coalition efforts can easily be reduced to supporting "lowest common denominator" demands. Coalitions also are more effective in coordinating efforts among those who are already committed to the goals of the movement than in bringing in new members or regenerating commitment among those who feel burned out (Arnold 1994).

Some feminist groups do, however, provide the interpersonal and moral support that activists need to sustain their commitment over the long haul. For example, in the "doldrums" after suffrage and before the revival of feminism, the National Women's Party provided its small cadre of loyalists a significant community context in which their feminist beliefs were accepted and their style of life endorsed, even when the rest of society was hostile to their message (Rupp and Taylor 1987). In the past three decades, a comparable "woman's community" has emerged, predominantly sustained by lesbian feminists and offering activists a place to live out some of their hopes for a woman-centered, woman-friendly environment (Taylor and Whittier 1992b). In such free spaces, feminists can find validation of their vision of the future and support for living outside the bounds of "acceptable" female behavior.

Because feminist groups are so numerous and varied, they also benefit the movement by serving as laboratories for developing feminist forms of organizational practice (Martin 1990). The early collectivist structures gave way to more hybrid forms of organization but not without leaving a legacy of idealized conceptions of what a feminist organization should be: participatory, nonhierarchical, democratic, autonomous and antibureaucratic (Ferguson 1984). Such idealization has often been used in very destructive ways: to trash women perceived as elitist; to resist organizational changes necessary for long-term survival; to exclude people unable to commit the time needed for participatory decision-making. Despite such bruising experiences, collectives hold out the promise of empowerment and self-discovery, encourage innovative thinking, and reward risk-taking. The positive and negative lessons learned in these encounters have diffused throughout the movement as activists moved from group to group, founded new organizations, and restructured old ones (Strobel 1994). As a result, feminist organizations are now typically hybrid types that use a flattened hierarchy and an unusually flexible division of labor and try to develop ways to unite the frequently separated spheres of home and workplace, reason and emotion (Ferree and Martin 1994).

This does not mean that feminist organizations have successfully resolved the tensions that arise from criticizing power relations while also trying to gain power in the interests of women. Because women are still not recognized as legitimate bearers of authority, they have difficulty exercising power within and across organizational settings. The struggle to understand the uses and misuses of power in feminist practice is a critical issue precisely because of the gains that women have made in reaching positions of authority and influence (Reinelt 1994). One activist argues that many feminist organizations are "running with their brakes on," that is, holding themselves back unnecessarily by self-defeating ways of thinking (Remington 1991). For example, the widespread use of the term "empowerment" allows feminists to avoid the apparently too-blunt word "power" but obscures awareness of the support their own leaders require—how, after all, can you "empower" the person you perceive to be already powerful? Thus women in leadership positions are often embarrassed about whatever institutional power they hold while at the same time they are deprived of the nurturance and constructive criticism they need to keep functioning effectively. Remington argues that the best possible use of the most talented and capable women in the movement will not be realized until feminist organizations discuss the responsible use of power rather than just the process of empowerment. This is what she calls the need to thrive, rather than merely survive (1990).

The multitude of contemporary feminist organizations provide ample opportunity for experiments such as those that Remington suggests. Because feminist organizations are where the ongoing work of the movement gets done, it is important for them to develop into thriving institutions that are good for the women who work in them as well as for the group called women as a whole.

Cultural Changes.   For many women, discovering the ideas of feminism was the first step toward "saving her own life"—escaping from stifling cultural traditions and expectations and rejecting the suspicion of madness that such an escape entailed. Literally millions of women went through some degree of consciousness-raising in the past three decades, discovering that they were not alone, that many of the problems they had defined as individual failings were socially generated and shared by other women, that the social arrangements that gave rise to such experiences could be challenged and perhaps even changed. The individual liberation of rejecting at least some portion of society's conventional demands finally allowed women to express anger, while thinking about the sources of their rage led to trenchant critiques of women's oppression in the family, the workplace, the health-care system, organized religion, and indeed, every area of social life.

The liberating potential of the movement has also affected men, both feminist and not. Most obviously, relationships between women and men have been modified by the transformations in attitudes, behaviors, and institutional structures described in this volume. The external and internal landscapes within which men and women develop a self-image and make choices have been irrevocably changed. And for a crucial subset of men, both today and in the past, the feminist movement has provided an opportunity for rethinking the meaning of masculinity and for enriching the study of the social construction of gender (Kimmel 1992).

The questioning, and ultimately the reframing, of women's experience has therefore touched nearly all elements of American culture. Feminist theorizing, particularly in the form of popular scholarship, provides an alternative way of thinking about the entire world, and new ideas are spread through the mass media and feminist presses, periodicals and bookstores. To a greater or lesser extent depending on specific location, local "woman's communities" provide an alternative way of actually living out these ideas. The feminist culture of some women's studies programs, many lesbian feminist communities, some service-provider networks, and other such bounded environments allows a wholly feminist subculture to flourish.

Within such subcultures, innovative metaphoric language can be used to symbolize a break with maleness (e.g., by spelling *women* as "wimmin" or taking a new name like Kathy Sarachild or Starhawk instead of the name inherited from male parents), to invoke images of female anger and power that are taboo in the larger culture (e.g., describing themselves as Amazons, furies, or witches), and to create symbolic statements that condense a more complex argument (e.g., "the personal is political" or "the master's tools will never dismantle the master's house"). Poets and political essayists such as Adrienne Rich, Audre Lorde, Marge Piercy, Mary Daly, and Robin Morgan have contributed powerfully to forming these and many other cultural resources for feminist communities.

Important as such free spaces are (whether found in the imagination or in actual communities) for realizing one's feminist ideals in "prefigurative politics" (Breines 1982), feminist cultural changes go beyond creating such secure but ghettoized places. Feminist challenges to mainstream (or "malestream") culture have created new possibilities for even those women and men who have not personally undergone any degree of feminist transformation. One of these new cultural realities is gender-consciousness (Rinehart 1992). The fact that many women identify collectively with a group called "women" and feel their fate bound up with that of other women changes the nature of political thinking. "Women" are now culturally defined as an interest group, a collective actor that is capable of taking positions on issues and asking the important question "Is this good for women?" about any piece of legislation, any personnel manager's decision, or any policy announcement. The political calculus employed by every decision-maker, feminist or not, shifts when it is apparent that women, collectively, have a voice (or many voices).

Perhaps even more profoundly, the nature of language itself has shifted—not without conscious and energetic efforts—to express this awareness that women cannot be ignored or subsumed under the pseudogeneric "man." The former invisibility of women is not, of course, remedied by a change of language alone. Thinking that remains focused on men alone produces such laughable phrases as "people and their wives." Nonetheless, the gender awareness born of this wave of feminist mobilization is often expressed by a sensitivity to word choice that makes it possible to talk and think, even unconsciously, in more gender-inclusive ways. One illustration of how this consciousness of language works is that students selected more pictures of women to illustrate a textbook chapter they were told was about "Urban Life" than for one they were told was about "Urban Man" (Schneider and Hacker 1973).

Feminist change at the level of discourse offers new ways of thinking about issues confronting women. Many of these concepts were so rapidly absorbed into the culture that they no longer seem recent inventions. Words and phrases such as "sexism," "sexual harassment," "comparable worth," "date rape," and "the feminization of poverty" named realities in women's lives that had been nameless and thus impossible to discuss. New words are constantly being created as well; "femicide," for example, is a coinage of the late 1980s (Radford and Russell 1992). With the language to talk about violence against women, the potential for finding new political solutions expands. Thus what Katzenstein (1994) terms "discursive politics," talking differently about issues, becomes a resource for instrumental and policy-focused changes.

In addition, discursive politics are a way in which the broader self, the collective identity of "women," is created for the movement as a whole. In that sense, collective identity is an end in itself, as Gamson puts it: "The creation of an ongoing collective identity that maintains the loyalty and commitment of participants is a cultural achievement in its own right, regardless of its contribution to the achievement of political and organizational goals" (1992, 57). It is a major achievement of the New Feminist Movement that this conception of who women are and what they want is broadly inclusive and diverse, that it refuses to separate gender from race, nationality, age, and other aspects of the human condition. The work toward this cultural accomplishment has been led by women of color in the United States and Third World women internationally, often in the face of initial incomprehension and hostility from white Western feminists.

The cultural changes that have been created in the past three decades have their limits as well. Taken-for-granted ideas about male dominance and superiority, while strongly challenged by feminists, have proved remarkably persistent. Any change in consciousness is an uphill struggle; it is hard to break free of "the umbilical cord of magic and myth" (Friere 1970) that justifies the status quo, or to question the various unconscious beliefs about nature, reality, and society that make up our cultural heritage. In these we swim, "like fish who do not know that the world is wet" (Bem and Bem 1970). The willingness of judges and jurors to accept woman-blaming, the commonplace hatreds directed at women that are tamely called "misogyny," the obviousness of the fact that women are not safe on the street at night or in their own home in the daylight, the pervasive "reasonableness" of seeing white men as automatically "qualified"; these and many other cultural beliefs are still very much with us as we enter the next millennium. But the cultural transformation that has occurred—and become part of an equally taken-for-granted reality—is nonetheless remarkable.

Feminism Enters the Twenty-first Century

To know how to evaluate future opportunities for change, we must first ask, How fundamental are the transformations that feminists seek? There is no one correct answer to that question, for the range of feminist visions is broad and varied. The historical roots of feminism in moral reform, liberal, and socialist worldviews continue to shape individuals' interpretations of what they want and how to get it. Although such diversity makes little practical difference to feminists who are defensively struggling merely to preserve their existing rights, it is very important when one envisions the future.

Sociologists typically distinguish between social movements on the basis of whether they are reformist or revolutionary, depending on how fundamental a challenge they pose to existing social arrangements. Some theorists have emphasized a movement's challenge to *ideas* about how society should be organized (e.g., Smelser 1963). In this view, movements that seek to change rules about how things should be done are called reform movements; while those that challenge values concerning what things should be done at all are called revolutionary. Other theorists focus on a movement's challenge to the persons and *institutions* holding power in the society (e.g., Tilly 1978). From their perspective, movements that change the balance of power among those already integrated in the system are called reform movements, and movements that attempt to dislodge existing power elites in favor of new contenders are called revolutionary. And neither of these frameworks should be confused with the popular notion that movements using violent tactics are revolutionary and those that are nonviolent are reformist.

Where, then, is the no-longer-new contemporary feminist movement going as it enters the next millennium? Feminists concerned about creating a new form of community—in the Socialist and radical traditions—seek fundamental value changes. Both socialist and radical feminists engage in deep analysis of the basic structures that support patriarchal values, believing that effective strategies for change need to be grounded in a proper understanding of the dynamics of the existing system. Career and liberal feminists, in contrast, do not focus on such values directly but rather emphasize the disjunction between mainstream American values of equality, self-development, individual achievement, and freedom on the one hand, and actual norms of male preference, discrimination, and restrictions on women's self-expression and freedom of movement on the other. From the perspective of ideological challenge, we would conclude that only radical and socialist feminists have a revolutionary vision for the future.

However, if we look at the challenge posed to existing establishments and controlling elites, the feminist revolution consists of the struggle for control over institutionalized forms of power in order to redirect them in ways that will meet the collective needs and interests of women. Neither career feminists nor radical feminists have this as a goal; they look primarily to the transformation of an individual woman and her consciousness as a means of releasing her potential and validating her experiences and perspectives. It is the liberal and socialist feminists who want immediate and far-reaching institutional change. They consider it important for women as a group to contend for power and to exercise the power they already hold in the service of institutional changes now and in the future.

In the liberal and socialist feminist view, access to the system for individuals (the career model) and building alternative institutions (the radical model) are helpful only insofar as they bring women into confrontation with existing power structures and whet their appetite for change. Because only liberal and socialist feminists see women collectively as contenders for control over existing social institutions and therefore engage directly in political struggles with mainstream elites, can we say that these two strands are revolutionary, and, in contrast, the career and radical feminists are reformist?

We believe that neither of these conclusions is satisfactory, because the basic model each relies on is flawed. Both conventional schemes for classifying revolutionary and reform movements not only are inconsistent with each other but also lack any developed theory relating changes in consciousness (norms and values) with changes in political arrangements (institutions and elites). A more adequate account of what feminist visions have to offer would have to begin with an understanding that social control in the realm of ideas (sometimes called "ideological hegemony") and social control over the realm of action (the degrees of monopoly of coercive force) are interrelated in complex and interlocking ways. Such a model would address social power that is invisible because it is so well institutionalized, as well as the direct use of sanctions, rewards, and physical force in society. This emergent model includes perceptions of injustice, legitimacy, authority, and the degree of belief in the possibility of ever achieving change (Gamson 1992). From such a perspective, it seems evident that fundamental, revolutionary challenges are best mounted simultaneously against social control in both the realm of ideas and the realm of institutionalized force. In this more integrated view, the career and radical feminist visions offer a new set of higher expectations to women, so that treatment once taken for granted is now perceived as unjust. At the same time, liberal and socialist strands complement these approaches by taking such higher expectations for granted and organizing action targeted directly at achieving a social order that offers more justice and freedom to women. Thus our expectation is that the feminist movement of the next millennium will be truly revolutionary to the extent that it manages to nurture all four types of proactive visions.

The real question remains whether any of these proactive possibilities will give significant direction to feminist activism, given the reactive posture forced upon the movement in the past fifteen years. Reactive politics are not necessarily bad politics, but they are the politics of pessimism. A reactive view of social change assesses the costs and benefits of any particular institution or policy with "all other things being equal," that is, unchanged, and looks first to the potential costs rather than the benefits. Activists are mobilized on the basis of spreading alarm about dangers in and threats to the status quo. In contrast, proactive politics are the politics of optimism. The proactive view assumes that everything can and eventually will change, and usually for the better; it highlights opportunities rather than costs and mobilizes activists on the basis of realizing a vision of the future and living out new possibilities.

Clearly, as we have shown, the New Feminist Movement has already experienced periods when proactive politics were dominant, as in the 1960s, and when reactive politics were central, as in the 1980s. What will the next decades bring? Perhaps hopes and expectations more tempered than the utopian schemes and the belief that the revolution was just around the corner that were so exhilarating in the 1960s, but perhaps with more imagination and vision than the long, hard struggles of the 1980s allowed. The future of American feminism will depend not only on the millions of women who are already activists of one sort or another, but also on the next generation of women whose influence is just beginning to be felt. Because feminism is not, and cannot be, some form of received wisdom handed down across generations but is an active interpretation of the realities of women's own lives and struggles, the feminism of the future will continue to be reborn differently in every generation.

Chronology

Executive Order 11375: Amends EO 11246 by adding sex discrimination as a prohibited practice and establishes a policy of "affirmative action" for women as well. Where government contracts exist, contractors must show a "good faith effort" to hire more women and minorities by stating their goals, timetables, and procedures. Enforcement is overseen by the Office of Federal Contract Compliance, and in the next decade a dozen contracts are withdrawn for noncompliance.

1968   Women protest at Miss America pageant. A sheep is crowned, but no bras are burned.

1969   First recent women's studies course officially taught at Cornell, following such rare predecessors as an 1892 course on the status of women taught at Kansas State.

EEOC guidelines no longer support "protective legislation" regulating women's hours, weight-lifting, or entry into construction trades and mining. Unions begin to drop their opposition to an equal rights amendment.

Chicago Women's Liberation Union (CLWU) founded; it becomes one of the longest lived and best known of the many "small groups" founded in these years.

1970   Women's Strike for Equality march in New York City draws unexpected crowd; mass media discover feminism.

Boston Women's Health Book Collective publishes the first newsprint edition of *Our Bodies, Ourselves.* The Feminist Press is founded and begins republishing out-of-print feminist classics and new writers. A mainstream press publishes *Sisterhood Is Powerful,* an anthology that made many alternative press articles available for a broad readership.

First coordinated women's studies programs are started at San Diego State and at Cornell.

1971   Supreme Court rules that "sex-plus" discrimination is illegal: rules for women with preschool children must apply to men with preschool children also.

President Nixon vetoes a bill providing public support for child-care centers.

1972　*Title IX of the Education Amendments:* Bars discrimination in all educational programs including athletics and specific university degree programs. First court case affirms right of men to enter nursing program.

Ms. magazine, National Women's Political Caucus, National Conference of Puerto Rican Women, and the academic journal *Feminist Studies* are all established.

Equal Rights Amendment (ERA) passed by both houses of Congress and sent to the states for ratification. Thirty states ratify by March 1973 (of the thirty-three needed for it to become part of the Constitution).

Rep. Shirley Chisholm attempts to run for President of the United States but her campaign draws little support from male-dominated African-American groups or feminist organizations and collapses under antifeminist and antiblack attacks.

Bay Area Women Against Rape formed; first rape crisis hot line opens in Washington, D.C.

Decade 2 (1973–82): Proliferation and Opposition

1973　Office workers organize 9-to-5 in Boston, Women Employed in Chicago, and Women Office Workers in New York City.

Roe v. *Wade* decision by Supreme Court affirms women's right to privacy in making reproductive choices, establishes a three trimester rule for level of state regulation.

Phyllis Schlafly founds STOP-ERA and begins a campaign against women's equal rights.

AT&T signs a $38 million settlement, promising to end race and sex discrimination in employment.

National Black Feminist Organization, Catholics for a Free Choice, and many other new feminist organizations are founded. First National Lesbian Conference held in Los Angeles.

Women's Educational Equity Act is passed by Congress, offering grants for development of nonsexist programs and teaching materials.

1974	Coalition of Labor Union Women (CLUW), National Congress of Neighborhood Women established, providing new working-class feminist networks.

Fourteen states now have state-level Equal Rights Amendments, but the federal amendment is stalled.

Eleven women irregularly ordained Episcopal priests and are officially recognized by their church two years later.

Lesbian Herstory Archives established in New York City; Olivia Records, *Quest,* and many other women's cultural groups founded. First National Women's Music Festival held at University of Illinois.

Mexican American Women's National Association founded.

Equal Credit Opportunity Act allows divorced women to get credit based on their married credit histories and prohibits discrimination in lending.

First women's studies research centers founded at Wellesley and at Stanford. Over fifty such centers exist today.

1975	Supreme Court outlaws automatic exclusion of women from jury duty and bans different ages of majority for men and women.

Congress requires military academies to admit women.

Alliance for Displaced Homemakers founded; it focuses attention on financial plight of divorced, middle-aged women with little experience in paid jobs.

First shelters for battered women emerge out of women's CR groups in Pittsburgh and Boston. First directory of the groups that are mushrooming around the country appears a year later.

First United Nations' International Women's Year Conference held in Mexico City, leading to an official

"Decade for Women." Planning for United States's own IWY conference begins.

Catholic bishops announce a "Pastoral Plan for Pro-Life Activities" ushering in an era of greater grassroots antiabortion mobilization.

Over two thousand attend a Socialist feminist conference under the auspices of the New American Movement (NAM) held in Yellow Springs, Ohio.

Signs: A Journal of Women in Culture and Society makes its debut.

1976   The Hyde Amendment restricts federal funding for abortion and demands parental/spousal consent for abortion when federal funds are used; it is affirmed by the Supreme Court the following year in *Harris* v. *McRae*.

Supreme Court rules that discrimination against "pregnant people" is not sex discrimination under the Civil Rights Act.

Diverse coalitions established: a feminist bookstore network, the National Alliance of Black Feminists, a Philadelphia fund-raising umbrella group "Women's Way," the National Women's Health Network, and Organization of Pan Asian American Women, among others.

NOW weathers two years of divisive struggles over leadership, establishes a formalized structure and professional staff.

1977   International Women's Year (IWY) Conference held in Houston; President Carter establishes a National Advisory Committee for Women (disbanded in 1979 when Bella Abzug is fired).

National Women's Studies Association founded; 276 Women's Studies programs exist.

NBC signs a $1.7 million agreement with EEOC for back pay for women. However, backlog of uninvestigated complaints at EEOC reaches a new high of 130,000 cases.

Alice Paul, last surviving leader of first wave feminist efforts, dies.

1978 The Pregnancy Discrimination Act counters the Supreme Court ruling, affirming that pregnancy must be treated "like any other temporary disability."

National Coalition Against Domestic Violence is founded; first Take Back the Night march is held in San Francisco.

After a massive march on Washington for the ERA, Congress extends deadline for ratification to 1982.

New York Times settles gender discrimination suit for $350,000 in back pay and damages.

1979 Supreme Court upholds veteran's preference in hiring, despite discriminatory effect on women. States have the right to hire the least qualified veteran before the most qualified nonveteran.

National Committee on Pay Equity founded to coordinate a growing number of state and municipal job evaluation and pay equity efforts.

National Coalition against Sexual Assault formed by rape crisis centers in twenty states.

Sister Theresa Kane publicly raises issue of sex discrimination with the Pope; Sonia Johnson excommunicated from Mormon Church for forming Mormons for ERA. In the early 1980s, Johnson conducts a hunger strike for the ERA and becomes president of NOW.

For first time, more women than men enter college.

Membership in NOW reaches 100,000.

President Carter holds a White House Conference on Families; New Right groups organize to defend "the" family from any such pluralism.

1980 Republican party drops endorsement of ERA and makes a stronger, less qualified "pro-life" stance part of its electoral platform. Ronald Reagan is elected president of the U.S., begins dismantling EEOC and challenging enforcement of Women's Educational Equity Act (WEEA).

Family Protection Act introduced; this attempt to over-turn WEEA and bar teaching about women in "nontra-ditional roles" or achieving gender equity is ultimately defeated.

Supreme Court allows cutoff of all federal Medicaid funds for abortion.

United Nations Mid-Decade Congress on Women held in Copenhagen.

Women's Pentagon Action weaves a "web of life" in a demonstration against violence and militarism.

1981 A federal court recognizes sexual harassment in form of a "hostile work environment" as a form of prohibited sex discrimination.

Supreme Court rules that women can be excluded from military draft.

Congresswomen's Caucus admits men, changes name to Congressional Caucus on Women's Issues, and begins push for a range of bills to improve women's economic position, including a bill for family and med-ical leave.

Sandra Day O'Connor is first woman appointed to Supreme Court.

Human Life Amendment introduced in Congress, would constitutionally define a fetus as a person.

National Institute for Women of Color, National Black Women's Health Project, National Black Women's Political Caucus, Kitchen Table: Women of Color Press, and National Coalition of 100 Black Women are all founded.

1982 ERA deadline for ratification passes, Phyllis Schlafly celebrates the defeat of the amendment.

Scholar and Feminist Conference at Barnard touches off debate about feminist responses to pornography.

Wisconsin passes first state lesbian and gay rights bill.

First convention of Older Women's League.

National Council for Research on Women, a consor-tium of centers, is founded.

Decade 3 (1983–93): Defensive Consolidation

1983   Supreme Court reaffirms *Roe* v. *Wade,* striking down
         some state restrictions that limit women's access to
         abortion; President Reagan announces that a pro-life
         position will be a major criterion for his appointments
         to the Court. NARAL membership rises to 150,000
         (from 26,000 in 1977).

         Gang rape of woman in New Bedford raises awareness
         of violence against women and becomes an instance of
         media racism.

         NOW's membership reaches 250,000.

         Women's Peace Camp established in Seneca Falls,
         New York, echoing the Greenham Common peace
         protests by women in England.

1984   Violent attacks on abortion and family planning clinics
         escalate; twenty-nine bombs and fires set this year.

         Reagan administration ruling blocks all U.S. aid to clin-
         ics abroad that discuss abortion; anti-abortion activists
         release the film, *The Silent Scream.*

         Grove City decision by Supreme Court weakens Title
         IX protection against gender bias in education.

         Guerrilla Girls begin protests against museums that
         exclude women artists.

         Geraldine Ferraro receives the Democratic party nomi-
         nation for Vice-President of the United States. Sonia
         Johnson tours United States as presidential nominee of
         the Citizen's Party, a consciousness-raising gesture.

1985   Conservative Judaism accepts women rabbis.

         EMILY'S List founded to raise money for Democratic
         women candidates for public office.

         Yale University clerical workers win recognition and
         successfully strike for pay equity. Maintenance work-
         ers, mostly male, support them.

         United Nations End-of-Decade Conference held in
         Nairobi. Assessment of national accomplishments and
         goals, entitled *Forward-Looking Strategies for the Year
         2000,* was issued.

Council of Presidents of major women's organizations is established in Washington, D.C., to coordinate lobbying efforts. It begins push for a Civil Rights Restoration Act; in later years it develops an annual "Women's Agenda."

1986   In *Meritor* v. *Vinson* the Supreme Court rules sexual harassment an illegal form of sex discrimination under Title VII. At the EEOC, over seven thousand complaints of sexual harassment are pending.

Operation Rescue launched to blockade abortion clinics.

NOW organizes a pro-choice March on Washington that draws at least 100,000 demonstrators.

In Gallup Poll, 56 percent of all women say yes to the question "Do you consider yourself a feminist?"

Family and Medical Leave Act first introduced in Congress and Council of Presidents begins lobbying support.

1987   Fund for a Feminist Majority founded.

Coalition efforts block appointment of Robert Bork to the Supreme Court.

Assessment of the United States's Plan of Action in the UN Decade for Women is completed, not by federal government but by nongovernmental organization, the National Women's Conference Committee. By its count, there are now over one thousand two hundred shelters for battered women, over six hundred rape crisis centers, and over one thousand displaced women's groups or service programs in the United States.

In *Garland* v. *Cal. Fed.* the Supreme Court rules that the Pregnancy Discrimination Act sets "a floor, not a ceiling" on benefits for pregnancy and childbirth and does not demand that women be treated the same as men.

1988   Supreme Court upholds ban on sex discrimination in private clubs where business is conducted but stops short of banning all-male clubs.

Abortifacient drug RU486 begins to be marketed in France.

Parental consent law in Indiana leads teenager Becky Bell to get an illegal abortion instead. She dies.

1989   In *Webster* decision, Supreme Court upholds state-level restrictions on abortion rights, which opens the way for a wave of new restrictive legislation.

Post-*Webster,* Students Organizing Student (SOS) and Women's Health Action and Mobilization (WHAM!), reproductive rights organizations, are founded. NOW's membership grows by forty thousand (or 25 percent), NARAL also experiences growth spurt; about 400,000 pro-choice demonstrators march in Washington.

Fourteen women engineering students are shot to death in Montreal by an antifeminist fanatic.

Ms. magazine collapses financially but is reinvented as an advertising-free publication.

Forty-five states and over one thousand five hundred municipalities and counties have adopted some sort of pay equity program.

1990   NOW creates a committee to explore forming a third political party.

Ohio Governor Celeste grants clemency to twenty-six women who assaulted or killed their batterers.

Americans with Disabilities Act (ADA) is passed; *Act for Better Childcare (ABC)* also becomes law.

National Women's Studies Association nearly dissolves in internal conflict. Over six hundred women's programs now exist.

1991   In *Rust* v. *Sullivan,* Supreme Court allows Bush administration rule prohibiting clinics that accept federal funds from mentioning abortion to their clients.

In *Johnson Controls* decision, Supreme Court blocks the exclusion or mandatory sterilization of women in high-paying jobs that involve high-risk chemical exposures.

Anita Hill's testimony in Senate Judiciary Committee's confirmation hearing for Clarence Thomas raises the issue and awareness of sexual harassment. Thomas appointed to Supreme Court despite the controversy.

Women's Action Coalition (WAC) founded.

1992 Pre-election, more than 500,000 demonstrators march in Washington for pro-choice position, setting new record.

National elections show a sudden burst in female representation; the number of women in Senate jumps from two to six, including the first African-American woman, Carol Moseley Braun.

Bill Clinton elected president, rescinds "gag rule" on abortion counselling, supports Food and Drug approval of RU486, and attempts to lift ban on gays and lesbians in military.

State Farm Insurance settles sex discrimination suit for $200 million, the largest damage award under Civil Rights Act.

1993 Ruth Bader Ginsburg, former counsel for ACLU's Women's Rights Project, appointed to Supreme Court; Janet Reno becomes first woman Attorney General.

Dr. David Gunn, a Florida abortion provider, is shot to death by an antiabortion activist.

Zoë Baird confirmation hearing shows double standard for appointees regarding childcare arrangements; Lani Guinier confirmation hearing casts doubt on Clinton commitment to civil rights.

Family and Medical Leave Act becomes law, requiring major employers to grant workers unpaid leave for family needs.

Bibliography

ABC/Washington Post. 1992. Poll conducted 3–7 June and archived at Roper Center. Storrs, Conn: University of Connecticut.

About Women on Campus. 1993. Students protest against failure to handle rape issues. *National Association for Women in Education* 2 (spring):1.

Academe. 1991. "Average college faculty salary by sex and academic rank." (March–April), no. 2.

Acker, J. 1989. *Doing comparable worth: gender, class and pay equity.* Philadelphia: Temple University Press.

————. 1990. Hierarchies, jobs, bodies: A theory of gendered organizations. *Gender & Society* 4:139–58.

Adams, C., and K. Winston. 1980. *Mothers at work: Public policies in the U.S., China, and Sweden.* New York: Longman.

Adamson, N., L. Briskin, and M. McPhail. 1988. *Feminist organizing for change: The contemporary women's movement in Canada.* Toronto: Oxford University Press.

Adler, M. 1979. *Drawing down the moon.* Boston: Beacon Press.

Ahrens, L. 1980. Battered women's refuges: Feminist co-operatives or social service institutions? *Radical America* (May–June): 41–47.

Altbach, E. H., ed. 1971. *From feminism to liberation.* Cambridge, Mass.: Schenkman.

American Association of University Women. 1992. *How schools shortchange girls: The A.A.U.W. Report.* New York: AAUP Educational Foundation.

American Council on Life Insurance. 1981. *Map '81.* Washington, D.C.: ACLI.

The American Enterprise. 1991. What women think about the feminist label. (November/December):92–93.

Amott, T. L. 1993. *Caught in the crisis: Women and the U.S. economy today.* New York: Monthly Review Press.

Amott, T. L., and J. A. Matthaei. 1991. *Race, gender, and work: A multicultural history of women in the United States.* Boston, Mass.: South End Press.

Anderson, J. 1994. Separatism, feminism and the betrayal of reform. *Signs* 19, no. 2: 437–49.

Andors, P. 1982. Cuban women twenty years later. *Guardian: Independent Radical Newsweekly* 34, no. 36: 21.

Angier, N. 1991. Women swell ranks of science but remain invisible at top. *New York Times*, 21 May, C1.

Arms, S. 1975. *Immaculate deception: A new look at women and childbirth in America*. Boston: Houghton Mifflin.

Arnold, G. 1994. Organizational dilemmas of feminist coalitions. In *Feminist Organizations: Harvest of the new women's movement*, edited by M. M. Ferree and P. Y. Martin. Philadelphia: Temple University Press.

Associated Press. 1988. Poll conducted 29 April–8 May and archived at Roper Center. Storrs, Conn.: University of Connecticut.

Association of American Colleges. 1980. On campus with women. *Project on the Status of Education of Women* 28 (fall): 4.

———. 1982. On campus with women. *Project on the Status of Education of Women* 12, no. 1:5,9.

Auzaldua, G., and C. Moraga, eds. 1981. *This bridge called my back: Writings by radical women of color*. Watertown, Mass.: Persephone Press.

Baca Zinn, M. 1990. Family, feminism, and race in America. *Gender & Society* 4 (March): 68–82.

Banks, O. 1981. *Three faces of feminism*. New York: St. Martin's Press.

Barnett, B. M. 1994. Black women's collectivist organizations: Their struggles during the "doldrums." In *Feminist organizations: Harvest of the new women's movement*, edited by M. M. Ferree and P. Y. Martin. Philadelphia: Temple University Press.

Baron, J. N., and A. E. Newman. 1990. For what it's worth: Organizations, occupations, and the value of work done by women and nonwhites. *American Sociological Review* 55:155–75.

Baron, J. N., B. S. Mittman, and A. E. Newman. 1991. Targets of opportunity: Organizational and environmental determinants of gender integration within the California civil service, 1979–1985. *American Journal of Sociology* 96:1362–1401.

Barrett, N. 1979. Women in the job market. In *The subtle revolution*, edited by R. Smith. Washington, D.C.: Urban Institute.

Barrett, M., and A. Philips. 1992. *Destabilizing theory: Contemporary feminist debates*. Stanford: Stanford University Press.

Barry, K. 1979. *Female sexual slavery*. New York: Prentice-Hall.

Bart, P. 1970. Portnoy's mother's complaint. *Transaction* 8, no. 12:69–74.

Beam, C., and D. Paul. 1992. A question of access: Is abortion really still legal? *Sojourner* 18 (September): 17–18.

Beckwith, B. 1984. He-man, she-woman: *Playboy* and *Cosmo* groove on genes. *Columbia Journalism Review* (January–February): 46–47.

Bellah, R. et al. 1985. *Habits of the heart.* Berkeley, Calif.: University of California Press.

Bem, S., and D. Bem. 1970. Case study of a non-conscious ideology: Training the woman to know her place. In *Beliefs, attitudes and human affairs,* edited by D. Bem, 89–99. Belmont, Calif.: Brooks/Cole.

Benedict, H. 1992. *Virgin or vamp: How the press covers sex crimes.* New York: Oxford University Press.

Bennetts, L. 1980. How women took charge at the Democratic convention. *Ms.* (November): 58–66.

Benson, D. J., and G. Thomson. 1982. Sexual harassment on a university campus: The confluence of authority relations, sexual interest, and gender stratification. *Social Problems* 29, no. 3:236–51.

Berch, B. 1982. *The endless day: The political economy of women and work.* New York: Harcourt, Brace, Jovanovich.

Bergmann, Barbara. 1986. *The economic emergence of women.* New York: Basic Books.

Berke, R. L. 1991. Concerned about role, women's caucus meets. *New York Times,* 14 July, 12.

Berkin, C. R. 1979. Not separate, not equal. In *Women of America: A history,* edited by C. R. Berkin and M. B. Norton, 273–88. Boston: Houghton Mifflin.

Berman, P. 1991. *Debating P.C.: The controversy over political correctness on campus.* New York: Dell.

Berry, M. F. 1986. *Why ERA failed.* Bloomington: Indiana University Press.

Bers, T. H., and S. G. Mezey. 1981. Support for feminist goals among leaders of women's community groups. *Signs* 6:737–48.

Bessmer, S. 1982. Anti-obscenity: A comparison of the legal and feminist approaches. In *Women, power, and policy,* edited by E. Boneparth. Elmsford, N.Y.: Pergamon.

Better, N. M. 1991. Dressing for success? Try lifting and tucking. *New York Times,* 26 May, 23.

Bickel, J. 1991. Women in medical school. In *The American woman, 1990–1991,* edited by S. Rix, 212–30. New York: Norton.

Bielby, W., and J. Baron. 1987. Undoing discrimination: Job integration and comparable worth. In *Ingredients for women's employment policy,* edited by C. Bose and G. Spitze, 211–29. Albany: State University of New York Press.

Blanchard, M. 1992. Speaking the plural: The example of *Women a Journal of Liberation. NWSA Journal* 4, no. 1:84–97.

Blau, F. 1979. Women in the labor force: An overview. In *Women: A feminist perspective,* edited by J. Freeman, 265–89. Palo Alto, Calif.: Mayfield.

Bloom, A. 1987. *The closing of the American mind.* New York: Simon & Schuster.

Blum, L. 1991. *Between feminism and labor: The significance of the comparable worth movement*. Berkeley: University of California Press.

Blumberg, R. L. 1984. *Civil rights: The 1960's freedom struggle*. Boston: Twayne.

Bly, R. 1990. *Iron John*. Reading, Mass.: Addison-Wesley.

Boles, J. 1979. *The politics of the ERA: Conflict and the decision process*. New York: Longman.

———. 1991. Form follows function: the evolution of feminist strategies. *The Annals of the American Academy of Political and Social Science* (May):38–49.

Bolotin, S. 1982. Voices from the postfeminist generation. *New York Times Magazine*, 26 October, 29ff.

Bookman, A., and S. Morgen. 1988. *Women and the politics of empowerment*. Philadelphia: Temple University Press.

Boston Women's Health Collective. 1976. *Our bodies, ourselves*. New York: Simon and Schuster.

Bourque, L. B. 1989. *Defining Rape*. Durham, N.C.: Duke University Press.

Boyer, D., and D. Fine. 1992. Sexual abuse as a factor in adolescent pregnancy and child maltreatment. *Family Planning Perspectives* 24:4–11.

Bradley, H. 1989. *Men's work, women's work: A sociological history of the sexual division of labor in employment*. Minneapolis: University of Minnesota Press.

Breines, W. 1979. A review essay. *Feminist Studies* 5:496–506.

———. 1982. *Community and organization in the new left, 1962–68*. New York: Praeger.

Breines, W., M. Cerullo, and J. Stacey. 1978. Social biology, family studies, and the anti-feminist backlash. *Feminist Studies* 4:43–67.

Brenner, J., and B. Laslett. 1991. Gender, social reproduction, and women's self-organization: Considering the U.S. welfare state. *Gender & Society* 5:311–33.

Brill, A. 1991. Womb versus woman: Politics of accusation and protection. *Dissent* (summer):395–99.

Bronfenbrenner, U. 1958. Socialization and social class through time and space. In *Readings in social psychology*, edited by E. E. Maccoby, T. M. Newcomb, and E. H. Harley, 400–25. New York: Holt.

Broverman, I., D. Broverman, F. Clarkson, P. Rosenkrantz, and S. Vogel. 1970. Sex role stereotypes and clinical judgement of mental health. *Journal of Consulting and Clinical Psychology* 34:1–7.

Brown, C. S. 1986. *Ready from within: Septima Clark and the civil rights movement*. Navarro, Calif.: Wild Tree Press.

Brown, R. M. 1984. In defense of traditional values: The anti-feminist movement. In *Women and the family: Two decades of change*, edited by B. B. Hess and M. B. Sussman. *Marriage and Family Review* 7, no. 3/4 (fall/winter).

Browne, A., and K. Williams. 1993. Gender, intimacy and lethal violence: Trends from 1976 through 1987. *Gender & Society* 7, no. 1:78–98.

Brownmiller, S. 1975. *Against our will: Men, women, and rape.* New York: Simon and Schuster.

Brush, L. D. 1990. Violent acts and injurious outcomes in married couples. *Gender & Society* 4:56–67.

Buechler, S. M. 1990. *Women's movements in the United States: Woman suffrage, equal rights, and beyond.* New Brunswick, N.J.: Rutgers University Press.

Bunch, C. 1980. What not to expect from the UN's women's conference in Copenhagen. *Ms.* (July):80–83.

Bunch, C., and S. Pollack, eds. 1983. *Learning our way: Essays in feminist education.* Trumansburg, N.Y.: Crossing Press.

Bunch-Weeks, C. 1970. A broom of one's own: Notes on the women's liberation program. In *The new woman: An anthology of women's liberation,* edited by J. Cooke, C. Bunch-Weeks, and R. Morgan, 185–210. Greenwich, Conn.: Fawcett.

———. 1990. Recognizing women's rights as human rights. *Response to the Victimization of Women and Children* 13, no. 4:13–16.

Burgess, A. W., ed. 1985. *Rape and sexual assault: A research handbook.* New York: Garland.

Burkhauser, R., and K. Holden. 1980. *A challenge to Social Security: The changing roles of women and men in American society.* New York: Academic Press.

Burris, V. 1983. Who opposed the ERA? The social bases of anti-feminism. *Social Science Quarterly* 64, no. 2:305–17.

Burstow, B. 1992. *Radical feminist therapy: Working in the context of violence.* Newbury Park, Calif.: Sage.

Burton, J. K. 1987. Dilemmas of organizing women office workers. *Gender & Society* 1, no. 4:432–47.

Caballero, C., P. Giles, and P. Shaver. 1975. Sex role traditionalism and fear of success. *Sex Roles* 1, no. 4:319–26.

Cagatay, N., C. Grown, and A. Santiago. 1986. The Nairobi women's conference: Toward a global feminism. *Feminist Studies* 12, no. 2:401–12.

Cancian, F., and B. Ross. 1981. Mass media and the women's movement: 1900–1977. *Journal of Applied Behavioral Science,* 17:9–26.

Cantor, M., and J. Cantor. 1992. *Prime time television: Content and control.* Newbury Park, Calif.: Sage.

Carden, M. L. 1974. *The new feminist movement.* New York: Russell Sage.

———. 1978. The proliferation of a social movement: Ideology and individual incentives in the contemporary women's movement. In *Research in social movements: Conflict and change,* Vol. 1, edited by L. Kriesberg, 179–96. Greenwich, Conn.: JAI Press.

———. 1981. The evolution of movement activity: Causes and effects. Paper presented at the annual meeting of the American Sociological Association.

Carroll, J. W., B. Hargrove, and A. T. Lummis. 1983. *Women of the cloth: A new opportunity for the churches.* New York: Harper & Row.

Cassell, J. 1977. *A group called women: Sisterhood and symbolism in the feminist movement.* New York: McKay.

Chafe, W. 1972. *The American woman: Her changing social, economic and political roles, 1920–1970.* New York: Oxford University Press.

———. 1977. *Women and equality: Changing patterns in American culture.* New York: Oxford University Press.

———. 1991. *The paradox of change: American women in the twentieth century.* New York: Oxford University Press.

Chancer, L. 1987. New Bedford Massachusetts: March 6, 1983 to March 22, 1984: The before and after of a group rape. *Gender & Society 1*, no. 3:239–61.

Chapman, J. 1993. *Feminism, politics and the reconstruction of gender.* New York: Routledge.

Cherlin, A. 1982. The interrelationship of feminist values and demographic trends. Paper presented at the annual meeting of the Eastern Sociological Society.

Cherlin, A., and P. Walters. 1981. Trends in U.S. men's and women's sex role attitudes: 1972–78. *American Sociological Review* 46:453–60.

Chesler, P. 1972. *Women and Madness.* New York: Avon.

———. 1986. *Mothers on Trial.* New York: McGraw Hill.

Chodorow, N. 1978. *The reproduction of mothering: Psychoanalysis and the sociology of gender.* Berkeley: University of California Press.

Chow, E. N-L. 1987. The development of feminist consciousness among Asian American women. *Gender & Society* 1, no. 3:284–300.

Christiansen-Ruffman, L. 1994. Women's conceptions of the political. In *Feminist organizations: Harvest of the new women's movement,* edited by M. M. Ferree and P. Y. Martin. Philadelphia: Temple University Press.

Chronicle of Higher Education. 1993. *Almanac,* 23 August.

Clark, J. 1991. Getting there: Women in political office. *Annals of the American Academy of Political and Social Science* 516:63–76.

Clymer, A. 1984. Poll sees gain equalling loss if Democrats pick a woman. *New York Times,* 30 April.

Coleman, J. S. 1957. *Community conflict.* Glencoe: The Free Press.

Collins E. G., and T. B. Blodgett. 1981. Sexual harassment: Some see it, some won't. *Harvard Business Review* 2:76–95.

Collins, P. H. 1990. *Black feminist thought: Knowledge, consciousness, and the politics of empowerment.* Boston: Unwin Hyman.

Coltrane, S. 1989. Household labor and the routine of production of gender. *Social Problems* 36:473–90.

Coltrane, S., and N. Hickman. 1992. The rhetoric of rights and needs: Moral discourse in the reform of child custody and child support laws. *Social Problems* 39 no. 4:400–20.

Combs, M. W., and S. Welch. 1982. Blacks, whites, and attitudes toward abortion. *Public Opinion Quarterly* 46:510–20.

Condit, M. 1990. *Decoding abortion rhetoric.* Champaign-Urbana: University of Illinois Press.

Conover, P. J., and V. Gray. 1983. *Feminism and the New Right: Conflict over the American family.* New York: Praeger.

Cook, E. A. 1989. Measuring feminist consciousness. *Women & Politics* 9, no. 3:71–88.

Corcoran, M. and G. Duncan. 1983. Why do women earn less? *Institute for Social Research Newsletter.* Ann Arbor, Mich: ISR

Costain, A. 1981. Representing women: The transition from social movement to interest group. *Western Political Quarterly* 34:100–13.

———. 1982. Femininity v. feminism: The battle of the 80s. *Second Century Radcliffe News,* 9 January.

———. 1991. After Reagan: New party attitudes towards gender. *Annals of the American Academy of Political and Social Science* 515: 114–25.

———. 1992. *Inviting women's rebellion: A political process interpretation of the women's movement.* Baltimore: Johns Hopkins University Press.

Costain, A., and W. D. Costain. 1987. Strategy and tactics of the women's movement in the United States: The role of political parties. In *The women's movements of the United States and western Europe,* edited by M. F. Katzenstein and C. M. Mueller, 196–214. Philadelphia: Temple University Press.

Cott, N. 1987. *The grounding of modern feminism.* New Haven: Yale University Press.

Cottle, C. E., P. Searles, R. J. Berger, and B. A. Pierce. 1989. Conflicting ideologies and the politics of pornography. *Gender & Society* 3:303–33.

Cox, N. 1976. *Counter-planning from the kitchen: Wages for housework.* New York: New York Wages for Housework Committee.

Crabtree, J. 1980. The displaced homemaker: middle-aged, alone, broke. *Aging* (January–February):17–20.

Crawford, V., J. Rouse, and B. Woods. 1990. *Women in the civil rights movement: Trailblazers and torchbearers.* New York: Carlson Press.

Dabbs Jr., J. M. 1992. Testosterone and occupational achievement. *Social Forces* 70:813–24.

Dalla Costa, M. 1972. Women and the subversion of the community. *Radical America* 6, no. 1:67–102.

Daly, M. 1978. *Gyn/ecology: The metaethics of radical feminism.* Boston: Beacon Press.

Daniels, A. K. 1991. Careers in feminism. *Gender & Society* 5:583–607.

Bibliography

Davis, A. 1981. *Women, race, and class.* New York: Random House.

Davis, F. 1991. *Moving the mountain: The women's movement in America since 1960.* New York: Simon & Schuster.

Davis, J. A., and T. W. Smith. 1990. *General social surveys, 1972–1990.* NORC ed. Chicago: National Opinion Research Center. Storrs, Conn.: The Roper Center for Public Opinion Research, University of Connecticut, distributor.

Davis, J., and D. G. Taylor. 1977. Short-term trends in American society: The NORC General Social Survey, 1972–77. Paper presented at the annual meeting of the American Sociological Association.

Deaux, K., and J. Ullman. 1983. *Women of steel.* New York: Praeger.

de Beauvoir, S. 1953. *The second sex.* New York: Knopf.

DeWitt, K. 1991. The evolving concept of sexual harassment. *New York Times,* 13 October, 1ff.

Degler, C. 1980. *At odds: Women and the family in America from the revolution to the present.* New York: Oxford University Press.

Deitch, C. 1982. The New Right, feminism, and abortion: Patterns of public opinion: 1972–80. Paper presented at the annual meeting of the American Sociological Association.

Densmore, D. 1968. *On celibacy.* Boston: No More Fun and Games. Mimeo.

Diamond, I. 1980. Pornography and repression: A reconsideration. *Signs* 5, no. 4:686–701.

———. 1983. *Families, politics, and public policy: A feminist dialogue on women and the state.* New York: Longman.

Diamond, I., and G. Orenstein. 1990. *Reweaving the world: The emergence of ecofeminism.* San Francisco: Sierra Club Books.

Dill, B. T. 1983. Race, class and gender: Prospects for an all-inclusive sisterhood. *Feminist Studies* 9, no. 1:131–50.

Dinnerstein, D. 1976. *The mermaid and the minotaur.* New York: Harper and Row.

Dionne, E. J. 1989. Struggle for work and family fuels movement. *New York Times,* 22 August:1–2.

DiPrete, T. A., and D. B. Grusky. 1990. Structure and trend in the process of stratification for American men and women. *American Journal of Sociology* 96:107–43.

Dobash, R. P., R. E. Dobash, M. Wilson, and M. Daly. 1992. The myth of sexual symmetry in marital violence. *Social Problems* 39: 71–91.

Donnerstein, E. 1980. Aggressive erotica and violence against women. *Journal of Personality and Social Psychology* 39:269–77.

Downie, S., ed. 1988. *Decade of achievement: 1977–1987: A report of a survey based on the national plan of action for women.* Beaver Dam, Wis.: National Conference Committee.

D'Souza, D. 1991. *Illiberal education: The politics of race and sex on campus.* New York: The Free Press.

Duchen, C. 1986. *Feminism in France: From May '68 to Mitterand.* Boston: Routledge.

Dugger, K. 1988. Social location and gender role attitudes: A comparison of black and white women. *Gender & Society* 2, no. 4:425–34.

Dull, D., and C. West. 1991. Accounting for cosmetic surgery: The accomplishment of gender. *Social Problems* 38:54–70.

Dunbar, R. 1970. Female liberation as the basis of social revolution. In *Sisterhood is powerful*, edited by R. Morgan. New York: Random House.

Durand, D. B., and M. W. Segal. 1992. Policies on women in the military. Workshop presentation for midyear meeting of Sociologists for Women in Society.

Dworkin, A. 1974. *Woman Hating.* New York: Dutton.

———. 1978. Safety, shelter, rules, and love: The promise of the ultra-right. *Ms.* (June):62ff.

Dzeich, B. and L. Weiner 1984. *The lecherous professor.* Boston: Beacon Press.

Easton, B. 1979. Feminism and the contemporary family. In *A heritage of her own: Toward a new social history of American women*, edited by N. F. Cott and E. H. Pleck. New York: Simon & Schuster.

Echols, A. 1989. *Daring to be bad: Radical feminism in America, 1967–1975.* Minneapolis: University of Minnesota Press.

Ehrenreich, B. 1983. *The Hearts of men.* Garden City, N.Y.: Doubleday.

Ehrenreich, B., and D. English. 1978. *For her own good: 150 years of experts' advice to women.* New York: Doubleday.

Eisenstein, Z. 1979. *Capitalist patriarchy and the case for socialist feminism.* New York: Monthly Review Press.

———. 1990. Specifying U.S. feminism in the 1990's: The problem of naming. *Socialist Review* 20, no. 2 (April/June):45–56.

Elshtain, J. B. 1981. Mr. Right is dead. *The Nation*, 14 November, 496–97.

———. 1982. Feminism, family and community. *Dissent* (Fall) 442–49.

England, P. 1992. *Comparable worth: Theories and evidence.* New York: Aldine de Gruyter.

Erickson, P. I., and A. J. Rapkin. 1991. Unwanted sexual experiences among middle and high school youth. *Journal of Adolescent Health* 12:319.

Estrich, S. 1993. Rape. In *Feminist jurisprudence*, edited by P. Smith. New York: Oxford.

Evans, S. 1979. *Personal politics: The roots of women's liberation the civil rights movement and the new left.* New York: Vintage.

Evans, S., and B. J. Nelson. 1989. *Wage justice: Comparable worth and the paradox of technocratic reform.* Chicago: University of Chicago Press.

Faludi, S. 1991. *Backlash: The undeclared war against American women.* New York: Crown.

Farrell, A.. 1994. Like a tarantula on a banana boat: *Ms.* magazine 1972–1989. In *Feminist organizations: Harvest of the new women's movement,* edited by M. M. Ferree and P. Y. Martin, Philadelphia: Temple University Press.

Farrell, S. 1991. It's our church too: Women's position in the Catholic church today. In *The social construction of gender,* edited by J. Lorber and S. Farrell, 228–54. Newbury Park, Calif.: Sage.

Ferguson, K. 1984. *The feminist case against bureaucracy.* Philadelphia: Temple University Press.

Ferree, M. M. 1974. A woman for president? Changing responses, 1958–1972. *Public Opinion Quarterly* 38:390–99.

———. 1976. The emerging constituency: Feminism, employment and the working class. Ph.D. diss. Harvard University.

———. 1980. Working class feminism: A consideration of the consequences of employment. *Sociological Quarterly* 21:173–84.

———. 1983a. The women's movement in the working class. *Sex Roles* 9:493–505.

———. 1983b. Housework: Reconsidering the costs and benefits. In *Women, Families and Public Policy,* edited by I. Diamond. New York: Longman.

Ferree, M. M., and E. J. Hall. 1990. Visual images of American society: Gender and race in introductory sociology textbooks. *Gender & Society* 4, no. 4:500–33.

Ferree, M. M., and P. Y. Martin. 1994. *Feminist organizations: Harvest of the new women's movement.* Philadelphia: Temple University Press.

Ferree, M. M., and F. D. Miller. 1984. Mobilization and meaning: Some social psychological contributions to the resource mobilization perspective. *Sociological Inquiry* 55:38–61.

Fierman, J. 1990. Why women still don't hit the top. *Fortune,* 30 July, 40–62.

Firestone, S. 1970. *The dialectic of sex.* New York: Morrow.

Fitzgerald, L. F., S. Shulman, N. Bailey, M. Richards, J. Swecker, Y. Gold, M. Ormerond, and L. Weitzman. 1988. The incidence and dimensions of sexual harassment in academia and the workplace. *Journal of Vocational Behavior* 32:152–75.

Flacks, R. 1971. *Youth and social change.* Chicago: Markham.

Flexner, E. 1959. *Century of struggle: The women's rights movement in the United States.* Cambridge: Harvard University Press.

Fox-Genovese, E. 1980. The personal is not political enough. *Marxist Perspectives* (Winter):94–113.

———. 1991. *Feminism without illusions: A critique of individualism.* Chapel Hill, N.C.: University of North Carolina Press.

Fraser, N. 1990. Struggle over needs: Outline of a socialist feminist critical theory of late capitalist political culture. *In Women, the state, and welfare,* edited by L. Gordon. Madison: University of Wisconsin Press.

Freedman, E. 1979. Separatism as strategy: Female institution building and American feminism. *Feminist Studies* 5:512–29.

Freeman, J. 1973. The origins of the women's liberation movement. *American Journal of Sociology* 78 (January):792–811.

———. 1975. *The politics of women's liberation.* New York: David McKay.

——— [Joreen, pseud.]. 1976a. Trashing: the dark side of feminism. *Ms.* (April):49ff.

———. 1976b. Something did happen at the Democratic national convention. *Ms.* (October):74ff.

———. 1987. Whom you know versus whom you represent: Feminist influence in the Democratic and Republican parties. In *The women's movements of the United States and western Europe*, edited by M. F. Katzenstein and C. McC. Mueller, 215–44. Philadelphia: Temple University Press.

———. 1993. Feminism vs. Family Values: Women at the 1992 Democratic and Republican Conventions. *PS* 26 (March):21–28.

Fried, M. G., ed. 1990. *From abortion to reproductive freedom: Transforming a movement.* Boston: South End Press.

Friedan, B. 1963. *The feminine mystique.* New York: Dell.

———. 1981. *The second stage.* New York: Summit.

Friere, P. 1970. *Pedagogy of the oppressed.* New York: Herder and Herder.

Fritz, L. 1979. *Dreamers and dealers: An intimate appraisal of the women's movement.* Boston: Beacon Press.

Fruchter, R., N. Fatt, P. Booth, and D. Seidel. 1977. The women's health movement: Where are we now? In *Seizing our bodies*, edited by C. Dreifus, 271–87. New York: Random House.

Gabin, N. 1982. They have placed a penalty on womankind: The protest actions of women auto workers in Detroit area UAW locals, 1945–47. *Feminist Studies* 8:372–98.

———. 1990. *Feminism in the labor movement: Women and the United Auto Workers, 1935–1975.* Ithaca, N.Y.: Cornell University Press.

Gallup Organization. 1986. Report of poll conducted for *Newsweek*, 5-11 February. Storrs, Conn.: The Roper Center, University of Connecticut.

Gallup Organization. 1987. The people, the press and politics. Report of poll conducted 25 April–10 May and archived at the Roper Center. Storrs, Conn.: University of Connecticut.

Gallup Organization. 1991. Report of poll conducted 14 October for CNN and archived at the Roper Center. Storrs, Conn.: University of Connecticut.

Gallup Organization. 1992. Report of poll conducted 1–3 October for CNN and archived at the Roper Center. Storrs, Conn.: University of Connecticut.

Game, A. 1991. *Undoing the social: Toward a deconstructive sociology.* Toronto, Canada: University of Toronto Press.

Gamson, W. 1968. *Power and discontent.* Homewood, Ill.: Dorsey.

———. 1975. *The strategy of social protest.* Homewood, Ill.: Dorsey.

———. 1992. The social psychology of collective action. In *Frontiers of social movement theory*, edited by A. Morris and C. Mueller, 53–76. New Haven: Yale University Press.

Garcia, A. 1989. The development of Chicana feminist discourse, 1970–1980. *Gender & Society 3*, no. 2:217–39.

Gaventa, J. 1980. *Power and powerless: Quiescence and rebellion in an Appalacian valley.* Urbana: University of Illinois.

Gearhart, S. 1979. *The wanderground.* Watertown, Mass.: Persephone Press.

Gelb, J. 1989. Feminism and politics: A comparative perspective. Berkeley: University of California Press.

Gelb, J., and M. Palley. 1982. *Women and public policies.* Princeton: Princeton University Press.

———. 1987. *Women and public policies.* (2nd ed.). Princeton: Princeton University Press.

General Social Survey. 1991. Report of poll archived at the Roper Center. Storrs, Conn.: University of Connecticut.

Gerlach, L., and V. Hine. 1970. *People, power and change.* Indianapolis: Bobbs-Merrill.

Gibbs, N. 1991. When is it rape? *Time*, 3 June, 48–55.

———. 1992. The war against feminism. *Time*, 9 March, 50–55.

Giddings, P. 1984. *When and where I enter: The impact of black women on race and sex in America.* New York: William Morrow.

Giele, J. Z. 1995. *Two paths to women's equality: Temperance, suffrage, and the origins of modern feminism.* New York: Twayne Publishers.

Gilder, G. 1973. *Sexual suicide.* New York: Time.

———. 1980. *Wealth and poverty.* New York: Basic Books.

Gilligan, C. 1982. *In a different voice.* Cambridge: Harvard University Press.

Ginsburg, F. 1989. *Contested lives.* Berkeley: University of California Press.

Gittell, M., and N. Naples. 1982. Activist women: Conflicting ideologies. *Social Policy* (summer):25–27.

Glass, J. 1990. The impact of occupational segregation on working conditions. *Social Forces* 68:779–96.

Glazer, N. 1982. The invisible intersection: Involuntary unpaid labor outside the home and women's work. Paper presented at the annual meeting of the Eastern Sociological Society.

———. 1990. The home as workshop: Women as amateur nurses and medical care providers. *Gender & Society* 4:479–99.

Glenn, E. N. 1992. From servitude to service work: Historical continuities in the racial division of paid reproductive labor. *Signs 18*, no. 1:1–43.

Goldberg, R. 1983. *Organizing women workers: Dissatisfaction, consciousness, and action.* New York: Praeger.

Goldberg-Ambrose, C. 1992. Unfinished business in rape law reform. *Journal of Social Issues* 48:173–86.

Goldin, C. 1990. *Understanding the gender gap: An economic history of American women.* New York: Oxford University Press.

Goleman, D. L. 1991. Do arrests increase the rates of repeated domestic violence? *New York Times,* 11 November, C8.

Gordon, L., ed. 1989. *Women, the state, and welfare.* Madison: University of Wisconsin Press.

Gordon, N. 1979. Institutional responses: The Social Security system. In *The subtle revolution,* edited by R. Smith, 223–56. Washington, D.C.: The Urban Institute.

Gordon, S. 1991. *Prisoners of men's dreams: Striking out for a new feminine future.* Boston: Little Brown.

Gornick, V., and B. Moran, eds. 1971. *Women in sexist society.* New York: Basic Books.

Graham, P. A. 1978. Expansion and exclusion: A history of women in American higher education. *Signs* 3:759–73.

Granovetter, M. 1973. The strength of weak ties. *American Journal of Sociology* 78:1360–80.

Grant, L., and K. B. Ward. 1991. Gender and publishing in sociology. *Gender & Society* 5:207–23.

Grauerholz, E. 1990. Sexual harassment in the academy: The experiences of faculty women. Department of Sociology, Purdue University, manuscript.

Greenberg, M. L. 1990. Another American tragedy: The death of Becky Bell. *On the Issues 27* (winter):10–13ff.

Greer, G. 1970. *The female eunuch.* New York: McGraw-Hill.

Grier, W., and P. M. Cobbs. 1968. *Black rage.* New York: Basic Books.

Griffin, S. 1971. Rape: The all-American crime. *Ramparts* 10:26–35.

———. 1979. *Women and nature: The roaring inside her.* New York: Harper and Row.

Grimstad, K., and S. Rennie, eds. 1975. *The new woman's survival sourcebook.* New York: Knopf.

Gross, A., R. Smith, and B. Wallston. 1983. The men's movement: Personal vs. political. In *Social movements of the sixties and seventies,* edited by J. Freeman, 71–81. New York: Longman.

Gurin, P. 1982. Group consciousness. *ISR Newsletter* (Institute for Social Research, University of Michigan), spring–summer, 4–5.

———. 1985. Women's gender consciousness. *Public Opinion Quarterly* 49 (summer):143–63.

Gutek, B., and B. Morash. 1982. Sex-ratios, sex role spillover and sexual harassment of women at work. *Journal of Social Issues* 38, no. 4:55–74.

Hacker, H. 1951. Women as a minority group. *Social Forces* 30 (October):60–69.

Haddad, R. 1979. The men's liberation movement: A perspective. Columbia, Md.: Free Men.

Hagan, J. 1990. The gender stratification of income inequality among lawyers. *Social Forces* 68:835–55.

Haignere, L. 1981. Admission of women to medical schools: A study of organizational response to social movement and public policy pressures. Ph.D. diss., University of Connecticut, Storrs.

Hall, E. J., and M. M. Ferree. 1986. Race differences in abortion attitudes. *Public Opinion Quarterly* 50, no. 2 (summer):193–207.

Hall, J. D. 1983. The mind that burns in each body: Women, rape, and racial violence. In *The powers of desire*, edited by A. Snitow, C. Stansell, and S. Thompson. New York: Monthly Review Press.

———. 1986. Women's history goes to trial: *EEOC* v. *Sears Roebuck and Company. Signs* 11, no. 4:751–52.

Hamilton, R. F., and L. L. Hargens. 1993. The politics of professors: Self-identifications, 1969–1984. *Social Forces* 71:603–28.

Harding, S. 1981. Family reform movements; Recent feminism and its opposition. *Feminist Studies* 7:57–75.

———. 1991. *Whose science? Whose knowledge?* New York: Cornell University Press.

Harlow, C. W. 1991. *Female victims of violent crime.* U.S. Bureau of Justice Statistics, NJC-126826: January.

Harris L., and Associates. 1991. A *survey of public attitudes toward Planned Parenthood and the Supreme Court decision in* Rust *v.* Sullivan. New York: Louis Harris and Associates, Inc.

Harrison, C. 1988. *On account of sex: The politics of women's issues, 1945–1968.* Berkeley: University of California Press.

Hawk, M. N. 1992. The treatment of chemically dependent mothers. Paper presented at the Conference on Social Change in Feminist Directions, midyear meeting of Sociologists for Women in Society.

Hayden, C., and M. King. 1966. A kind of memo. *Liberation* 11:35–36.

Heilbrun, C. 1988. *Writing a woman's life. N*ew York: Norton.

Henshaw, S. K. 1991. The accessibility of abortion services in the United States. *Family Planning Perspectives* 23:246–52.

Hess, B. 1983a. New Faces of Poverty. *American Demographics* (May):26–31.

———. 1983b. Protecting the American family: Public policy and the New Right. In *Families and change: Social needs and public policy*, edited by R. G. Genovese. South Hadley, Mass.: J. F. Bergin.

Hewitt, E., and S. Hiatt. 1973. *Women priests: Yes or no.* New York: Seabury.

Hewlett, S. A. 1986. *A lesser life: The myth of women's liberation in America.* New York: Warner.

Heywoode, T. 1977. Working class feminism. Paper presented at the annual meeting of the Society for the Study of Social Problems.

Himmelstein, J. L. 1984. The new right. In *The new Christian right*, edited by R. C. Liebman and R. Wuthnow. Hawthorne, N.Y.: Aldine.

———. 1990. *To the right: The transformation of American conservatism.* Berkeley: University of California Press.

Hoban, P. 1992. Big WAC Attack. *New York*, 3 August, 30–35.

Hochschild, A., with A. Machung. 1989. *The second shift: Working parents and the revolution at home.* New York: Viking.

Hole, J., and E. Levine, 1971. Rebirth of feminism. New York: Quadrangle.

Holm, J. 1982. *Women in the military: An unfinished revolution.* Ignacio, Calif.: Presidio Press.

hooks, b. 1981. *Ain't I a woman: Black women and feminism.* Boston: South End Press.

———. 1984. *Feminist theory from margin to center.* Boston: South End Press.

———. 1989. *Talking back: Thinking feminist, thinking black.* Boston: South End Press.

———. 1990. *Yearning: Race, gender and cultural politics.* Boston: South End Press.

Horner, M. 1969. Why bright women fail. *Psychology Today* 36, no. 6:36ff.

Howe, F., and C. Ahlum. 1973. Women's studies and social change. In *Academic women on the move*, edited by A. Rossi and A. Calderwood. New York: Russell Sage.

Huber, J. 1976. Toward a sociotechnological theory of the women's movement. *Social Problems* 23:371–88.

Hull, G., P. Scott, and B. Smith. 1982. *All the women are white, all the blacks are men, but some of us are brave: Black women's studies.* Old Westbury, N.Y.: The Feminist Press.

Hunt, J. G., and L. L. Hunt. 1982. The dualities of careers and families. *Social Problems* 29:499–510.

Hyde, C. 1994. Feminist social movement organizations survive the new right. *In Feminist organizations: Harvest of the new women's movement*, edited by M. M. Ferree and P. Y. Martin. Philadelphia: Temple University Press.

Inglehardt, R. 1977. *The silent revolution: Changing values and political styles among western publics.* Princeton, N.J.: Princeton University Press.

Jacobs, J. A. 1989. *Revolving doors: Sex segregation and women's careers.* Stanford, Calif.: Stanford University Press.

Jacobs, J. A., and R. J. Steinberg. 1990. Compensating differentials and the male-female wage gap: Evidence from the New York State comparable wage study. *Social Forces* 69:439–68.

Jacobs, R. H. 1991. *Expanding social roles for older women.* Southport Institute for Policy Analysis, Southport, Conn.

Jacobson, M., and W. Koch. 1978. Attributed reasons for support of the feminist movement as a function of attractiveness. *Sex Roles* 4:169–74.

Jaffe, F., B. Lindheim, and P. R. Lee. 1981. *Abortion politics: Private morality and public policy*. New York: McGraw-Hill.

Jaffee, D. 1989. Gender inequality in workplace autonomy and authority. *Social Science Quarterly* 70:375–90.

Jaquette, J. 1989. *The women's movement in Latin America: Feminism and the transition to democracy*. Boston: Unwin Hyman.

Jayawardena, K. 1986. *Feminism and nationalism in the Third World*. Atlantic Highlands, N.J.: Zed Books.

Jeffords, S. 1989. *The remasculinization of America: Gender and the Vietnam war*. Bloomington: Indiana University Press.

Jensen, I., and B. Gutek. 1982. Attributions and assignment of responsibility for sexual harassment. *Journal of Social Issues* 38, no. 4:121–36.

Johnson, J. 1981. Program enterprise and official co-optation in the battered women's shelter movement. *American Behavioral Scientist* 24:827–42.

Johnson, L. 1982. Weaving a web of life: Women's Pentagon Action, 1981. *Win* 18, no. 2:16–20.

Johnson, M., 1980. Women and elective office. *Society* 17, no. 4:63–69.

Johnston, D. 1992. Survey shows number of rapes far higher than official figures. *New York Times*, 24 April.

Jones, K., and P. A. Roos. 1991. The feminization of sociology. Paper presented at the annual meeting of the American Sociological Association.

Joseph, G., and J. Lewis. 1981. *Common differences: Conflicts in black and white feminist perspectives*. Garden City, N.Y.: Doubleday.

Kahn, K. F., and E. N. Goldenberg. 1991. The media: Obstacle or ally of feminists? *Annals of the American Academy of Political and Social Science* (May):104–13.

Kamen, P. 1990. Feminism, a dirty word. *New York Times*, 23 November, A37.

———. 1991. *Feminist fatale*. New York: Donald Fine.

Kaminer, W. 1990. *A fearful freedom: Women's flight from equality*. Reading, Mass.: Addison-Wesley.

———. 1991. On the devaluation of rights: A critique within feminism. *Dissent* 38:388–94.

Kanter, R. M. 1977. *Men and women of the corporation*. New York: Basic Books.

Katzenstein, M. F. 1990. Feminism within American institutions: Unobtrusive mobilization in the 1980's. *Signs* 16, no. 1:27–54.

———. 1994. Discursive politics and feminist activism in the Catholic Church. In *Feminist organizations: Harvest of the new women's movement*, edited by M. M. Ferree and P. Y. Martin. Philadelphia: Temple University Press.

Katzenstein, M. F., and C. M. Mueller, eds. 1987. *Women's movements of the United States and Western Europe: Consciousness, political opportunity and public policy*. Philadelphia: Temple University Press.

Katzman, D. M. 1978. *Seven days a week: Women and domestic service in industrializing America.* New York: Oxford University Press.

Kelly, L. 1988. *Surviving sexual violence.* Minneapolis: University of Minnesota Press.

Kessler-Harris, A. 1976. Women, work and the social order. In *Liberating women's history,* edited by B. A. Carroll. Urbana, Ill.: University of Illinois Press.

———. 1990. *A woman's wage: Historical meanings and social consequences.* Lexington, Ky.: University of Kentucky Press.

Killian, L. 1972. The significance of extremism in the black revolution. *Social Problems* 20:41–49.

Kimmel, M., ed. 1987. *Changing men: New directions in research on men and masculinities.* Newbury Park, Calif.: Sage.

———. 1992. *Against the tide: "Profeminist" men in the United States, 1776–1990,* a documentary history. Boston, Mass.: Beacon Press.

King, Y. 1988. The ecology of feminism and the feminism of ecology. Communities 75:32–38.

Klandermans, B., and D. Oegema. 1987. Potentials, networks, motivations and barriers. *American Sociological Review* 52:519–31.

Klatch, R. E. 1986. The new right and its women. *Society* (March/April):30–38.

Klotzberger, N. 1973. Political action by academic women. In *Academic women on the move,* edited by A. Rossi and A. Calderwood. New York: Russell Sage.

Kluegel, J., and E. Smith. 1982. Whites' beliefs about blacks' opportunities. *American Sociological Review* 47, no. 4:518–31.

Knoke, D. 1990. The mobilization of members in women's associations. In *Women, politics and change,* edited by L. Tilly and P. Gurin. New York: Russell Sage.

Koedt, A. 1970. The myth of the vaginal orgasm. In *Notes from the second year,* edited by S. Firestone and A. Koedt. New York: New York Radical Feminists.

Kolbert, E. 1991. Sexual harassment at work is pervasive, survey suggests. *New York Times,* 11 October, 1ff.

Komarovsky, M. 1962. *Blue collar marriage.* New York: Random House.

Koss, M. P. 1988. Hidden rape: Sexual aggression and victimization in a national sample of students in higher education. In *Rape and sexual assault. vol. 2,* edited by A. W. Burgess. New York: Garland.

———. 1992. The underdetection of rape: Methodological choices influence incidence estimates. *Journal of Social Issues* 48:61–76.

Koss, M. P., and M. R. Harvey. 1991. *The rape victim: Clinical and community interventions.* Newbury Park, Calif.: Sage.

Koziara, K. S., and P. J. Insley. 1982. Organizations of working women can pave the way for unions. *Monthly Labor Review* (June): 53–55.

Kramer, J. 1970. The founding cadre. *New Yorker*, 28 November, 52–140.

Kurz, D. 1989. Social science perspectives on wife abuse: Current debates and future directions. *Gender & Society* 3:489–505.

L'Hommedieu, E. 1991. Walking out on the boys: Interview with Dr. Francis Conley. *Time*, 8 July, 52–53.

Langer, E. 1973. Notes for the next time: A memoir of the 1960s. *Working Papers*, Fall, 48–83.

———. 1976. Why big business is trying to defeat the ERA: The economic implications of inequality. *Ms.* (May):64ff.

Lasch, C. 1977. *Haven in a heartless world: The family besieged.* New York: Basic Books.

Laws, J. L. 1975. The psychology of tokenism: An analysis. *Sex Roles* 1, no. 1:51–67.

Lederer, L., 1980. *Take back the night.* New York: William Morrow.

Lee, G. M. 1971. One in sisterhood. In *Asian Women*, Editorial Staff, 119–21. Berkeley, Calif.: University of California Press.

LeGrande, L. 1978. Women in labor organizations: Their ranks are increasing. *Monthly Labor Review* (August):8–14.

Leidner, R. 1993. Constituency, accountability, and deliberation: Reshaping democracy in the National Women's Studies Association. *NWSA Journal* 5, no. 1:4.

Lemert, C. 1991. The end of ideology, really. *Sociological Theory* 9:164–72.

Leon, C. B. 1982. Occupational winners and losers, 1972–80. *Monthly Labor Review* (June):18–28.

Lewin, T. 1992. Hurdles increase for many women seeking abortions. *New York Times*, 15 March, 1ff.

Lewis, D. 1977. A response to inequality? Black women, racism and sexism. *Signs* 3:339–61.

Liebman, R. C., and R. Wuthnow, eds. 1983. *The new Christian right.* Hawthorne, N.Y.: Aldine.

Lindsey, K. 1980. Women's commissions in exile. *Ms.* (February): 23–25.

Livingston, J. 1982. Responses to sexual harassment on the job. *Journal of Social Issues* 38, no. 4:5–22.

Lopate, C. 1974. Pay for housework? *Social Policy 5* (September–October):27–31.

Lorber, J. 1989. Mothers or MDs? Women physicians and the doctor patient relationship. *In Feminist Frontiers II*, edited by L. Richardson and V. Taylor. New York: Random House.

Lord, L. 1982. Pornography and militarism. Women against Violence in Pornography and Media Newspage 6, no. 10:1–3.

Lorence, J. 1991. Growth in service sector employment and MSA gender earnings inequality: 1970–1980. *Social Forces* 69:763–83.

Lowell, L. 1980. Abortion: A question of survival. *Win*, 1 August, 15–28.

Luker, K. 1984. *Abortion and the politics of motherhood.* Berkeley: University of California Press.

Lundberg, F., and M. F. Farnham. 1947. *Modern woman: The lost sex.* New York: Universal Library.

Lunneborg, P. 1990. *Women changing work.* New York: Bergin & Garvey.

Luttrell, W. 1984. Beyond the politics of victimization. *Socialist Review* 14, no. 1:42–47.

McAdam, D. 1988. *Freedom summer.* New York: Oxford University Press.

McAllister, P. 1982. *Reweaving the web of life: Feminism and nonviolence.* Philadelphia: New Society Publishers.

McCarthy, J. D., and M. Zald. 1977. Resource mobilization and social movements: A partial theory. *American Journal of Sociology* 82 (May):1212–41.

McGuire, M. 1982. Feminist strike in San Jose. *Win* 18, no. 9:4–7.

Machung, A. 1989. Talking career, thinking job: Gender differences in career and family expectations of Berkeley seniors. *Feminist Studies* 15, no. 1 (spring):35–58.

McIntosh, M., A. Wong, N. Cagatay, U. Funk, H. Safa, L. Ahmed, D. Izraeli, K. Ahooja-Patel, and C. Bunch. 1981. Comments on Tinker's "A feminist view of Copenhagen." *Signs* 6, no. 4:771–89.

MacKinnon, C. 1987. *Feminism unmodified: Discourses on life and law.* Cambridge: Harvard University Press.

MacKinnon, C. 1993. Sexual harassment: Its first decade in court. In *Feminist Jurisprudence*, edited by P. Smith. New York: Oxford.

Maitland, S. 1982. *A map of the new country: Women and Christianity.* New York: Routledge.

Malamuth, N. M., R. J. Sockloski, M. P. Koss, and J. S. Tanaka. 1991. Characteristics of aggressors against women: Testing a model using a national sample of college students. *Journal of Consulting and Clinical Psychology* 59:670–81.

Malamuth, N., and M. P. Koss. 1991. Unpublished study funded by National Institute of Mental Health. Quoted in D. Goleman, New studies map the mind of the rapist. *New York Times*, 10 December, C1ff.

Malos, E. 1978. Housework and the politics of women's liberation. *Socialist Revolution* 37:41–72.

———. 1980. *The politics of housework.* London: Allison & Busby.

Manegold, C. 1992. No more nice girls: In angry droves, radical feminists just want to have impact. *New York Times*, 12 July.

Mansbridge, J. 1986. *Why we lost the ERA.* Chicago: University of Chicago Press.

Marano, C. 1980. Displaced homemakers: Critical needs and trends. Paper presented at Agricultural Outlook Conference, U.S. Department of Agriculture, Washington, D. C.

Margolis, Diane Rothbard. 1993. Women's movements around the world: Cross-cultural comparisons. *Gender & Society* 7, no. 3:379–99.

Marshall, S. E. 1991. Who speaks for American women?: The future of antifeminism. *Annals of the American Academy of Political and Social Science* 514:50–62.

———. 1994. Confrontation and cooptation in anti-feminist organizations. In *Feminist organizations: Harvest of the new women's movement*, edited by M. M. Ferree and P. Y. Martin. Philadelphia: Temple University Press.

Martin, D. 1976. *Battered wives*. San Francisco: Glide.

Martin, P. Y. 1990. Rethinking feminist organizations. *Gender & Society* 4:182–206.

———. 1993. Rape crisis centers, feminism and the politics of rape processing in the community. Paper presented at the annual meeting of the American Sociological Association.

Martin, S. E. 1980. Breaking and entering: Policewomen on patrol. Berkeley: University of California Press.

———. 1989. Sexual harassment: The link joining gender stratification, sexuality and women's status. In *Women: A feminist perspective*, 3d ed., edited by Jo Freeman. Palo Alto, Calif.: Mayfield.

Mason, K. O., and L. L. Bumpass. 1975. U.S. women's sex role ideology, 1970. *American Sociological Review* 40:1212–19.

Mason, K. O., J. Czajka, and S. Arber. 1976. Change in U.S. sex role attitudes, 1964–74. *American Sociological Review* 41:537–96.

Mason, K. O. and Y-H. Lu. 1988. Attitudes toward women's familial roles: Changes in the U.S., 1977–1985. *Gender & Society* 2, no. 1 (March):39–57.

Mathews, D. G., and J. S. DeHart. 1990. *Sex, gender, and the politics of ERA: A state and the nation.* New York: Oxford University Press.

Matthews, N. 1989. Surmounting a legacy: The expansion of diversity in a local anti-rape movement. *Gender & Society* 3:519–33.

———. 1994. Feminist clashes with the state: The case of state-funded rape crisis centers. In *Feminist organizations: Harvest of the new women's movement*, edited by M. M. Ferree and P. Y. Martin. Philadelphia: Temple University Press.

Maxwell, S., and P. Y. Martin. 1992. Rape crisis centers and mainstream organizations: Circumstances, discourse, and practice. Paper presented at Feminist Organizations Conference.

McNamee, S. J., C. L. Willis, and A. M. Rochford. 1990. Gender differences in patterns of publications in leading sociology journals, 1960–1985. *The American Sociologist* (summer):99–115.

Mead, M. 1935. *Sex and temperament in three savage societies.* New York: William Morrow; New York: Dell, 1963.

Mellow, G. O. 1989. Sustaining our organizations: Feminist health activism in an age of technology. In *Healing technology: Feminist perspectives,* edited by K. S. Ratcliff, et al. Ann Arbor: University of Michigan Press.

Melucci, A. 1989. *Nomads of the present: Social movements and individual needs in contemporary society,* edited by J. Keane and P. Mier. Philadelphia: Temple University Press.

Meyer, M. H. 1990. Family status and poverty among older women: The gendered distribution of retirement income in the United States. *Social Problems* 37:551–63.

Mies, M., and K. Jayawardena. 1981. *Feminism in Europe.* The Hague: Institute of Social Studies.

Miller, F. 1983. The end of SDS and the emergence of Weathermen: Demise through success. In *Social movements of the sixties and seventies,* edited by Jo Freeman, 279–300. New York: Longman.

Millett, K. 1970. *Sexual politics.* Garden City, N.Y.: Doubleday.

Milkman, R. 1979. Women's work and economic crises. In *A heritage of her own,* edited by N. F. Cott and E. H. Pleck. New York: Simon & Schuster.

———. 1982. Redefining "women's work": The sexual division of labor in the auto industry during World War II. *Feminist Studies* 8:336–71.

Mohanty, C., A. Russo, and L. Torres. 1991. *Third world women and the politics of feminism.* Bloomington: University of Indiana Press.

Molm, L. 1978. Sex role attitudes and the employment of married women: The direction of causality. *Sociological Quarterly* 19, no. 4:522–33.

Morgan, M. 1973. *The total woman.* New York: Pocket Books.

Morgan, R. 1973. Lesbianism and feminism: Synonyms or contradictions. Originally published in *The lesbian tide;* reprinted in Morgan, *Going too far.*

———. 1980. *Going too far.* New York: Random House.

———. 1982. *The anatomy of freedom.* New York: Doubleday.

Morgan, R., ed. 1970. *Sisterhood is powerful: An anthology of writings from the women's liberation movement.* New York: Vintage.

Morgen, S. 1986. The dynamics of cooptation in a feminist health clinic. *Social Science and Medicine* 23 no. 2:201–10.

———. 1994. It was the best of times, it was the worst of times: Emotional discourse in the work cultures of feminist health clinics. In *Feminist organizations: Harvest of the new women's movement,* edited by M. M. Ferree and P. Y. Martin. Philadelphia: Temple University Press.

Morris, A. 1984. *The origins of the civil rights movement: Black communities organizing for change.* New York: The Free Press.

Morris, M. 1973. Newspapers and the new feminists: Blackout as social control. *Journalism Quarterly* 50:37–42.

Morrison, T. 1992. *Race-ing justice, en-gender-ing power.* New York: Pantheon.

Moskos, C. 1990. Army women. *Atlantic Monthly* (August):71–79.

Mottl, T. 1978. The analysis of countermovements. *Social Problems* 27:620–35.

Moynihan, D. P. 1965. *The Negro family: The case for national action.* Washington, D.C.: U.S. Government Printing Office.

Ms. 1982. (July/August):265.

Mueller, C. 1980. Feminism and the new woman in public office. Paper presented at the annual meeting of the Eastern Sociological Society.

———. 1983a. In search of a constituency for the new religious right. *Public Opinion Quarterly* 47, no. 2:213–28.

———. 1983b. Women's movement success and the success of social movement theory. Paper presented at the conference on the Women's Movement in Comparative Perspective, Cornell University.

———. 1988. The empowerment of women: Polling and the women's voting bloc. In *The politics of the gender gap,* edited by C. Mueller, 16–36. Newbury Park, Calif.: Sage.

———. 1990. Ella Baker and the origins of participatory democracy. In *Women in the civil rights movement: Trailblazers and torchbearers,* edited by V. Crawford, J. Rouse and B. Woods. New York: Carlson Press.

———. 1992. Building social movement theory. In *Frontiers of social movement theory,* edited by A. Morris and C. Mueller, 3–25. New Haven: Yale University Press.

Mueller, C., and T. Dimieri. 1982. The structure of belief systems among contending ERA activists. *Social Forces* 60:657–75.

Murphy, J. 1989. Should pregnancies be sustained in brain-dead women? A philosophical discussion of postmortem pregnancy. In *Healing technology: Feminist perspective,* edited by K. S. Ratcliff, et al. Ann Arbor: University of Michigan Press.

Myrdal, G. 1944. *An American dilemma.* New York: Harper and Row.

National Abortion Federation. 1992. *Incidents of violence and disruption against abortion providers.* Mimeo.

National Coalition against Domestic Violence. 1991. Letter to members. Washington, D.C.

National Committee on Pay Equity. 1992. *Newsnotes.* Washington, D.C.: NCPE.

National Opinion Research Center. 1991. *Family Planning Perspectives* 23, no. 4:148.

National Victim Center. 1992. *National women's study.* Washington, D.C.

Nazzari, M. 1983. The woman question in Cuba: Some structural constraints on its solution. *Signs* 9, no. 2:246–63.

NEA 1993 Almanac of Higher Education. Washington, D.C.: National Educational Association, 1993.

Nelson, B., and N. Chowdraty. 1993. *Women and politics worldwide.* New Haven: Yale University Press.

Ng, R. 1988. *The politics of community services: Immigrant women, class and state.* Toronto: Garamond.

O'Brien, D. J. 1975. *Neighborhood organizations and interest groups.* Princeton, N.J.: Princeton University Press.

Ochs, C. 1977. *Behind the sex of God.* Boston: Beacon Press.

O'Connell, M. 1991. Women in the state police. Unpublished.

———. 1991. Late expectations: Childbearing patterns of American women for the 1990s. U.S. Bureau of the Census, *Current Population Reports,* Series P-23, no. 176. Washington, D.C. U.S. Government Printing Office.

O'Farrell, B., and S. Harlan. 1982. Craftworkers and clerks: The effect of male coworker hostility on women's satisfaction with non-traditional jobs. *Social Problems* 29, no. 3:252–64.

Okin, S. M. 1991. Economic equality after divorce: "Equal rights" or special benefits? *Dissent* (summer):383–86.

Olson, M. 1968. *The logic of collective action.* New York: Schocken.

O'Neill, W. 1969. *Everyone was brave: The rise and fall of feminism in America.* Chicago: Quadrangle Books.

Oppenheimer, V. 1982. *Work and the family: A study in social demography.* New York: Academic Press.

O'Reilly, J. 1982. Phyllis Schlafly's last fling. *Ms.* (September):46ff.

Ozawa, M. N., ed. 1989. *Women's life cycle and economic insecurity: Problems and prospects.* New York: Greenwood.

Padavic, I., and B. F. Reskin. 1990. Men's behavior and women's interest in blue-collar jobs. *Social Problems* 37:613–28.

Paglia, C. 1990. *Sexual personae: Art and decadence from Nefertiti to Emily Dickinson.* New Haven, Conn.: Yale University Press.

Paige, J. 1971. Political orientation and riot participation. *American Sociological Review* 36 (October):810–20.

Palmer, P. M. 1983. White women/black women: The dualism of female identity and experience in the U.S. *Feminist Studies* 9, no. 1:151–70.

Paludi, M., and R. Barickman. 1991. *Academic and workplace sexual harassment: A resource manual.* Albany: SUNY Press.

Payne, C. 1989. Ella Baker and models of social change. *Signs* 14, no. 4:885–89.

Pearce, D. 1978. The feminization of poverty: Women, work and welfare. *Urban and Social Change Review* (February):1–17.

———. 1979. The feminization of poverty: women, work and welfare. In *Working women and families,* edited by K. F. Feinstein, 103–24. Beverley Hills: Sage.

Petchesky, R. 1980. Reproductive freedom: Beyond a woman's right to choose. *Signs* 5, no. 4:661–85.

———. 1981. Antiabortion, antifeminism, and the rise of the New Right. *Feminist Studies* 7:206–46.

———. 1984. *Abortion and woman's choice: The state, sexuality and reproductive freedom.* Boston, Mass.: Northeastern University Press.

Peterson, E. 1963. American women: A report. Washington, D.C.: U.S. President's Commission on the Status of Women.

Pettigrew, T. F. 1979. The ultimate attribution error: Extending Allport's cognitive analysis of prejudice. *Personality and Social Psychology Bulletin* 5:461–71.

Pfister, B. 1993. Building the next feminism: Facing the questions of equity and inclusion in the 1990s. *Democratic Left* 21, no. 2:14–17.

Piercy, M. 1970. The Grand Coolie Damn. In *Sisterhood is powerful*, edited by R. Morgan. New York: Random House.

Pinard, M. 1968. Mass society and political movements: A new formulation. *American Journal of Sociology* 73 (May):682–90.

Piven, F. F., and R. Cloward. 1977. *Poor people's movements.* New York: Pantheon.

Pleck, E. 1990. The unfulfilled promise: Women and academe. *Sociological Forum* 5:517–24.

Pleck, J. 1979. Men's family roles: Three perspectives and some new data. *The Family Co-ordinator* (October):481–88.

Pogrebin, L. C. 1982. Anti-Semitism in the women's movement. *Ms.* (June):45ff.

Radford, J., and D. Russell. 1992. *Femicide: The politics of woman-killing.* New York: Twayne.

Randall, M. 1982. Nicaragua: A struggle for dignity. *Guardian: Independent Radical Newsweekly* 34, no. 2:510–11.

Ransford, H. E., and J. Miller. 1983. Race, sex, and feminist outlooks. *American Sociological Review* 48 (Fall):46–59.

Reid, E. 1975. Between the official lines. *Ms.* (November):88ff.

Reinelt, C. 1994. Moving on to the terrain of the state: The politics of battered women's shelters in Texas. In *Feminist organizations: Harvest of the new women's movement*, edited by M. M. Ferree and P. Y. Martin. Philadelphia: Temple University Press.

Remington, J. 1990. *The need to thrive: Women's organizations in the Twin Cities.* St. Paul: Minnesota Women's Press.

Renzetti, C. 1987. New wave or second stage? Attitudes of college women toward feminism. *Sex Roles* 16, no. 5/6:265–77.

Reskin, B., and P. Roos. 1990. *Job queues, gender queues.* Philadelphia: Temple University Press.

Rich, A. 1976. *Of woman born: Motherhood as experience and institution.* New York: Norton.

———. 1980. Compulsory heterosexuality and lesbian existence. *Signs* 5, no. 4:631–60.

Ries, P., and A. J. Stone, eds. 1992. *The American woman, 1992–93: A status report.* New York: Norton.

Rinehart, S. T. 1992. *Gender consciousness and politics.* New York: Routledge.

Roach, J. L., and J. K. Roach. 1978. Mobilizing the poor: Road to a dead end. *Social Problems* 26, no. 2:160–71.

Roach, S. L. 1990. Men and women lawyers in in-house legal departments: Recruitment and career patterns. *Gender & Society* 4:207–19.

Robertson, N. 1992. *Girls in the balcony: Women, men and the New York Times.* New York: Random House.

Robinson, D. A. 1979. Two movements in pursuit of equal employment opportunity. *Signs* 4:413–33.

Robinson, J. 1987. *The Montgomery bus boycott and the women who started it.* Knoxville: University of Tennessee Press.

Roiphe, K. 1993. Rape hype betrays feminism: Date rape's other victim. *New York Times Magazine*, 13 June, 26ff.

Rollins, J. 1985. *Between women: Domestics and their employers.* Philadelphia: Temple University Press.

Romero, M. 1992. *Maid in the U.S.A.* New York: Routledge.

Roos, P. A., and K. Jones. 1993. Shifting gender boundaries: Women's inroads into academic sociology. Unpublished manuscript, Department of Sociology, Rutgers University, New Brunswick, N.J.

Roper Organization, Inc. 1980. *The 1980 Virginia Slims American women's opinion poll.* Storrs, Conn.: Roper Center.

———. 1985. *The 1985 Virginia Slims American women's opinion poll.* Storrs, Conn.: Roper Center.

———. 1990. *The 1990 Virginia Slims American women's opinion poll.* Storrs, Conn.: Roper Center.

Rosen, E. I. 1987. *Bitter choices: Blue collar women in and out of work.* Chicago: University of Chicago Press.

Rosenberg, J., W. R. F. Phillips, and H. Perlstadt. 1991. Now that we are here: Discrimination, disparagement, and sexual harassment: The experience of women lawyers. Paper presented at the annual meeting of the Eastern Sociological Society.

Rosenfeld, R. A., and K. B. Ward. 1991. The contemporary U.S. women's movement: An empirical example of competition theory. *Sociological Forum* 6:471–99.

Rosenfelt, D., and J. Stacey. 1987. Second thought on the second wave. *Feminist Studies* 13:341–61.

Rossi, A., ed. 1973. *The feminist papers: From Adams to De Beauvoir.* New York: Columbia University Press.

———. 1977. A biosocial perspective on parenting. *Daedalus* 106:1–31.

———. 1982. *Feminists in politics: A panel analysis of the first national women's conference.* New York: Academic Press.

Roth, S. 1993. Women in U.S. labor unions: The impact of CLUW. Paper presented at the annual meeting of the Eastern Sociological Society.

Rothman, B. K. 1982. In *Labor: Women and power in the birthplace*. New York: W. W. Norton.

———. 1989. *Recreating motherhood*. New York: Norton.

———. 1991. Beyond Patriarchy. *Tikkun* 5:91–92.

Rothschild-Whitt, J. 1979. The collectivist organization: An alternative to rational-bureaucratic models. *American Sociological Review* 44:509–27.

Ruddick, S. 1980. Maternal thinking. *Feminist Studies* 6, no. 3:343–67.

Ruether, R. 1983. *Sexism and God-talk: Toward a feminist theology*. Boston: Beacon Press.

———. 1986. *Women-Church: Theology and practice*. San Francisco: Harper & Row.

Runciman, W. G. 1966. *Relative deprivation and social justice*. London: Routlege & Kegan Paul.

Rupp, L. 1979. Women's place is in the war: Propaganda and public opinion in the U.S. and Germany, 1939–1945. In *Women of America: A history*, edited by C. R. Berkin and M. B. Norton. Boston: Houghton Mifflin.

Rupp, L., and V. Taylor. 1987. *Survival in the doldrums: The American women's rights movement, 1945 to the 1960's*. Columbus: Ohio State University Press.

Russell, D. 1975. *The politics of rape: The victim's perspective*. New York: Stein & Day.

Russo, N. F., et al. 1991. Gender and success related attributions: Beyond individualistic conceptions of achievement. *Sex Roles* 25:331–50.

Ruzek, S. 1978. *The women's health movement*. New York: Praeger.

Ryan, B. 1989. Ideological purity and feminism: The U.S. women's movement from 1966 to 1975. *Gender & Society* 3:239–57.

———. 1992. *Feminism and the women's movement: Dynamics of change in social movement, ideology and activism*. New York: Routledge.

Ryan, M. P. 1979. *Womanhood in America*. 2d ed. New York: New Viewpoints.

———, 1981. *The cradle of the middle class*. New York: Cambridge University Press.

Rytina, N. 1981. Occupational segregation and earning differences by sex. *Monthly Labor Review* (January):49–52.

Sacks, K. B. 1988. *Caring by the hour: Women, work and organizing at Duke Medical Center*. Urbana: University of Illinois Press.

Sanday, P. R. 1990. *Fraternity gang rape: Sex, brotherhood, and privilege on campus*. New York: New York University Press.

Sapiro, V. 1991. "The gender gap and women's political influence." *Annals of the American Academy of Political and Social Science* 515:23–37.

Sargent, L. 1981. *Women and revolution*. Boston: South End Press.

Sayers, J. 1982. *Biological politics: Feminist and antifeminist perspectives.* London: Tavistock.

Scharf, L. 1980. *To work and to wed: Female employment, feminism and the Great Depression.* Westport, Conn.: Greenwood Press.

Scheppele, K. 1977. Feminism as a response to sociological ambivalence. Paper presented at the annual meeting of the American Sociological Association.

Schlesinger, M., and P. Bart. 1981. Collective work and self identity: The effect of working in a feminist illegal abortion collective. In *Workplace democracy and social change,* edited by F. Lindenfeld and J. Rothschild-Whitt. Boston: Porter-Sargent.

Schmittroth, L. 1991. *Statistical record of women worldwide.* Detroit: Gale Research.

Schneider, B. 1982. Consciousness about sexual harassment among hetero-sexual and lesbian women workers. *Journal of Social Issues* 38, no. 4:75–94.

———. 1988. Political generations in the contemporary women's movement. *Sociological Inquiry 58, 1 (winter):4–21.*

———. *1991.* Put up and shut up: Workplace sexual assaults. *Gender & Society* 5:533–48.

Schneider, J., and S. Hacker. 1973. Sex role imagery in the use of the generic "man" in introductory textbooks: A case of the sociology of sociology. *American Sociologist* 8:12–18.

Schrager, C. 1993. Questioning the promise of self-help: A reading of *Women who love too much. Feminist Studies* 19, no. 1:177–92.

Schreiber, E. M. 1978. Education and change in American opinions on a woman for president. *Public Opinion Quarterly* 42:171–82.

Schreiber, R., and R. Spalter-Roth. 1994. Outsider issues and insider tactics: Strategic tensions in the women's policy network in the 1980s. In *Feminist organizations: Harvest of the new women's movement,* edited by M. M. Ferree and P. Y. Martin. Philadelphia: Temple University Press.

Scott, H. 1974. *Does socialism liberate women? Experiences from Eastern Europe.* Boston: Beacon Press.

Scott, J. 1988. Deconstructing equality versus difference. *Feminist Studies* 14, no. 1:33–50.

———. 1989. Conflicting beliefs about abortion: Legal approval and moral doubts. *Social Psychological Quarterly* 52:319–26.

Scully, D. 1990. *Understanding sexual violence: A study of convicted rapists.* Boston: Unwin Hyman.

Seals, B., P. Jenkins, and J. Manale. 1992. Sexual harassment. Paper present-ed at midyear meeting of Sociologists for Women in Society.

Sealander, J., and D. Smith. 1986. The rise and fall of feminist organizations in the 1970's: Dayton as a case study. *Feminist Studies* 12:321–42.

Searles, P., and R. Berger. 1987. The feminist self-defense movement: A case study. *Gender & Society* 1, no. 1:61–84.

Seidman, S. 1991. The end of sociological theory: The postmodern hope. *Sociological Theory* 9:131–46.

Shaffer, H. 1981. *Women in the two Germanies.* Elmsford, N.Y.: Pergamon.

Shapiro, V. 1991. Feminism: A generation later. *Annals of the American Academy of Political and Social Science* 514:10–22.

Sheppard, N. 1992. *WAC Talk.* "Women talk to WAC" Undated Suppplement.

Showalter, E. 1979. Feminism's awkward age: The deflated rebels of the 1920s. *Ms.* (January):64–79.

Shulman, A. K. 1980. Sex and power: Sexual bases of radical feminism. *Signs* 5, no. 4:590–604.

Sidel, R. 1978. *Urban survival: The world of working class women.* Boston: Beacon Press.

Simon, R., and J. Landis. 1989. The polls: Women's and men's attitudes about a woman's place and role. *Public Opinion Quarterly* 53:265–76.

Simonds, W. 1994. Feminism on the job: Ideology and practice in an abortion clinic. In *Feminist organizations: Harvest of the new women's movement,* edited by M. M. Ferree and P. Y. Martin. Philadelphia: Temple University Press.

Simons, M. 1979. Racism and feminism: A schism in the sisterhood. *Feminist Studies* 5:384–401.

Smelser, N. 1963. *A theory of collective behavior.* New York: The Free Press.

Smith, D. 1976. Sexual aggression in American pornography: The stereotype of rape. Paper presented at the annual meeting of the American Sociological Association.

———. 1987. *The everyday world as problematic: A feminist sociology.* Boston, Mass.: Northeastern University Press.

Smith, E. R., and J. R. Kluegel. 1984. Beliefs and attitudes about women's opportunity: Comparisons with beliefs about blacks and a general model. *Social Psychology Quarterly* 47, no. 1:81–95.

Smith, P. 1993. *Feminist jurisprudence.* New York: Oxford.

Smith, T. W. 1991. Data from National Opinion Research Center cited in *Family Planning Perspectives* 23:148.

Snow, D., et al. 1986. Frame alignment processes, micromobilization, and movement participation. *American Sociological Review* 51, no. 4 (August):464–81.

Snow, D., and R. Benford. 1988. Ideology, frame resonance, and participant mobilization. *International Social Movement Research* 1:197–217.

Sokoloff, N. 1981. *Between money and love: The dialectics of women's home and market work.* New York: Praeger.

———. 1992. *Black and white women in the professions.* New York: Routledge.

Solomon, A. 1991. From CR to PR: Feminist theatre in America. In *Contemporary American theatre*, edited by B. King. New York: St. Martin Press.

Spalter-Roth, R., and R. Schreiber. 1994. Outsider issues and insider tactics: Strategic tensions in the women's policy network in the 1980s. In *Feminist organizations: Harvest of the new women's movement*, edited by M. M. Ferree and P. Y. Martin. Philadelphia: Temple University Press.

Spelman, E. 1988. *Inessential Woman: Problems of exclusion in feminist thought.* Boston, Mass.: Beacon Press.

Spitze, G., and Huber, J. 1982. Effects of anticipated consequences on ERA opinion. *Social Science Quarterly* 63:323–32.

Spock, B. 1945. *The common sense book of baby and child care.* New York: Duell, Sloan, and Pearce.

Spretnak, C., ed. 1982. *The politics of women's spirituality: Essays on the rise of spiritual power within the feminist movement.* New York: Doubleday.

Stacey, J. 1983. The new conservative feminism. *Feminist Studies* 9:559–83.

———. 1987. Postindustrial conditions and postfeminist consciousness in the Silicon Valley. *Socialist Review* 17, no. 6(96):7–28.

———. 1989. *Brave new families.* New York: Basic Books.

Staggenborg, S. 1989. Stability and innovation in the women's movement: A comparison of two movement organizations. *Social Problems* 36:75–92.

———. 1991. *The Pro-Choice movement.* New York: Oxford University Press.

———. 1994. Can feminist movements be successful? In *Feminist organizations: Harvest of the new women's movement,* edited by M. M. Ferree and P. Y. Martin. Philadelphia: Temple University Press.

Standard Periodical Directory. 15th ed. 1992. New York: Oxbridge Communications.

Steinberg, R. 1987. Radical challenges in a liberal world: The mixed success of comparable worth. *Gender & Society* 1, no. 4:466–75.

Steinem, G. 1983. An appeal to young women. Address to NWPC Annual Meeting, San Antonio, spring, 1983, cited in *Comment*, 14 no. 2.

Stember, C. H. 1976. *Sexual Racism.* New York: Harper & Row.

Stiehm, J. 1982. Women, men, and military service: Is protection necessarily a racket? In *Women, power, and policy* edited by E. Boneparth, 282–93. New York: Pergamon.

———. 1989. *Arms and the enlisted woman.* Philadelphia: Temple University Press.

Stimpson, C. 1971. Thy neighbor's wife, thy neighbor's servants: Women's liberation and black civil rights. In *Woman in sexist society*, edited by V. Gornick and B. K. Moran. New York: Basic Books.

Strasser, S. 1982. *Never done: A history of American housework.* New York: Pantheon.

Straus, M. A. 1992. Sociological research and social policy: The case of family violence. *Sociological Forum* 7:211–37.

Stricker, F. 1979. Cookbooks and lawbooks. In *A heritage of her own*, edited by N. F. Cott and E. H. Pleck. New York: Simon & Schuster.

Strobel, Margaret. 1990. Women's Liberation Unions. In *Encyclopedia of the American left*, edited by M. J. Buhle, P. Buhle, and D. Georgakas, 841–42. New York and London: Garland.

———. 1994. Organizational learning in the Chicago women's liberation union. In *Feminist organizations: Harvest of the new women's movement,* edited by M. M. Ferree and P. Y. Martin. Philadelphia: Temple University Press.

Sugarman, S. D., and H. Hill, eds. 1990. *Divorce reform at the crossroads.* New Haven, Conn.: Yale University Press.

Swerdlow, M. 1989. Men's accomodations to women entering a nontraditional occupation: A case of rapid transit operatives. *Gender & Society* 3:373–87.

Swidler, A. 1986. Culture in action: Symbols and strategies. *American Sociological Review* 51 (April):273–86.

Tangri, S., Burt, M., and Johnson, L., 1982. Sexual harassment at work: Three explanatory models. *Journal of Social Issues* 38, no. 4:33–54.

Tarrow, S. 1983. Struggling to reform: Social movements and policy change during cycles of protest. *Western Societies Occasional Papers* no. 15, Center for International Studies, Cornell University.

———. 1989. *Democracy and disorder: Protest and politics in Italy, 1965–1975.* New York: Oxford University Press.

Tax, M. 1980. The rising of the women: Feminist solidarity and class consciousness, 1880–1917. New York: Monthly Review Press.

Taylor, V. 1989a. The future of feminism: A social movement analysis. In *Feminist frontiers II*, edited by L. Richardson and V. Taylor. New York: Random House.

———. 1989b. Social movement continuity: The women's movement in abeyance. *American Sociological Review* 54:761–75.

Taylor, V., and L. Rupp. 1993. Women's culture and lesbian feminist activism: A reconsideration of cultural feminism. *Signs* 19, no. 1:32–61.

Taylor, V., and N. Whittier. 1992a. Theoretical approaches to social movement culture: The culture of the women's movement. Paper presented at the Workshop on Culture and Social Movements, June 18–20, San Diego.

———. 1992b. Collective identity in social movement communities: Lesbian feminist mobilization. In *Frontiers of social movement theory,* edited by A. Morris and C. Mueller, 104–30. New Haven: Yale University Press.

———. 1993. The new feminist movement. In *Feminist frontiers III,* edited by L. Richardson and V. Taylor. New York: McGraw-Hill.

Theodore, A. 1986. *The campus troublemakers: Academic women in protest.* Houston, Tex: Cap and Gown Press.

Thompson, E. P. 1963. *The making of the English working class.* New York: Random House.

Thornton, A., and D. Freedman. 1979. Changes in the sex role attitudes of women, 1962–1977: Evidence from a panel study. *American Sociological Review* 44:832–42.

Thornton, A., D. Alwin, and D. Camburn. 1983. Causes and consequences of sex role attitudes and attitude change. *American Sociological Review* 48:211–27.

Tiano, S. 1981. The separation of women's remunerated and household work. Paper given at American Sociological Association Annual Meeting.

Tierney, K. 1982. The battered women's movement and the creation of the wife-beating problem. *Social Problems* 29:207–20.

Tiffany, J. 1982. Militant women for peace: International actions by women against militarism and nuclear technology. *New Women's Times* 8 no. 6:12–14.

Tillet, R., and D. Krafchek, 1991. Factsheet on women's political progress. *National Women's Political Caucus.*

Tilly, C. 1978. *From mobilization to revolution.* Reading, Mass.: Addison Wesley.

Tinker, I. 1981. A feminist view of Copenhagen. *Signs* 6:531–37.

Tobin, S. 1983. Why not a feminist? *The Feminist Special* (spring):6–9.

Treiman, D., and H. Hartmann. 1981. *Women, work and wages: Equal pay for jobs of equal value.* Washington, D.C.: National Academy Press.

Trimberger, E. K. 1979. Women in the old and new left: The evolution of a politics of personal life. *Feminist Studies* 5:432–50.

———. 1991. *Intimate warriors: Portrait of a modern marriage, 1899–1944.* New York: Feminist Press at CUNY.

Trimberger, E. K., and P. Dennis. 1979. Women in the old and new left: The evolution of a politics of personal life. *Feminist Studies* 5:432–50.

Tuchman, G. 1978. *Making news: A study in the construction of reality.* New York: Free Press.

Tudiver, S. 1986. The strength of links: International women's health networks in the eighties. In *Adverse effects: Women and the pharmaceutical industry,* edited by Kathleen McDonnell, 187–214. Toronto: Women's Press.

U.S. Bureau of the Census. 1975. *Historical Statistics of the United States: Colonial times to 1970.* Washington, D.C.: U.S. Government Printing Office.

———. 1981. *Statistical Abstract of the United States, 1981.* Washington, D.C.: U.S. Government Printing Office.

———. 1982. Fertility of American women: 1980. *Current Population Reports,* P-20, No. 369 (Advance Report; March)

———. 1983a. Money income and poverty status of families and persons in the U.S. 1982. *Current Population Reports,* P-60, No. 140 (July).

———. 1983b. *Statistical Abstract of the United States, 1982–83.* Washington, D.C.: U.S. Government Printing Office.

———. 1983c. Child support and alimony, 1981. *Current Population Reports* P-23, No. 124. (Advance Report May).

———. 1983d. Household and family characteristics, March, 1982. *Current Population Reports,* P-20, No. 381 (May).

———. 1983e. Childcare arrangements of working mothers: June 1982. *Current Population Reports,* P-23, No. 129. (November).

———. 1990a. Women owned businesses up 57 percent over 5 years. *Census and You,* 25 no. 12:1–2.

———. 1990b. Work and family patterns of American women. *Current Population Reports,* P-23-165. Washington, D.C.: U.S. Government Printing Office.

———. 1991a. Money income of households, families, and persons in the United States: 1990. *Current Population Reports,* P-60, no. 174 (September). Washington, D.C.: U.S. Government Printing Office.

———. 1991b. Late expectations: Childbearing patterns of American women for the 1990s. Martin O'Connell. *Current Population Reports,* P-23, no. 176. Washington, D.C.: U.S. Government Printing Office.

———. 1991c. *Statistical abstract of the United States, 1991.* Washington, D.C.: U.S. Government Printing Office.

———. 1991d. Annual report. Fertility of American women: June 1990. *Current Population Reports,* P-20, no. 454.

———. 1991e. Child support and alimony: 1989. *Current Population Reports,* P-60, no. 173.

———. 1992a. Poverty in the United States: 1991. *Current Population Reports,* 60–181. Washington, D.C.: U.S. Government Printing Office.

———. 1992b. *Statistical Abstract of the United States, 1992.* Washington, D.C. U.S. Government Printing Office.

———. 1993. Educational attainment in the U.S. 1992. *Current Population Reports,* P-20, no. 462 (July).

U.S. Bureau of Labor Statistics. 1990. *BLS Update.* Washington, D.C.: U.S. Government Printing Office.

———. Unpublished data quoted in *The American woman, 1992–93: A status report,* edited by P. Reis and A. J. Stone, 301. New York: Norton.

U.S. Department of Labor. 1982. The female-male earnings gap: A review of employment and earnings issues. *Bureau of Labor Statistics* Report 673. Washington, D.C.: U.S. Government Printing Office.

U.S. Department of Education. 1993. National Center for Education Statistics. *Digest of Education Statistics.* Washington, D.C.:U.S. Government Printing Office

U.S. Merit Systems Protection Board. 1981. *Sexual harassment in the workplace: Is it a problem?* Washington, D.C.: U.S. Government Printing Office.

Vandepol, A. 1982. Dependent children, child custody, and mothers' pensions: The transformation of state-family relationships in the early 20th century. *Social Problems* 29:221–35.

Vanek, J. 1974. Time spent in housework. *Scientific American* (November):116–20.

Van Gelder, L. 1970. The trials of Lois Lane. In *Sisterhood is powerful* edited by R. Morgan. New York: Vintage.

———. 1978. Four days that changed the world: Behind the scenes at Houston. *Ms.* (March):54ff.

Vanneman, R., and T. F. Pettigrew. 1972. Race and relative deprivation in the U.S. *Race* 13 no. 4:461–86.

Van Zoonen, L. 1992. The women's movement and the media: Constructing a public identity. *European Journal of Communications* 7:453–76.

Verba, S., and N. Nie. 1972. *Participation in America.* New York: Harper and Row.

Verba, S., G. Orren, and G. D. Ferree. 1984. *Equality in America.* Cambridge, Mass.: Harvard University Press.

Viguerie, R. 1980. *The New Right: We're ready to lead.* Falls Church, Va.: Viguerie.

Vogel, L. 1990. Debating difference: Feminism, pregnancy and the work place. *Feminist Studies* 16 (spring):9–32.

———. 1993. *Mothers on the job: Maternity policy in the American workplace.* New Brunswick, N.J.: Rutgers University Press.

Voter Research and Surveys. 1990. *Final 1990 General Election Exit Polls.* Survey conducted 6 November 1990 by Voter Research & Surveys, a consortium of ABC News, CBS News, CNN, and NBC News. New York: Voter Research & Surveys.

Wakefield, N. 1990. *Postmodernism: The twilight of the real.* London: Pluto Press.

Walker, K., and M. Woods. 1976. Time use: A measure of household production of family goods and services. Paper presented at the annual meeting of the American Home Economics Association.

Wallace, M. 1982. A black feminist's search for sisterhood. In *But some of us are brave*, edited by G. Hull, P. Scott, and B. Smith, 5–12. Old Westbury, N.Y.: Feminist Press.

Wallis, C. 1989. Onward, women! *Time,* 4 December, 80–89.

Walshok, M. L. 1981. *Blue collar women: Pioneers on the male frontier.* Garden City, N.Y.: Anchor Books.

Wandersee, W. D. 1988. *Women on the move: American women in the 1970s.* Boston: Twayne.

Ware, S. 1981. *Beyond suffrage: Women in the New Deal.* Cambridge, Mass.: Harvard University Press.

WEAL, 1983. *Washington Report.* (June–July):3.

Weber, M. 1922. *Wirtschaft und Gesellschaft.* Tüebingen: Mohr. English edition: 1947. *The theory of social and economic organization,* translated by A. M. Henderson and T. Parsons. New York: Oxford University Press.

Weinbaum, B. 1978. *The curious courtship of women's liberation and socialism.* Boston: South End Press.

Weinbaum, B., and A. Bridges. 1979. The other side of the pay check: Monopoly capital and the structure of consumption. In *Capitalist patriarchy and the case for socialist feminism,* edited by Z. Eisenstein, 190–205. New York: Monthly Review Press.

Weisstein, N. 1970. Kinder, Kirche, and Küche as scientific law: Psychology constructs the female. In *Sisterhood is powerful,* edited by R. Morgan. New York: Random House.

Weitz, R., and D. Sullivan. 1986. The politics of childbirth: The re-emergence of midwifery in Arizona. *Social Problems* 33, no. 3:163–75.

Weitzman, L. J. 1985. *The divorce revolution: The unexpected social and economic consequences for women and children in America.* New York: The Free Press.

Welch, S. 1975. Support among women for the issues of the women's movement. *The Sociological Quarterly* 16:216–27.

Wells, R. V. 1979. Women's lives transformed: Demographic and family patterns in America, 1600–1970. In *Women of America: A history,* edited by C. R. Berkin and M. B. Norton. Boston: Houghton Mifflin.

Whittier, N. 1994. Turning it over: Personnel change in the Columbus Ohio women's movement 1969–1984. In *Feminist organizations: Harvest of the new women's movement,* edited by M. M. Ferree and P. Y. Martin. Philadelphia: Temple University Press.

Wilkie, J. R. 1981. The trend toward delayed parenthood. *Journal of Marriage and the Family* 43, no. 3 (August):583–91.

Williams, C. 1989. *Gender differences at work: Women and men in nontraditional occupations.* Berkeley, Calif.: University of California Press.

Willis, E. 1970. Women and the left. In *Notes from the second year,* edited by A. Koedt and S. Firestone. New York: New York Radical Feminists.

Wilson, J. 1973. *Introduction to social movements.* New York: Basic Books.

Wirthlin Group. 1991. Public opinion poll cited in A. Clymer, Abortion foes say poll backs curb on advice. *New York Times,* 25 June, A23.

Withers, J. 1988. Art essay: The guerrilla girls. *Feminist Studies* 14, no. 2:284–300.

Withorn, B. 1980. Helping ourselves. *Radical America* (May–June):25–38.

Wolf, N. 1991. *The beauty myth: How images of beauty are used against women.* New York: William Morrow.

Women's Action Almanac, 1980. New York: William Morrow.

Women's Bureau, U.S. Dept. of Labor. 1990. Data reported in *New York Times*, 5 May 1991, sec. 3, p. 6.

Wright, R. 1991. Gender differences in computer careers. Paper presented at the annual meeting of the Eastern Sociological Society.

Wyatt, G. E. 1992. The sociocultural context of African American and White American women's rape. *Journal of Social Issues* 48:77–92.

Wyatt, G. E., S. D. Peters, and D. Guthrie. 1988. Kinsey revisited: Part I. Comparisons of the sexual socialization and sexual behavior of white women over 33 years. *Archives of Sexual Behavior* 17:201–39.

Yankelovich, D. 1981. *New rules: Searching for self-fulfillment in a world turned upside down.* New York: Random House.

Yankelovich Clancy and Shulman. 1989. Survey on women, work and family for *Time* and *Cable News Network*, 1 December. Archived at Roper Center. Storrs, Conn.: University of Connecticut.

———. 1992. Survey on problems facing women today for *Time* and *Cable News Network*, 20 February.

Yllo, K., and M. Bograd, eds. 1988. *Feminist perspectives on wife abuse.* Newbury Park, Calif.: Sage.

Yount, K. R. 1989. 'Harrazzment' among male underground coal miners: The impact of workplace structure and gender. Paper presented at the annual meeting of Sociologists for Women in Society.

Zald, M. 1988. The trajectory of social movements in America. *Research in Social Movements, Conflict and Change* 10. Greenwich, Conn.: JAI Press.

Zald, M., and B. Useem. 1987. Movement and countermovement interaction: Mobilization, tactics, and state involvement. In *Social movements in an organizational society,* edited by M. N. Zald and J. D. McCarthy, 247–72. New Brunswick, N.J.: Transaction.

Zelizer, V. A. R. 1985. *Pricing the priceless child: The changing social value of children.* New York: Basic Books.

Index

Page numbers in italics refer to illustrations.

The Authors

Myra Marx Ferree, professor of sociology and women's studies at the University of Connecticut, has been interested in feminism since she read Millett's *Sexual Politics* as an undergraduate. Her Ph.D. dissertation (Harvard, 1976) was on working-class women's responses to feminism. Her research since then has concentrated on the micropolitics of gender (the division of labor, power, satisfaction, and perceived equity in the household), public opinion on women's issues (attitudes toward a woman for president, race differences in abortion attitudes, and gender beliefs of Cuban immigrant women), and comparative feminism. Her studies of the women's movement include intensive research on the development of feminism in West Germany, including the difficulties it has faced as the country has recently expanded to encompass the former German Democratic Republic. She is the co-editor, with Patricia Yancey Martin, of an overview of American feminist organizations (*Feminist Organizations: Harvest of the New Women's Movement*, 1994) and with Beth Hess of a handbook of feminist social science research (*Analyzing Gender*, 1987). She is currently beginning work on a collaborative project on abortion discourse in the mass media in the United States and Germany. Professor Ferree is past chair of both the Section on Sex and Gender and the Section on Collective Behavior and Social Movements of the American Sociological Association.

Beth B. Hess, professor of sociology at County College of Morris, has been interested in feminism since she read Millett's *Sexual Politics* as a young wife and mother in suburban New Jersey. Having graduated from Radcliffe College in 1950, she returned to academe in 1963, earning the Ph.D. from Rutgers University in 1971. A member of Sociologists for Women in Society since 1972, she has brought her feminist concerns to her many journal articles, book chapters, and professional presentations in the fields of gerontology, friendship, social policy, and undergraduate education. In addition to the explicitly feminist books she has written with Myra Marx Ferree, she has co-edited four editions of *Growing Old in America* (1991) with Elizabeth W. Markson and coauthored five editions of *Sociology* (1995) with Elizabeth W. Markson and Peter J. Stein. Organizational offices she has held include chair of the Behavioral and Social Science Section of the Gerontological Society, president of Sociologists for Women in Society, president of the Eastern Sociological Society, vice president of the Society for the Study of Social Problems, and secretary of the American Sociological Association.